郭广昌
与
复星

（汉英双语）

郭宏文　著

朱源　徐坤　赵天予　刘雯倩　译

中国出版集团

中译出版社

图书在版编目（ＣＩＰ）数据

郭广昌与复星 = GUO GUANGCHANG & FUSON：汉英对照 / 郭宏文著；朱源等译. -- 北京：中译出版社，2021.9

（"中国著名企业家与企业"丛书. 第二辑）

ISBN 978-7-5001-6750-1

Ⅰ. ①郭… Ⅱ. ①郭… ②朱… Ⅲ. ①郭广昌－生平事迹－汉、英②制药工业－工业企业管理－经验－中国－汉、英 Ⅳ. ① K825.38 ② F426.77

中国版本图书馆 CIP 数据核字（2021）第 188739 号

出版发行：中译出版社
地　　址：北京市西城区车公庄大街甲4号物华大厦6层
电　　话：（010）68005858，68358224（编辑部）
传　　真：（010）68357870
邮　　编：100044
电子邮箱：book@ctph.com.cn
网　　址：http://www.ctph.com.cn

策划编辑：刘永淳　范　伟
责任编辑：范　伟　郑　南
封面设计：潘　峰

排　　版：孙艳武
印　　刷：山东华立印务有限公司
经　　销：新华书店

规　　格：710毫米×1000毫米　1/16
印　　张：23.75
字　　数：350千字
版　　次：2021年9月第1版
印　　次：2021年9月第1次

ISBN 978-7-5001-6750-1　　　　定价：89.00元

目　录

序　言

在中国工商界，提起郭广昌和他所创建的复星，几乎所有的人都耳熟能详，赞许有加。即使是在全球工商界，也有许许多多的人了解郭广昌，了解他所创建的复星。

郭广昌的人生经历是一部跌宕起伏的传奇，是一个励志创业的经典范例，是一棵引领成长的参天大树，是一盏商海旅途的指路明灯……

郭广昌 1967 年出生于浙江省东阳市农村的一个贫困家庭，1985 年毕业于东阳中学后，他以优异的成绩考入了复旦大学哲学系。1989 年毕业时，他因在校表现优异被留校任教。1992 年，他联手复旦大学的同事，也是复旦大学的校友梁信军，毅然决然地辞去复旦大学的教师工作，用借来的 3.8 万元，踏上了创业的新征程，从此一发而不可收。他们所创办的复星，从最初的市场调查和咨询行业做起，逐步进入房地产、百货、钢铁、金融等行业，最终成为国际化的大型民营企业。2018 年，复星国际总收入达到 1,094 亿元，同比增长 24.2%；总资产达到 6,388.8 亿元，同比增长 20%。2018 年，郭广昌的身价达到 617 亿元，由复星直接和间接控股的公司有 100 多家。

在许多人看来，郭广昌的人生和创业历程，与马云惊人地相似。他们是浙江同乡，郭广昌是金华东阳人，马云是杭州人，他们后来都成为浙商的优秀代表，成为中国企业家的优秀代表；他们大学毕业后都曾担任教师，郭广昌从复旦大学毕业留校任教，马云从杭州师范学院毕业后在杭州电子工业学院任教；他们都从教师岗位上辞职创业，并走向成功，郭广昌创办了当今著名的复星，而马云创办了当今响当当的阿里巴巴……

翻看郭广昌的人生履历就会发现，在人生历程的关键时刻，他几次做出重大抉择，成就了人生的转折。

第一次重大抉择是 1982 年初中毕业时，郭广昌毅然放弃读师范学校的机会，改读高中。这一抉择，成了他人生的第一次转折。他出生于一个贫苦的农民家庭，像大多数的农家父母一样，他的父母也希望自己的儿子通过努力，早日改变农民身份。因此，初中毕业时，父母让他报考师范学校，当一名吃"皇粮"的老师。他没有违背父母的意愿，以优异的成绩被师范学校录取。可拿到师范学校的录取通知书后，郭广昌感觉自己就像拿到人生的判决书。他觉得，自己不能一辈子就待在东阳做一名乡村教师，而是应该去圆自己的大学梦。于是，郭广昌决定：放弃师范学校，改读高中。最终，他读完三年高中后，以优异的成绩，考入了上海复旦大学，成为哲学系的一名学生。大学生活，无疑为他后来的成功与辉煌打下了坚实的知识和思想基础。

第二次重大抉择，是 1992 年受邓小平南方谈话的影响，郭广昌放弃出国深造的机会，毅然辞职"下海"创业。进入上海复旦大学后，从东阳来到上海的郭广昌，发现了一片家乡东阳所无法比拟的广阔天地。在大学期间，他把更多的时间和精力放在了接触社会上。大学期间，他做了两件让同学感到惊讶的事情：1987 年暑期，他一个人不声不响地骑自行车，沿大运河考察一路骑到北京；1988 年暑假，他组织十几名同学策划了"黄金海岸 3000 里"活动，骑着自行车从上海出发沿海考察，终点到达海南。这两件事，帮助他在一定程度上了解了社会、认识了自己，表现出的魄力和组织能力直接影响到他毕业时被学校留在了校团委。留校工作后，一颗年轻的心，让他更加渴望看到更广阔的天空。于是，他打算出国留学，并为此积极做准备，先后通过了 TOEFL 和 GRE 考试，还筹钱准备好了出国所需经费。1992 年发生的一件事情却改变了郭广昌的计划，这件事就是邓小平的南方谈话。郭广昌认为，邓小平南方谈话后，上海必将成为投资和创业的热土。在国内可以大有作为，何必一定要到国外去？于是，郭广昌不仅放弃了出国的念头，而且还决定辞职，自己去打拼一番事业，在上海滩开创自己理想的新天地。也就是在那一年，25 岁的郭广昌在上海"下海"经商，并掘到了人生的第一桶金。

第三次重大抉择，是 1995 年将企业名称由"广信"正式更名为"复星"后，郭广昌摒弃传统民营企业家族式用人的管理模式，携手复旦校友大力实施人才战略。其实，早在创业初始，郭广昌就深刻认识到企业的竞争，归根结底是人才的竞争。他说："青年人最需要的不是个人英雄主义，而是集体英雄主义。我们这些人，能力上可能每人只能打 70 ~ 80 分，但是我们要做能力的加法和乘法。在复星，我们最大的愿望，是培养一批志同道合的青年企业家群体和一个朝气蓬勃的青年创业团队。"在人才引进和培养上，郭广昌不断深化"以发展吸引人、以事业凝聚人、以工作培养人、以业绩考核人"的用人观念。他一直强调复星的每个人都要有企业团队精神，每个在复星工作的员工都应该把复星当作自己的另一个家，每个人都是这个大家庭的一个成员。公司的运营就像一场球赛，赛场上如果有一个人掉链子，是难以赢得比赛，这就需要每个人都团结努力，公司才能更好地发展下去。

从 1992 年依靠 3.8 万元创业，到 1995 年资产超过 1 亿元，郭广昌和复星人仅仅用了 3 年时间。

1998 年 8 月，复星旗下的复星医药在上海证券交易所挂牌上市，复星一次性募集资金 3.5 亿元，实现了将产业与资本市场成功对接，由此也拉开了复星借用资本进一步扩张产业的序幕。

2001 年 11 月 28 日，刚刚成立不到一个月的复星投资，就与豫园商城签署了控股权转让托管协议，复星投资成为豫园商城新的第一大股东。豫园商城是最早的 A 股上市公司之一，商城旗下有"老庙黄金"和"亚一金店"这样的全国黄金珠宝零售招牌。2002 年，已经变成复星旗下企业的豫园商城，纯经营收入 5 亿元，让复星仿佛拉住了一头"现金奶牛"。

2003 年，豫园商城和复星产业投资等四家公司合资成立德邦证券，意味着复星拿到了德邦证券的控股权。随后，豫园商城与复星产业投资再度联手，与山东招金集团共同投资设立了招金矿业。很快，招金矿业于 2006 年登陆香港联交所主板。同年，复星集团、南钢集团、复星产业投资和广信科技四家企业，合资成立南京钢铁联合有限公司，简称南钢联。随后，南钢联收购了江苏省最大的国有钢铁企业——南京钢铁股份，占据 60% 的股份，相当于复星间接控股南钢股份。

2007 年 7 月，由郭广昌持股 58% 的复星国际在香港联交所主板上市，融资额达 132 亿港元，成为当年香港联交所第三大首次公开募股，同时也是香港联交所历史上第六大首次公开募股。

随后，复星明确提出，要做"世界一流的投资集团"，开始稳步推进全球化进程。

2010 年 6 月，复星出资 2,500 万欧元，注资法国老牌旅游度假村运营商——地中海俱乐部，占股 7.1%；2015 年 3 月，复星出资 9.58 亿欧元，完成对地中海俱乐部的整体收购，持股比例达 98%。

2012 年 9 月，复星与美国保德信金融集团，合资成立复星保德信人寿。

2013 年 12 月，复星以 7.25 亿美元的价格，收购了纽约第一大通曼哈顿广场大楼。这栋大楼，是洛克菲勒家族两栋地标性建筑之一。收购这一建筑，旨在扩张复星在全球主要金融中心的业务；同月，复星与世界银行集团旗下的国际金融公司，在香港地区合资成立了鼎睿再保险公司。

2014 年 1 月，复星出价 10.38 亿欧元，在竞标中击败了强大对手——美国投资基金阿波罗全球管理公司，一举收购了葡萄牙保险公司 Fidelidade 80% 股权，到 2015 年年初，复星持有股份增至 85%；当年，复星又通过 Fidelidade，成功收购了葡萄牙最大的私营医疗集团 Luz Saude。

2014 年 6 月，复星以 5,680 万欧元的价格，收购了葡萄牙电网公司 REN 的 3.9% 国有股份。

2014 年 8 月，复星以 4.64 亿美元的价格，投标购买了美国特种险企业 Ironshore 的伤亡及财产险种，该险种约占 Ironshore 公司 20% 的股份。

2014 年 10 月，在连续两次提高收购报价后，复星最终击败全球 500 强企业——美国联合健康，以 4.6 亿欧元的价格，收购了葡萄牙医疗保健服务商 ESS 96.07% 的股权。

2014 年 11 月，复星旗下的全资附属公司超越能源出价 4.39 亿澳元（约合 23.6 亿人民币），收购澳大利亚洛克石油有限公司 92.6% 的股份，成为该公司的第一大股东。

2015 年 7 月，复星宣布完成对美国劳工险公司 Mea-dowbrook 的收购。

2016 年 7 月，复星收购英格兰足球英冠联赛球队股权。

2017 年 10 月，复星医药以 10.91 亿美元的出价，完成对印度仿制药企业 Gland Pharma 的收购，拥有该企业 74% 的股权。

2018 年 2 月，复星与英国生物医药投资公司 Arix Bioscience 签署战略合作协议；同月，复星在法国巴黎宣布，收购法国历史最悠久的高级定制时装品牌 Lanvin，成为控股股东，而现有股东仅保留公司少量股权……

郭广昌带领着复星人，正以"中国动力嫁接全球资源"为核心，加速推进复星的全球化布局，助推全球经济的融合协调发展，一个优秀的企业家和一个伟大的企业永远令人期待！

第一章

出身贫寒，
志向高远学习优异

出生农家,少小立志干事业

位于浙江省东阳市中南部的横店镇是国家可持续发展实验区、国家影视产业实验区、浙江省高新技术实验区。这个人口不到9万的江南小镇,先后荣获了"国家卫生镇""全国文明镇""第一批中国特色小镇"等20多项国家级荣誉称号。2010年,横店镇被浙江省列为首批小城市培育试点镇;2018年5月,横店镇荣登"全国最美特色小城镇50强"榜单;2018年10月,横店镇在"全国综合实力千强镇前100名"榜单上排名第29位。

但是,40多年前的横店却是一个令人难以想象的贫困之地。这里山多地少,偏僻落后,人们的生活普遍比较贫困。1975年,当时的横店乡人均年收入只有75元。那时,当地流传着这样一首民谣:"抬头望见八面山,薄粥三餐度饥荒,有女不嫁横店郎。"这首民谣是横店当时贫困落后状况的一个真实写照。

今天的横店早已今非昔比。到2015年,横店镇的农民人均年纯收入就已经达到了30,020元,是40年前的400.27倍。也就是说,2015年一位农民的年收入额,是1975年400位农民的年收入额总和。横店镇能够取得今天这样的翻天覆地的变化,是横店人紧紧抓住了改革开放这一巨大的历史机遇,苦干实干加巧干、咬定青山不放松的结果。在创造奇迹、创造辉煌的过程中,催生了像横店集团这样的一批优秀企业、横店集团董事局主席徐文荣和横店集团控股有限公司总裁徐永安父子这样的一批优秀企业家。横店集团作为横店镇的本土企业,到2018年,已发展成为拥有5家上市公司、200多家生产与服务型企业、5万余名员工的特大型民营集团,成为具有新时代影响力的品牌企业。而复星创始人、董事长郭广昌就是从横店走出去的一位杰出的优秀企业家。

1967 年，郭广昌出生于东阳市横店镇一户普通的农村家庭。在他的血液中，流淌着前辈人朴实坚韧、低调务实的性格特质。就是这种特质，后来驱动着他走出农村，去探寻自己的梦想，实现和创造自己的人生价值。

童年时代，郭广昌的家里比较贫困，如果用家徒四壁来形容虽然有点夸张，但也不是太过分。家境的清贫，非但没让郭广昌变得自卑而消沉，反而让他养成了自强自立、不屈不挠的个性品质。郭广昌是家里唯一的男孩，他有两个姐姐。郭广昌从小就懂得为父母分忧解难，是一个非常懂事的孩子。他常对母亲说，我是家里的男人，家里的事情就是我的事情，一旦有了什么事情，我来替您扛着。

郭广昌的家境虽然比较贫困，由于父母勤劳肯干，善于持家，家里的三个孩子从没挨过饿。他的父亲是一名石匠，经常跟随乡里集体工程队的大队人马去外地做一些施工项目，挣点小钱来贴补家里。他的母亲是生产队的一名菜农，会栽种、侍弄很多种蔬菜。当回忆起小时候的生活经历时，郭广昌记忆犹新地说："虽然家里比较贫困，到了春天我妈妈偶尔也会出去借粮食，但是她很能干，种了许多红薯什么的，总能想办法让我们吃饱。也许是小时候的红薯吃多了，直到今天，我一闻到红薯的味道就会反胃。"

郭广昌的父母非常明白教育能够改变一个人命运的道理，即使家庭条件很艰苦，也会尽量想办法供孩子们读书。当时，作为农民的孩子，要想离开农村，能够出人头地，出路只有两条：一是靠读书；二是当兵或者外出做建筑工人。郭广昌的父母很会激发自己儿子的能动性，把这两条出路摆在了郭广昌的面前，让他自己做出选择。

面对父母给他出的选择题，他深知父母的用心良苦，毅然决然地选择了读书。而他的选择,恰恰符合了父母和两个姐姐的心愿。至此,郭广昌的父母和他的两个姐姐,都满心欢喜地表示一定会支持他的选择。

郭广昌回忆:"那个时候,我们东阳人普遍有重男轻女的思想。这种思想,看似偏向于男孩子,同时也是男孩子的一种压力。也就是说,如果你是一个男孩,家里不需要你烧饭,也不需要你洗衣服,更不需要你干家务,但要求你必须要有出息,要出人头地。因为你是男人,未来你就是这个家庭的支柱。"

郭广昌虽然是家里最晚出生的孩子,但他是家里的独子,因此,郭广昌得到了全家给予的"特殊待遇",是一家人的掌上明珠。一家人的一致愿望就是让郭广昌一心一意读好书,其他的事情都不用管。那时,郭广昌的母亲经常提醒郭广昌:"孩子,你一定要争气,咱家是一个穷人家,只有好好读书,你才能有出息,咱一家人才会有希望。"

而事实上,郭广昌确实没有让父母亲和姐姐们失望,学习成绩一直很好。在读初中期间,由于郭广昌家住农村,离家太远,因此只好住在学校的集体宿舍里。有弊就有利,由于郭广昌在课余没有太多的事情可做,便爱上了读书。那时,学校里有一个小小的图书室,郭广昌经常泡在图书室里,有时一泡甚至长达几个小时,几乎到了痴迷的程度。

读初中时的第一个暑假,郭广昌想像其他同学一样,打着行李卷回到家里,帮助父母做一些力所能及的事情。结果,郭广昌的想法被自己的父母和姐姐们坚决地阻止了。在亲人们的心里,只希望郭广昌能够一心一意地读好书。亲人们对他说:"你把书读好,比你干再多的农活都更让我们高兴。"显然,郭广昌拗不过父母和两个姐姐。感受着父母和两个姐姐对自己的莫大支持,郭广昌在心中默默发誓,长大后一定要成就一番事业,以此来回报家乡和亲人。

有一天，郭广昌在学校的图书室里，意外地读到了海德格尔的《存在与时间》，让他一下子对哲学产生了浓厚的兴趣。而随着阅读量的增加，他对哲学的理解越来越深厚，并变得越来越善于思考，善于提出相应的问题。逻辑思维的基础也开始逐步建立，很快超越了身边多数同龄的孩子。当时，让他最引以为自豪的就是作文课，老师总是请他讲解文章中引用的哲学理论。正是这个原因，郭广昌树立了要成为一名伟大哲学家的理想，立志要干一番大事业。

改读高中，改变一生的决定

人生的道路随时都有可能面临着选择，而往往一个决定就会改变人的一生。中国著名作家柳青在他的长篇小说《创业史》中写道："人生的道路虽然漫长，但紧要处常常只有几步，特别是当人年轻的时候。没有一个人的生活道路是笔直的、没有岔道的。"

1982年春天，即将初中毕业而且成绩优异的郭广昌，在报考时面临着一次足以改变他一生命运的选择：目标是上师范学校，还是上高中？这个在如今看来不需要思考的问题，却让当时的郭广昌以及他的家人纠结万分。

1977年，中国正式恢复了停止十余年的高考制度。当时，所有的大学生毕业后，国家都会统一分配工作，大学成为许多年轻人和莘莘学子改变命运的最佳途径。但那时全国的大学资源和招生名额极其有限，面对数以百万计的考生，"千军万马挤独木桥"的现状无疑是对那个时代学生高考的一种写照。正因为此，当时的某一个农村家庭如果能培养出个大学生，一定会高兴得不得了,放鞭炮、请客吃饭几乎都是必不可少的。

1982 年的时候,初中生是可以报考师范学校的,而且毕业后国家负责统一分配工作。因为家里比较贫困,郭广昌的父母都希望儿子能报考师范学校,3 年后就可以分配工作。而读高中,毕业还要参加高考,前途未卜,工作也是遥遥无期。父母认为,郭广昌读师范学校,不仅早早就锁定了教师这份稳定又受人尊重的工作,能够及早地自食其力,而且师范学校还免收学费,并附带一些额外的补贴,这也相当于直接减轻了家庭的经济负担。

郭广昌迎合了父母的意愿,做出报考师范学校的决定,并以优异的考试成绩,被师范学校录取。成绩发布后,全家人都为之高兴,他的父母更是整日的笑容满面。

成绩公布后,郭广昌的心里却有一种说不出的惆怅。在村里,大家都知道郭广昌是一个孝子,从小就听父母的话,心里更懂得感恩。1993 年,郭广昌创业淘得第一桶金时,他所做的第一件事情,就是在老家东阳市横店镇买了一块地,给父母建起一幢 5 层的楼房,让二老居住。而在当时,在选择报考志愿这件事上,他深知就读师范学校能够实现父母对他一直以来的期待,使自己早日成为一名吃"皇粮"的人,从而缓解家庭贫困的窘境,因此报考了师范学校。可是,谁又能理解怀有"鸿鹄之志"的郭广昌的内心是一种什么样的心情呢?很快,师范学校的录取结果公布了,郭广昌毫无悬念地被金华师范学校录取。对此,他的父母和姐姐都非常高兴,而唯独他自己一点也高兴不起来。

当一名老师教书育人,本是一个既受人尊重又有稳定收入的工作,对于许多农村孩子来说是一件求之不得的事情。可在郭广昌看来,一旦成为一名教师,就有可能要一直在家乡从事这份工作。而他的脑海里,时不时地浮现出在书本中读到的那些伟大人物的形象，这些人物和他们不凡的经历，总是让他热血沸腾，成为他的榜样、他的目标、他的旗帜、他的力量源泉。他甚至想，如果自己是一名老师，也许会教育学生将来也像自己一样当一名老师。师生也许会这样对话：上学为了啥？为了将来当老师。将来当老师为了啥？为了教学生。教学生为了啥？为了让学生将来当老师。

想到这些，郭广昌渐渐地明白了，当一名老师教书育人本身没有任何问题，但他的志向绝不仅仅是教学生读书。这就好比中国现代文学大师鲁迅最初选择的是学医，后来弃医从文一样。中国儒家经典书籍《礼记·大学》中说："身修而后家齐，家齐而后国治，国治而后天下平。"郭广昌觉得，这个世界还有太多太多的知识等着他去认知和探索，他的修身之路还很长，未来也一定有更大的使命在等待着他，他理应在更大的舞台上去做更多的事情，去帮助更多的人。

经过一番思考，郭广昌更加明确了自己的目标。他虽然对父母和姐姐一直支持他专注于读书所付出的一切心存感激，但他的眼界和志向，已经远远超出了他们最初的期望。在这个人生最关键的岔道口上，郭广昌终于做出了这样的选择：放弃读师范学校，改读高中，然后报考大学。

感到时机已经成熟后，郭广昌就把自己的决定当面告诉了父母和姐姐们。为了说服让他们接受自己的决定，郭广昌确实动了一番脑筋。他说：我很想早点参加工作，为家庭撑起一片天，但是，如果我去读师范学校，三年毕业后做一名中学或者小学教师，所挣的工资，也只是能够改善一下家里的生活条件，不会让家里发生太大的变化。接着，他又谈起了自己"修身、齐家、治国、平天下"的理想，列举了许多伟大的人物舍小利、取大利，舍眼前、求长远的例子。结果，他越说越激动，越讲越滔滔不绝。

此时，郭广昌父母的内心也同样是非常矛盾的。他们理解自己孩子的想法，这一点，无疑让他们深感欣慰。是啊，哪个家长不希望自己的儿子有个大出息呢？但另一方面，由于是农家出身和文化知识所限，他们对郭广昌所讲的人物实例和外面的世界知之甚少，有些似懂非懂的感觉。家里一直以来的贫困状况，压得他们有些喘不过气来，总觉得儿子读师范学校是他们能看得清、摸得着的最好出路。

当郭广昌一股脑地把自己的理想和抱负全部吐露出来后，一家人几乎是鸦雀无声。这样的局面僵持了几分钟后，母亲和两位姐姐各自说了一句"我没意见"后，便拿起农具下地干活去了。郭广昌的父亲也站起来，走到儿子身边，轻轻地拍了他两下，然后目光坚定地说：决定走这条路，那就无论如何也要把它走完。今后遇到多大的困难和挫折，我们一家人都会支持你。说完，郭广昌的父亲也干活去了。

父亲的话，一下子打消了郭广昌的顾虑和纠结。在万分感激父亲的理解和支持的同时，他也更坚定了自己的信念。他深知，自己的这次决定，不只事关自己一个人的梦想，也关系着全家人未来的福祉。君子一言，驷马难追，他必须坚定地朝着自己的目标迈进。几天后，郭广昌带着一床被子和十几斤米，到县城的东阳中学报到，正式开启了高中阶段的全新学习生活。

高中时代，文弱书生有主见

唐代著名文学家王勃在《滕王阁序》中写道："穷且益坚，不坠青云之志。"这句话的意思是说，一个人的处境越是艰难，就越是坚韧不拔，越是不丢失高远之志。

1982 年 9 月，郭广昌放弃读师范学校的机会，毅然进入坐落在县城的东阳中学读书，从此，他开始用实际行动，加倍地努力学习，践行着他对全家人的承诺。高中的三年生活，他几乎每天都在重复着相同的学习和生活规律：晨跑——晨读——早饭——上课——午饭——上课——晚饭——晚自习——晚十点就寝。这样的作息规律，每天都不会发生大的变化。

那段高中时光，使郭广昌的意志品质得到了极大的锻炼，从此，他养成了能够沉下心静心做事的习惯。他认为，取得学习成功的关键是要弄清楚自己想要做什么，想要达到什么目的。只有这样，才能有计划、有激情地为之努力，并自我激励。

发奋苦读的精神，不仅让郭广昌的学习成绩优异，还让他能够挤出时间，阅读大量的课外书籍。他在初中时就已经养成了良好的读书习惯，东阳中学的图书室，又成了他充分利用课余时间的理想场所。东阳中学的藏书比他读初中的学校要多得多，书籍的门类也更为广泛。随着阅读的累积和视野的拓展，郭广昌除了一如既往地喜欢哲学方面的书籍外，历史、文学、传记类的书籍也成了他喜爱的读物。通过阅读，他不断开阔眼界，增长见识，看问题的角度、深度和广度都在发生明显的改变，逐步形成了自己独立的世界观、人生观和价值观。当时，身边大多数学生还不十分清楚自己为什么要读书，将来应该做什么，而郭广昌已经有了比较清晰的方向和目标。

读高中时，郭广昌身材比较清瘦，平时他态度温和，言语也不多，看上去一副标准的文弱书生相，可在骨子里，郭广昌非常有主见。在课堂上，一旦到了讨论环节，他就变得能言善辩起来，不仅语言逻辑缜密，而且思维活跃，总是有着与众不同的见解。他不怕被同学们质疑，总喜欢有人与他辩论，这样，他就会把自己平时在阅读中所积累的知识和体会，恰到好处地发挥出来，用以佐证自己的观点。他年纪虽小，却给人一种满腹经纶的感觉。

当时，有一次班级搞活动，活动结束后，班主任老师要求每一名学生都要写一篇总结或感想之类的文章。很快，全班的学生都交上文章，唯独郭广昌没交。当老师把他叫到办公室谈话时，他竟然直言不讳地说："我觉得没必要写这个总结，再说也没什么可总结的，与其凭空说大话、套话，还不如缄默不言。"

郭广昌坦诚直率的话语，让班主任老师很是惊讶。就在那一天，班主任老师与他促膝长谈。他们谈学习，谈人生，谈社会，谈了许多许多。郭广昌觉得，他人生第一次这么酣畅淋漓地表达自己的想法。班主任老师也就此发现了这位平时不显山、不露水的少年，竟有着远远超过同龄人的知识和思想，有些问题甚至比老师想得还透彻。

交谈中，班主任老师问郭广昌平时都读些什么书。郭广昌有些不好意思地说了他近期读的几本书，而这些书，都是有关哲学和历史方面知名的著作。老师听了，感到非常惊讶。老师忽然明白了，原来，郭广昌利用课余时间一直在读书，难怪他能有那么多一针见血的观点，有不同于一般人看问题的视角。

最后，班主任老师又问郭广昌将来想做什么，郭广昌毫不掩饰地说出了自己"修身、齐家、治国、平天下"的人生目标。当这样一个目标从郭广昌的口中说出来时，老师并不觉得他的目标不切实际，反而让他更坚信这个学生的未来一定会有所作为。他鼓励郭广昌要再接再厉，朝着自己的目标迈进。班主任老师还提醒他别因为喜欢阅读耽误了学习功课，一定要通过自己的努力考上重点大学。

不负众望，考取复旦哲学系

高中时代是一个人学习成长的关键时期。初中毕业放弃了读师范学校机会、放弃了提前就业"吃皇粮"机会的郭广昌，毅然决然地选择了读高中，然后报考大学，向着更加高远的目标进发。事实证明，郭广昌的选择是非常正确的。

三年的高中生活，让郭广昌学到了许多，也懂得了许多。这些学到的和懂得的，都极大地丰富了他的精神世界，让他更有信心去赢得未来。他更加明确了做人的目标与准则，懂得了许多做人的道理，懂得了如何处理好与同学之间的关系，让自己变得越来越成熟。他学会了如何独立有效地解决问题。在学习方面，他积累了一套适合自己的学习方法，善于给自己制订学习计划，安排学习时间。在紧张的学习生活中，他总能寻找到其中的快乐。在精神提升方面，他能够恰到好处地与他人沟通交往，对人充满理解和宽容，磨砺出坚强、自信、自尊、爱集体、爱祖国的精神品质。他充满自信，又能坦然地面对失败。高中三年，他无时不在进步，随着成绩的提高，道德品质和身体素质也同时在逐步提高。

三年时间过得很快，郭广昌迎来了高考前的冲刺阶段，并开始填报高考志愿。此时，郭广昌对自己的选择早已胸有成竹，就是不被大多数学生和家长看好的哲学专业。

后来，有许多人直言不讳地问郭广昌为什么要报考哲学专业，他给出的答案是："1985 年前后，改革开放全新的思想观念已经影响到了东阳，我以中学生特有的幼稚和热情开始进行自己的思考。那时，读的较多的文章都是鲁迅先生的。鲁迅说：光有良好的体魄，没有健全的头脑，这也是民族的悲哀。我深深地被那种要启发国民思想的热情所激励，认为改革开放初期的主要问题，也是如何解放国民思想的问题，所以，我在填报大学志愿时，把哲学专业作为自己的第一选择。"

其实，郭广昌高中的最后一年是中国改革开放的一个转折点。1984年，中国改革开放的总设计师邓小平首次亲临深圳特区视察，肯定了在深圳建立经济特区的政策，为中国进一步改革开放奠定了基础。那一年，受此指引和鼓舞而创业的柳传志、王石、张瑞敏等草根企业家，也在后来被称为改革开放后的第一代企业家，被冠以"84派"的美誉。

郭广昌不仅早就选定了报考的专业，同样早就选定了报考的院校。按照郭广昌的学习成绩，他可以报考国内任意一个国家重点院校，但他既没选择北京大学，也没选择清华大学，而是报考了上海复旦大学。毫无疑问，复旦大学是中国最好的大学之一，也是除了坐落在首都北京的北大和清华之外的最好的大学。郭广昌从小就对上海这座国际大都市充满了向往，因为上海聚集了很多优秀的外国人，素有"东方巴黎"之称，是中国经济比较发达、科学技术比较先进、人才资源非常丰厚的城市。正是报考了复旦大学，郭广昌便将自己的命运与"上海"紧紧地捆绑在了一起。

后来的实践证明，郭广昌报考复旦大学的这一选择，比他当初放弃读师范学校而选择读高中更加睿智。在郭广昌看来，上海是一座有着全球化基因的城市，"海纳百川、追求卓越、开明睿智、大气谦和"就是对上海城市精神的高度概括。如果说是故乡东阳横店赐予了他自强不息、坚韧不拔的个性品质，那么，上海作为郭广昌的第二故乡，便是赋予了他远见卓识的大局观和战略观。自从他踏入这座城市，迅速在接下来的不到十年的时间里，成长为中国乃至全球商界的一颗耀眼的明星。

正如人们所预料的那样，在不久之后到来的高考中，郭广昌不负众望，以全班第一的成绩，如愿考取了复旦大学哲学系，给高中三年的寒窗苦读画上了一个圆满的句号。此时，郭广昌依然怀揣着"修身、齐家、治国、平天下"的伟大理想，他相信大学四年的学习生活，一定会让他的理想插上腾飞的翅膀。

第二章

四年大学，
学业有成下海创业

专注哲学，先悟道而后习术

1985年9月，郭广昌怀着无比憧憬的心情，背着母亲为他准备好的行囊，乘火车来到了上海这座中国最大的城市，成为复旦大学哲学系的一名新生，从而掀开了他人生旅程的崭新一页。

当时，作为曾经的远东金融中心和时尚文化之都，上海虽然没有20世纪30年代的繁华景象，但依然是全国最大的经济中心和老工业基地。

初次来到上海的郭广昌，很快就被"中西合璧"的海派风格的建筑所吸引。面对此起彼伏的楼群，车水马龙的大街，摩肩接踵的人流，郭广昌的心情非常激动，几天都难以平静。他甚至自嘲当时的感觉，就好像是出了国一样，一切都是那么新鲜。

但郭广昌是一个很理性的人，他很快就把心思收拢在学业上。

郭广昌选择就读哲学系，完全是选择了先"悟道"而后"习术"。郭广昌认为，与学习其他专业相比较，哲学专业看似虚无缥缈，哲学知识却存在于生活中的方方面面。哲学除了能让人们迅速看透事物的本质外，还能拓宽视野，提升格局。"视野"是指通过眼睛所能看到的事物，同时也指人的思想和知识领域；"格局"是指人的认知层次。但这条道路走起来并不容易。在"悟道"的过程中，由于事先缺乏一个清晰的目标，可能会让人的思想停留在抽象的意识层面，出现"纸上谈兵"的问题。如果这样，哲学就可能真的变成了"无用之学"。

郭广昌一直清楚地记得他入学时的情景。他到复旦大学报到时，迎接他的并不是什么"欢迎新同学入学"的标语，而是一条"我不入地狱，谁入地狱"的标语口号。显然，这是哲学系师哥师姐们对哲学认识的一种诠释。这条标语虽然看起来有些惊悚，但郭广昌并不觉得特别的惊讶，相反却一下子消除了郭广昌心中的忐忑，因为他觉得自己"找到组织"了，可以全身心地投身到哲学知识的海洋中。从他在初中读到第一本哲学著作时，就喜欢上了哲学，一直梦想着考入大学攻读哲学专业。显然，他已经做好了应对各种困难的心理准备。

后来，郭广昌在回忆入学时的场景时说："当时，这条标语，远比国政系的'欢迎未来的政治活动家'等标语更让我心潮澎湃。于是，我全身心地投入到那种要成为'失败的英雄'的悲壮情绪中，想的也是如何去完成'五四'所未能完成的启蒙任务。所以，在当时的复旦校园里，穿着一身旧军装、三五成群地大谈如何超越马克思的人中，就有一个是我，这也是当时复旦一景。"那时，郭广昌确实把"我不入地狱，谁入地狱"当成了激励自己的警句，让他萌生出学好哲学的责任感。

郭广昌认为，相比于大多数专业来说，哲学研究的是一些虚无且无先验可循的问题，而且没有人知道这些问题在什么时候会有答案，甚至其中的许多问题在几代人的有生之年，都未必能得到解答。这些问题，就好比一个黑洞，你想去一探究竟，但不确定这个洞有没有出口。可这恰恰是哲学的迷人之处。人们不断通过思辨和实验，来揭开未知的谜团，一步步探寻事物的本质。即便是坠入地狱，也将在地狱中得到修炼，成为他所说的"失败的英雄"。

事实上，郭广昌所说的"失败的英雄"，一点儿都不"失败"。哲学研究的过程本身就是一个成长的过程，它既拓宽了人们的视野，也打开了人们的格局。视野是看问题的角度和宽度，格局是看问题的高度和深度。有了角度和宽度、高度和深度，才能在面对问题，尤其是那些之前从未遇到过的问题时，做到先于他人一步透过现象看到本质，从而迅速做出准确的决断。

在钻研哲学的过程中，郭广昌无形搭建了自己的底层思维逻辑。这种底层思维逻辑，让郭广昌在大学期间更注重阅读，更加注重涉猎各个学科领域的知识。在复旦大学的图书馆里，几乎每天都能看到他的影子，每个门类科室里，都留着他的借阅记录。那时，他并不是凭兴致翻阅，而是在相关学科中，总结发现诸多的共通点，许多理论在不同的学科中都存在，只是诠释的方法不同。后来，郭广昌总结说，他大学时代所读的书籍，在某种程度上预示了他今天千亿级体量的产业帝国里，所覆盖的各种看似不那么相关的领域。无论这些领域的产品或客户有多少交集，都至少能在商业逻辑和运营管理上找到相当程度的趋同。

大学四年的哲学修身和与书为伴，让郭广昌对社会、对生活有了更多的涉猎和理解。他说："可能有人说哲学是无用之学，哲学系也的确没有教我学会任何一项基础的技能，但它教会了我思考和学习的方法。正是因为与书为伴，所以我的大学生活特别充实，也让我的内心特别丰富。也正是因为有了广泛阅读的基础，让我有了更多对个人、对社会以及对国家未来的思考。在我当年所涉猎的众多书籍中，对我影响颇为深远的，就是《礼记大学》。书中的许多哲学思想，都成为我后来的立业之本，尤其是那句'修身、齐家、治国、平天下'让我思考了良久。人们常说，大学是一个人的世界观、价值观、人生观建立并确定的时期。我想，作为一个处于改革开放之际的中华男儿，我的未来之路必然任重道远。"

千里骑行，青岛啤酒结情缘

郭广昌进入上海复旦大学就读哲学专业之前，还从来没离开过东阳，到上海是他人生第一次出远门。进入复旦后，郭广昌总是梦想着到上海以外的地方去看一看。

1987 年大二的暑假，郭广昌终于有了离开上海出去转一转的机会。这次机会，就是独自一人去祖国的首都北京做一次调研。实际上，这是他自己创造的机会。这次调研比较特殊，因为他选择的交通工具既不是火车，也不是汽车，而是自行车。郭广昌这一次是独自一人骑行去北京。

从上海启程长途骑行去北京，就算是在道路基础设施比较完善的今天，也依然是一次不小的挑战。当时，郭广昌骑着自行车去北京做调研，并非为了挑战自我，也不是为了健身，他这么做的原因很简单，就是手头没钱买车票。他觉得，单程几十块的火车票太贵，与其把钱花在买车票上，还不如用这些钱买辆自行车，然后一路骑过去，不仅可以欣赏到了沿路许许多多的风景，还能得到一辆自行车。

20 世纪 80 年代的中国，一户人家如果有一辆自行车，是一件脸面上非常有光的事情。在大学的校园里，一名男生能够骑着自行车载着一名女生，穿梭在林荫小道上，会吸引许多羡慕甚至嫉妒的目光。能够拥有一辆属于自己的自行车是许许多多在校大学生的梦想，郭广昌也毫不例外。幸运的是，他骑行去北京做调研的想法得到一位好友母亲的大力支持，这位母亲慷慨地借给郭广昌 200 块钱。就这样，郭广昌拥有了人生的第一辆自行车。郭广昌后来回忆说："买下自行车的那一刻，我的内心比后来买一辆法拉利要高兴得多，并骄傲地宣称：'古有赤兔千里走单骑，今有自行车陪我行万里'。"

有了自行车后,郭广昌给自己精心设定了一条骑行路线,就是沿着大名鼎鼎的京杭大运河一路前行。这条全长 1,794 公里的人工运河,是世界上开凿最早、长度最长的一条人工河道,长为苏伊士运河的 9 倍,巴拿马运河的 22 倍,其自身价值堪比长城。京杭大运河作为中国古代联系南北的水运要道,北起北京通州,南至浙江杭州,途经六个省市,在茫茫 2,500 多年历史的长河中,见证了一个又一个王朝的更迭兴衰。小时候,郭广昌在书中读到过这条充满故事的京杭运河。借这次进京的机会,他一定要亲眼看一看这一千年历史文化遗产的真实容颜。

就这样,郭广昌骑着自己的自行车,踏上了长达 1,000 多公里的北上征程。他边骑行,边欣赏着沿途的美丽风光。每经过一个城市,他就停下来看一看,并主动热情地与当地老百姓聊天,了解他们的生活情况,体会他们的内在心情。他还不时地拿出日记本和钢笔,记录所获得的相关信息,也记录下自己的内心感想。看到眼前斑驳的河岸和古老的石桥,郭广昌的脑海中总能浮现出一幅幅在书中所读到的历史画面,让他感慨时代的变迁,感慨个人在历史的长河里不过是沧海一粟。

骑行了整整 20 天后,郭广昌带着厚厚的考察笔记,终于抵达了京杭大运河的终点——北京通州。20 天的旅途劳顿,郭广昌已经是相当疲惫了。他的皮肤已经晒得黝黑,小腿和大腿无处不在酸痛。但回想这一路上所看到的、听到的和学到的东西,他觉得实在是不虚此行。

郭广昌稍事休息后,又骑着自行车前往八达岭长城,兴致勃勃地与万里长城进行了一次亲密的接触,领略了"不到长城非好汉"的恢宏气魄。

完成了北京的调研任务后,郭广昌在返程之前把自行车卖了,变成了返回上海的旅资。在回程的路上，他感觉自己腰包里的钱还比较充裕，而且从青岛坐船回上海比坐火车便宜，就特意绕道去了青岛。到了青岛后，郭广昌所做的第一件事就是买了回上海的船票。买完票剩下的钱只够郭广昌吃一顿饭。郭广昌觉得，既然自己已经来了，就一定要不枉此行，尝一尝有名的青岛啤酒。于是，郭广昌来到青岛码头的一个小卖部里，寻找目标。

青岛啤酒创办于1903年，后来发展成为享誉全球的中国名牌啤酒。20世纪80年代，由于物资短缺，啤酒都是凭票供应的。在上海复旦大学，能和同学们分着喝一瓶光明牌啤酒，就足以让郭广昌的内心非常高兴。这一次他来到了啤酒之乡青岛，大名鼎鼎的青岛啤酒就在自己的眼前，他下定决心无论如何也要奢侈一回。于是，他用剩下的钱买了一瓶青岛啤酒，在码头度过了一晚。他美美地喝着那瓶啤酒，心里想，如果以后能够天天喝上这么好喝的青岛啤酒，那可真是太爽了。

郭广昌的这个愿望，不仅在几年后就得到了实现，而且令人意想不到的是，2018年，他所创建的复星，一举收购了日本朝日集团所拥有的青岛啤酒17.99%的股权，一跃成为青岛啤酒的第二大股东。为了纪念这一历史性的收购，青岛啤酒专门定制了一款名为"鸿运当头，复星高照"的红瓶包装啤酒。后来，这款啤酒成了复星招待宾客的专用啤酒。

如今，提起那一次北京骑行以及喝青岛啤酒的故事，郭广昌依然感慨万千。他说："30多年过去了，我每次到海外出差，总要在当地找一家中餐厅犒劳一下自己。期间，毫无例外地，青岛啤酒总是必点的佐餐酒水，因为海外的每家中餐厅，都供应着来自中国的青岛啤酒。30多年的潮起潮落，很多让国人充满记忆的品牌遗憾地消失了，但是，青岛啤酒品牌依旧充满活力，成为大家随时都能喝到的饮品，这是我20岁那年骑行来青岛时所绝对无法想象的。"

显然,20 岁的那一瓶青岛啤酒,让郭广昌与青岛啤酒结下了不解之缘。

奔赴海南,寻找希望的土地

时光暂且穿越到 30 年后。

2018 年 1 月 21 日,海南日报报业集团与复星携手,在三亚举行签约仪式,宣布共同启动"我与海南·30 年·30 人"海南建省办经济特区 30 周年大型主题活动。海南日报党委书记、社长、总编辑郭志民,复星国际董事长郭广昌,三亚市副市长许振凌等出席签约启动仪式。海南日报报业集团与复星共同主办此次主题活动,目的就是通过寻访 30 年来与海南大特区命运息息相关或有着不解之缘的各界代表人物,讲述他们闯海创业、追逐梦想、见证奇迹的动人故事,解码他们通往成功之路上的独特特区基因,挖掘他们投身改革浪潮,敢闯敢试、敢想敢干、敢为人先的"特区精神",为海南建省办经济特区 30 周年献礼,为海南下一个 30 年大改革、大开放、大发展凝聚强大精神力量。这次大型主题活动主要设计了四项内容:30 年 30 人——大型系列人物寻访;中国梦 海南情——"我与海南 30 年"大型作品征集;复星之夜——30 年 30 人发布盛典;30 年 30 人特别主题沙龙。

在主题活动签约仪式上,郭广昌与海南日报报业集团总经理翁朝健深情相拥,让人感到他们之间的关系非同一般。事实也确实如此。30 多年前,他们就相识于复旦大学哲学系,而且是同一个宿舍上下铺的室友。他们能在主题活动签约仪式上再度聚首,他们的心中无不充满了激动和感慨。

1985 年,翁朝健与郭广昌同时考入复旦大学哲学系。翁朝健是海南省文昌市人,进入复旦后,同学们都亲切地叫他"阿健"。大学四年,郭广昌一直睡在翁朝健的上铺。那时,他们常常从老庄、程朱聊到王阳明;从尼采、康德、萨特聊到马克思、恩格斯……他们还聊到中日围棋擂台赛聂卫平横扫日本"超一流",聊到中国女排豪取"五连冠",聊到1986世界杯马拉多纳的"上帝之手"……显然,他们是无话不说的好兄弟。

1988年的夏天,郭广昌做了一个比上一年暑假去北京更疯狂的决定,就是骑着自行车去海南。那一年,海南正式被中央批准建省办经济特区,吸引了10万之众怀揣着梦想的有志青年,从全国各地聚集到海南,希望在这里打拼出一片新天地。

得知海南建立经济特区的这一消息,郭广昌心潮澎湃,热血沸腾。于是,他倡议并发起了一次骑行去海南的活动。这一次,他与12名复旦大学的同学,拿着上海永久牌自行车厂赞助的3,000块钱和复旦大学团委的一封介绍信,每人骑着一辆自行车从上海出发,沿着东南的海岸线一路南下。郭广昌一行途经中国改革开放最早设立的四个经济特区——厦门、汕头、深圳、珠海,最终目标是海南经济特区。他们一边骑行、一边调研,行程达3,000多公里。

到达海南后,郭广昌一下子被眼前的景象惊呆了。尽管这里的基础设施还不发达,整个海口也只有一个红绿灯,但他依然用"燃情岁月"四个字来描述当时的画面。他后来回忆说:"那时,海南四处热火朝天,10万人才下海南,'闯海墙'前日日都是人头攒动,其中很多都是大学生。他们找不到工作,就在街上卖馄饨,在椰子树下摆地摊。可即便是卖椰子,他们的脸上也都充满着对未来的期望,那一张张朝气蓬勃的脸让我印象太深刻了……"

应该说,1988年的海南之行,郭广昌很大的成分是出于好奇,是一个年轻人的一种探奇。但海南改革开放所迸发出来的勃勃朝气,深深地吸引了郭广昌。在海南的所见所闻,对他形成了巨大的冲击,让他对经济特区有了全新的认识。

这一次在海南的生活虽然比较短暂,却给郭广昌留下了深刻的印象,对这片开放的土地也有了不一样的感情。到了大四那年的春节,郭广昌没有回家,又一次跑到海南,在同学翁朝健的家里过年。这一年,他第一次吃到了海南的特色美食——文昌鸡。翁朝健一家人热情款待让郭广昌体会到了海南人的好客淳朴,他因此对这片土地充满了好感,爱上了这片土地。他在内心由衷地立下誓言:"如果有一天能够为海南做点什么,我一定会出力。我相信有一天条件成熟,这颗种子一定会发芽。"

1989 年毕业前夕,郭广昌在给翁朝健的毕业纪念册上,深情地写下了这样一段话:"阿健,一生中真正值得回味的美好记忆不多,对我来说那个寒假你一家的热情,文昌鸡的风味,还有白云、蓝天、椰林组成的南岛风光,是我永远难忘的。当我踏上归程时,我心里默念着:总有一天我会再来寻找一片属于我的土地!"

当时,在许多人看来,郭广昌能够写出这样的话,或许只是一种年少的轻狂。但实际上,郭广昌确实从来都没有忘记这段给翁朝健的留言。因此,他在创业成功后,多次来到海南进行考察,并一步步在海南展开发展的布局。2007 年,复星投资海南矿业并帮助它成功上市。2007 年 8 月 15 日,复星设立了海南省复星光彩教育奖励基金,专门用于奖励当地品学兼优的高中生。这个奖励基金设立 10 多年来,已经有 4,800 多人次的海南学生因此受益。2016 年,复星投资兴建的地中海俱乐部三亚度假村顺利开业。2018 年4 月,复星投资 100 多亿元、历时 6 年打造的一站式旅游休闲度假综合体项目——三亚·亚特兰蒂斯正式开业。这是一个海南旅游 3.0 标杆项目，共拥有 1,314 间客房，还拥有亚洲最大的水族缸、精彩绝伦的水上乐园与海豚湾剧场。在盛大的开业仪式上，郭广昌在发言过程中几度哽咽，他非常感慨 30 年前埋下的为海南做点事的种子，到今天，不仅生根发芽，还长成了参天大树。这其中凝聚了太多人的心血和爱心，而郭广昌也是期待了太久。

如今，有很多人都会好奇地问郭广昌：为什么对海南的发展预判得那么准？对此，郭广昌饶有兴致地回答说："13 亿中国人，只有一个海南，一个三亚，怎能不倍加珍惜？分享大家一个健康的秘诀，不要一直待在工作的地方，来三亚度个假吧！"

辞去工作，下海从商创新业

1989 年，郭广昌凭借着在校期间的优秀表现，毕业时获得了留在复旦大学工作的机会，成为复旦大学团委的一名老师。对于许许多多的应届毕业生来说，留校任教是一件求之不得的事情。以这样的方式毕业，不仅让郭广昌彻底走出了农村，留在了上海这座中国最大的城市，还获得了一份令人羡慕的稳定又体面的工作。尤其是对于他远在东阳农村的家庭来说，这已经远远超出了入学时的预期。

后来，在复旦大学团委工作期间中，郭广昌结识了比他小两届、同样也是留校任教的梁信军。正是这样的结缘，让梁信军成为与郭广昌一同创立复星的联合创始人之一。梁信军家乡在浙江台州，是一名地地道道的"学霸"级人物。1987 年，他以台州市高考理科状元的身份，被录取分数线极高的复旦大学遗传工程系录取。入学后，他学业成绩依然非常优异，年年都会拿到学校的最高奖学金。

梁信军留校后，与郭广昌很快成了工作上的好伙伴，生活中的好朋友。他们之间，既是棋逢对手，又是英雄相惜。那段时间，他们一起带着学生，做了不少社会实践和市场调查活动，以此来开阔学生的视野，活跃学生的思维。当时，中国的改革开放刚刚过去10年，各行各业发生了翻天覆地的变化。他们的所见所闻，让他们逐步意识到学校只是一个教书育人的地方，要想干出一番大事业，就必须走出这个相对的舒适区，到改革开放的最前线。在相互的交流之中，两个人都产生了一种"空有一身本领，却无用武之地"的感受。

为此，郭广昌还一度萌生了出国留学的念头，目标是美国。但到美国去学习什么呢？是继续攻读哲学？还是和当时许多出国的人一样，假留学之名，实为打工赚钱？做好了去美国的一切准备后，郭广昌最终冷静下来，打消了出国留学的想法。

众所周知，中国两千多年的封建专制文化，使"官本位"这种思想意识深入中国社会的各个层面。"官本位"是一种"以官为本、以官为贵、以官为尊"为主要内容的价值观。为此，走仕途成为知识分子的最好选择，而经商是让人看不起的，属于走投无路的选择，尤其弃官从商，更是让人难以理解。

1992年的春天，邓小平的南方谈话，以其"东方风来满眼春"的强大力量彻底改变了郭广昌的人生轨迹。在1992年以前，中国改革开放虽然取得了不小的成绩，但关于姓"资"还是姓"社"的意识形态之争，始终"你方唱罢我登场"，热热闹闹地进行着，导致改革开放总是不够坚决、放不开手脚。邓小平的南方谈话，完全打开了这一思想桎梏，中国从此不再空谈意识形态，树立了发展才是硬道理的理念。

邓小平在讲话中明确提出："非公有制经济是社会主义市场经济的重要组成部分。"这句话，不仅给中国的民营企业正了名，也让郭广昌和梁信军二人做出了"下海从商"的决定。正是在邓小平南方谈话的激励下，二人经过短期筹划，从各自名字中分别取一字，在上海市工商局注册成立了"广信科技发展有限公司"，主打业务就是市场调查和咨询，注册资金仅仅 3.8 万元。

当时，他们放弃复旦大学教师的工作，自己白手起家进行创业，这是大多数人无法理解的行为。为此，他们起初没有将这一决定告诉家人，而是悄悄地做起来再进行公开。梁信军后来回忆说："尽管家人知道后还是比较理解和支持的，但自己的社会地位明显下降。在碰到熟人时，常有人说他'小梁，你变了，你变成商人了，变得唯利是图了'。"如今，中国已经形成了尊重企业家、鼓励创新创业的社会氛围，这与改革开放所带来的中国经济腾飞和老百姓生活水平的提高是分不开的。

选择"下海从商"这条道路后，郭广昌终于从"形而上"的空中楼阁，降落到"形而下"的广袤平原，有了脚踏实地的感觉。留校任教后，眼看离"齐家"的目标已经不远，可郭广昌却主动选择了回到起点，修身的地点变成了社会这所大学。在郭广昌的眼里，商业一定能造福社会，改变社会，让人们的生活更美好。有了这样的理念，他便把当初"修身、齐家、治国、平天下"的九字理想，改成了"修身、齐家、立业、助天下"。

广信科技咨询公司诞生后，郭广昌在公开信中说，我和信军等几个人创办了一家小企业，叫作"广信"。名字还不错，也很好懂，"广"是我，"信"就是信军。1993 年，郭广昌依靠帮助元祖食品做调查报告这个项目挖到第一桶金,成功赚到了30万元。随后,他们又陆续接下了太阳神等项目,很快就赚到了100万元。

1995年,郭广昌将广信更名为复星。随着汪群斌和范伟的加盟,当时处于起步阶段的房地产行业和生物医药行业,先后成了郭广昌创业发展的新选择。

作为"92派"(邓小平的南方谈话后成长起来的一批企业家)的代表人物,郭广昌一直以"如履薄冰、如临深渊、战战兢兢、兢兢业业"的心态不懈地努力着。但事实上,郭广昌在财富之路上走得并不孤独。复星创建初期,郭广昌与和他一同创业的梁信军、汪群斌、范伟和谈剑4人,并称为"复星5人组",甚至还被称为"复旦5虎",因为这5个人都是复旦校友。为此,梁信军说:"我们5个人就像5根手指,哪一根也少不得。5根手指攥紧,就是一只拳头。而且,我们几个人除了在学校建立起了良好的关系外,浙商的精神也在我们几个人身上有所体现,而由这种共同的文化演绎而成的企业文化,则是我们5个人同心的最大基础。"

第三章

复星起航，
开启创业崭新时代

出师顺利，首次投标成赢家

人生拥有无数个第一次，郭广昌也是如此。如今的郭广昌虽然身居富豪之列，但他始终保持着谦虚谨慎的儒商本色。在许许多多的场合，郭广昌总是谦虚地说："我们复星还是一个小公司。"这种谦虚的背后，是这家原始注册资本仅有 3.8 万元的广信科技发展有限公司，一次次地取得了用小资金换取大资产的传奇业绩。

广信科技成立之初，就带着比较锐利的开路先锋色彩。在复旦大学工作的几年间，郭广昌经常带着学生做假期调查。期间，专业的社会统计方法加上实践经验的积累，为广信科技的诞生打下了一定基础。广信科技成立时，全国同类咨询公司不超过 10 家，而上海就有 4 家。作为行业排头兵，广信科技以敏锐的目光，迅速占领了上海的咨询市场。而随着越来越多的企业进驻上海，对上海的需求调查无疑为广信科技的立足提供了机遇。

然而，创业的过程是非常艰难的。郭广昌骑着一辆自行车跑业务，这一标志性的作风，后来被众多的创业同盟者津津乐道。那时，广信科技确实是个小得不能再小的公司。一间不足 15 平方米的小平房里，摆着公司最贵重的家当——一台 586 计算机。而公司跑业务的"公车"，就是郭广昌经常骑着的那辆 28 式大横梁自行车。

面对艰苦的创业条件，郭广昌没有丝毫的退缩。其实，他在离开复旦大学时，就已经下定了决心："只要选择了就不能后退，后退是懦夫才做的事。我郭广昌是顶天立地的男人，我要用自己的智慧开创未来。"在这种信念的支撑下，郭广昌每天骑着那辆自行车，不停地穿行在上海的大街小巷。汗水从他的额上流下，流进他的眼中，甚至模糊他的视线，可他的心却一直是清新明亮的。

通俗讲，市场调查和咨询这个行业，就是古时候行军打仗时的军师角色。20世纪90年代初的中国，做这一行的人并不多，正因为是冷门，郭广昌才选择在这个行业开始创业。他说："创业要选择新的行业，老行业不需要创业，而是需要创新，但创业也不能选择太新的东西，领先半步是先锋，领先一步就有可能成为先烈了。"

1993年，刚刚进入上海市场的台湾元祖食品公司，正在谋求进一步的多元化发展，急需一家专业化的咨询公司为他们出谋划策。为此，元祖公司发布了一个寻求咨询的招标公告，并期待能得到一个满意的招标结果。

看到元祖公司寻求咨询的招标公告后，郭广昌的心情非常激动。在他的心里，一直在寻找着这样的一个机会。他骑着自行车立即赶回公司，把招标公告这个消息告诉了几位同仁。几个人听了，都显得异常兴奋。大家马上行动起来，共同准备公司的资质材料。很快，郭广昌就带着材料到元祖公司报名竞标。

在元祖公司的招标办公室里，已经有三家咨询公司先于广信科技通过了资质审查。看到这一阵势，作为广信科技的法定代表人，郭广昌的心里有些紧张。他强迫自己镇静下来，把公司的资格证明和相关经营材料，递交给了元祖公司负责审查的工作人员。他一直表现得小心翼翼，因为这个机会对他、对公司来说，都太重要了。元祖公司的工作人员接过材料，粗略地扫了一眼，就放到了一边。与另外三家公司递交的材料相比，广信科技的材料只有几页，没有优势可言。因此，郭广昌在心里一遍遍地劝慰自己："不要太紧张，也不要看得太重。"

郭广昌虽然在心里劝慰自己，但实际上却掩盖不了期盼的心情。他甚至在走出办公室的门口时,脚竟然绊到了门槛,一个趔趄差点摔倒,是身后的梁信军伸手把他扶住。

值得庆幸的是,两天后,元祖公司的电话打到了广信科技的办公室,告知广信科技通过了资质审查,可以准备相应的材料参加竞标。接完电话,郭广昌和梁信军都激动不已。郭广昌很快有一种预感,这个机会一定属于广信科技。想到这个,他的心脏一阵剧烈的跳动。

公开竞标的那一天,天气非常炎热。郭广昌和梁信军带着公司另外两名工作人员一起来到了元祖公司的会议室。元祖公司的市场部负责人现场发给他们一些元祖公司的背景、发展规划等资料,然后简单说明了此次招标的目的,要求广信科技在20分钟之内,阐述对元祖公司项目的理解和开展调查的方法。

在广信科技之前,已经有两家咨询公司遭到淘汰。元祖公司市场部负责人陈述完毕后,郭广昌和梁信军耳语了几句,便从包里拿出一摞纸来。这些纸上,是广信科技为元祖公司制定的市场调查计划,包括对象抽取、样本采集、调查方法、调查周期等,都做了详细的说明。郭广昌随即把这份市场调查计划书提交给对方,然后言简意赅地做了介绍和说明。

郭广昌介绍自己和梁信军的基本情况以及广信科技的由来,他们放弃稳定体面的复旦大学老师的工作而出来创业的魄力,让元祖公司的人刮目相看。尤其是他们所展示的调查计划很有见地。交谈中,元祖公司的市场负责人发现,眼前这两个年轻人不仅见识广博、思路清晰,而且对中国的发展现状有着相当深刻的见解。最后,元祖公司认为,很值得给这两位有志青年一次机会。20分钟后,元祖公司当场宣布,与广信科技展开合作。

成功中标后,郭广昌的心情马上平静下来。他意识到,中标只是一个起点，接下来必须脚踏实地地开展工作，确保对方满意。

广信咨询，收入首超一百万

广信科技与元祖公司签订了合作协议后，郭广昌带领公司员工随即投入到紧张的工作之中。他身先士卒，事必躬亲，从设计调查问卷，到走上街头发放调查问卷、开展现场访谈、收集调查问卷，每个细节都做到尽职尽责。在设计调查问卷的过程中，郭广昌与梁信军一起亲自拟定调查问题，其他相关人员负责归类分析元祖公司之前的运营模式和销售业绩。在郭广昌看来，调查问卷的问题不能太多，太多了，被调查者就不会有耐心逐一认真答完。元祖公司做这个市场调查目的是尽可能全面了解上海的食品饮料市场。如何既能将市场了解得全面一些，又不让被调查者感到不耐烦，是摆在郭广昌面前的一个实实在在的课题。

这一次能够中标为元祖公司做市场调查，让郭广昌懂得了什么是活学活用和现学现用。在整个学生时代尤其是大学时代所历练出来的超强学习能力和领悟能力，让他总能快速地理解和掌握一门新知识，并快速运用到自己的工作中。郭广昌所具备的这种素质，就是新兴人才的一大特点。在他看来，没有强大的学习能力，就无法跟上瞬息万变的时代发展步伐。

当签约后的第6个工作日结束时，调查问卷的制定提前完成。这个问卷每个问题都非常巧妙地涉及消费者在购买食品时所关注的购买点，并结合了元祖公司关心的需求比例和问卷的趣味性。不仅内容全面而丰富，整个问卷只设计了10个问题。这样，在发放问卷时，可现场与被调查者进行访谈，从而掌握第一手调查资料，确保得到全面准确的分析结果。

发放调查问卷的第一天早上 7 点，人们才刚刚起床准备吃早餐时，郭广昌就已经站在了上海鲁迅公园门口，对过往的行人进行书面和口头调查。他对过此路段的每一个人，都进行耐心友好地询问，并做出相关解释。郭广昌脸上的笑容让每一位被调查者都觉得非常轻松，没有不耐烦的感觉，一些人还主动地问郭广昌一些问题。在与这些被调查者的交谈之中，郭广昌得到了许多启发，获得了许多新的想法。

郭广昌从早上 7 点一直忙到天黑，中午只吃了一块面包，喝了一瓶水。他这种忘我的工作精神，深深地感染着公司的其他员工。傍晚收工统计后，当天郭广昌足足发放了 1 万份调查问卷，相当于每个小时发出了七八百份。

收工后，郭广昌甚至顾不上吃饭，开始兴奋地翻看收回来的调查问卷，脸上难掩内心的喜悦，心里充满了对被调查者的感激之情。翻看着一份又一份填写整齐的调查问卷，郭广昌不禁萌生了一个新的想法。

第二天，郭广昌按照自己的计划早早上了街。他事先买了许多小礼品，把准备好的一张桌子摆在一个临街的路口，而不是鲁迅公园门口。桌子上放着一块告示牌，牌子上面写着："填问卷送礼品。"这一招，吸引了更多好奇的行人驻足询问，行人们填问卷的积极性一下子被调动起来。仅仅半天时间，他所准备的礼品就全部发完了，而 1 万份调查问卷也几乎填完了。

正当郭广昌沉浸在胜利的喜悦中，3 名治安巡逻员走到他的面前。他们二话没说，把属于郭广昌的所有东西都装上了巡逻车。郭广昌一看急了，因为桌子不要紧，可那已经填好的近 1 万份问卷是无价之宝，便立即上前与治安巡逻员进行沟通。对方看他戴着眼镜，是个知识分子的形象，就让他跟他们走一趟，然后再返还调查问卷。

与治安巡逻员来到街道治安管理办公室后，对方对郭广昌说，现在是市场经济了，各种经济模式都在兴起，只要大家不触犯法律不违反规定，都是国家鼓励的。但发放问卷这种活动，应该和街道管理处打声招呼，不然，大批人群密集在闹市区，既不便于管理，也不安全。

郭广昌连连道歉，并保证下一次做调查，一定先办理申请审批手续。郭广昌的态度，赢得了治安巡逻员的同情和理解，很快把调查问卷还给了他。拿着两袋子调查问卷，郭广昌第一次尝到了失而复得的滋味。

郭广昌离开时，有一名治安巡逻员很关切地对他说："我看你也是个读书人，怎么不好好在办公室里待着，跑到大街上干这种粗活来了？"在这位治安巡逻员看来，读书人就应该安分地待在办公室里，过安稳的日子，不应该跑到外面来受苦遭罪。就是这句话，让郭广昌一辈子都记忆犹新。

当天晚上，郭广昌又投入到问卷的整理之中。那些回收的问卷以及通过聊天得来的信息，充分地体现了一种市场发展趋势，就是具有本地特色的产品，经过精加工，必将受到人们的极大欢迎，而来自全国各地的食品通过精加工后，达到精细化，这也将受到人们的欢迎。

一个月后，郭广昌和他的团队按照合同的约定，为元祖公司按期做出了一份详细全面的调查报告。报告重点提出了三条建议：一、传统的月饼太大，大多数人一次吃不完，建议可以做小；二、在豆沙、五仁等传统口味之外开发新的口味；三、月饼的食用价值正逐渐被送礼价值取代，可以将月饼的包装设计得更华丽，让送礼更体面。总之，随着人们生活水平的提高，新时代的月饼既要好吃，又要有"面子"。

令人意想不到的是，这份调查报告所采取的调查方式和使用的专业术语，都让元祖公司大加赞赏。尤其是当这份资料翔实、分析独到的调查报告送到元祖公司老总面前时，老总给予了极高的评价，并当即决定，在原有合同数额的基础上，追加两万元调研费，作为对广信科技发展有限公司的一种认同。

在郭广昌的心里，元祖公司老总主动追加的那两万元，其自身价值，甚至超过了合同所约定的 28 万元全款。在他看来，那两万元是对广信科技这个品牌的认可与信赖。

正是因为郭广昌和公司所有员工树立了诚信、优质的服务品牌，广信科技的业务开始繁忙起来，包括太阳神、乐凯胶卷、天使冰王等许多国内知名品牌商，纷纷找上门来，展开相应的合作。到 1993 年年底，广信科技发展有限公司的业务收入一举突破了 100 万元大关，这 100 万元，来之容易，也来之不易。

房产销售，营收再超一千万

1993 年年底，当广信科技的业务收入首次超过 100 万元时，无论是郭广昌，还是广信科技，都已经让人刮目相看。那时的 100 万元，是现在的 100 万元所无法比拟的。

就在广信科技做得风生水起的时候，郭广昌却突然宣布广信科技退出市场调查和咨询行业，去另寻出路。郭广昌说："当门庭若市的时候，差不多也就是门可罗雀的时候了。"

事实也确实如此。市场调查和咨询行业在经过两年多的无限风光之后，随着越来越多同行公司的加入，获得利益的空间越来越小。后来，业界高度评价郭广昌当初选择退出咨询行业是多么的远见卓识。

当初在复旦大学教师岗位上选择下海从商，郭广昌曾立下了这样一句誓言："只有懦夫才后退，我绝不后退。"也就是从那时起，郭广昌这个看上去并不十分健壮的男子汉，在商海中始终扮演着开路先锋的角色。从开展市场调查和咨询业务开始，郭广昌的每一次进入和退出，无疑都在走别人没有走过的路。

随着广信科技越做越大，后来被称为"复星五人组"的其余三位——汪群斌、范伟、谈剑，也先后加入广信科技的创业队伍中来。汪群斌、范伟二人与梁信军是同届同学，均毕业于复旦大学遗传工程系；而谈剑则是"复星五剑客"中唯一的女生，1993年毕业于复旦大学计算机科学系。由于他们五个人均是复旦大学的学子，"广信"正式更名为"复星"，所取的就是"复旦之星"的意思。

公司"添人进口"并更改名称后，公司的综合实力得到增强，开始在业务上主打医药牌，并开始涉足房地产。没多久，郭广昌摇身一变，成为上海首批房地产开发商之一。

起初，复星做的是房地产销售。那时，中国的房地产行业还没有市场化，与后来火爆的房地产市场根本无法相提并论。全国住房状况大致分为三个体系：一是福利分房，就是单位所建房屋以福利的方式无偿分配给职工居住；二是内销商品房，就是由政府下属的城建公司建设，土地免费，面向当地企业和居民，售价较低；三是外销商品房，就是由国内外的房地产公司开发建设，土地由批租获得，面向华侨、外籍人士和港澳台人士，价格较高，但档次也明显高很多。

复星接手的第一个楼盘是一个滞销楼盘，房屋根本卖不动。当时，人们的工资水平较低，大家都指望福利分房或是购买低价的内销房，因此形成了福利分房和内销房长期供给不足。而外销房不仅价格高，还要限定购房者的身份，因此出现了库存积压的问题。郭广昌所接手的第一个楼盘，就是这种外销房。由于房地产销售的工作本身不需要资本注入，提成又比较可观，是个典型的"空手套白狼"行为。

接手了滞销的楼盘后，郭广昌制定了针对楼盘特点的广告宣传方案，然后重装上阵，展开了强大的销售攻势。结果，强大的广告宣传取得了奇效，那个滞销的楼盘不久就宣告售罄。销售滞销楼盘这件事，让郭广昌对政策和市场有了一个全新的认识。

房地产销售的关键一环就是寻找买家，寻找客户。郭广昌觉得，能够买房的客户，应该具备两个基本条件：一是收入较高；二是有比较强烈的住房需求。具备这两个条件的客户，应该是有"海归"背景的高收入群体。可这样的客户上哪儿去找呢？如果上报纸登广告，不仅价格贵，而且看报纸的读者也不是目标客户，势必造成无效投放。

就在这时，梁信军给郭广昌提了一个超级建议。他说："顺藤摸瓜呗！每个出国留学的人都记录在案的，应该能查到。"好一个"顺藤摸瓜"，这其中的含义也许只有郭广昌了然于心。当年，他萌生出国留学的念头时，需要排队办签证，没人能跳过这一步。

第二天，郭广昌和梁信军通过相关部门，几经周折在老同学介绍下顺利地得到了资料。

回来后，郭广昌把楼盘资料和配套设施以及售后服务等具体情况，制作成简洁明了的宣传册。然后带领公司所有的员工，按照获得资料上的登记地址，兵分五路，各自分别负责一个片区，将宣传册分发到有留学生的家庭。

这一办法，果然收到立竿见影的效果。原本滞销的楼盘，逐渐开始门

41

庭若市起来。正是因为给这个楼盘做代理，1994年年底，复星的营业收入首次超过1,000万元，开启了企业发展的一个新起点。复星几乎是白手起家，从年收入首次超过100万元，到年收入首次超过1,000万元，仅仅用了不到三年时间。就这样，郭广昌很快从许多人质疑的目光中走了出来。

生物制药1亿元销售不是梦

应该说，从郭广昌决定从商那一刻起，他就从来没有怀疑过自己把握财富的能力，对任何事情的孜孜以求，总会让他的所得大大地超过期望。

郭广昌有着非同寻常的市场嗅觉，一直恪守着"走到市场中去，体验鲜活的市场需求"。了解他的人都知道，他的市场运作手段，如果总结起来看，就是能租的不买、能租的不建，充分利用现成的资源搞经营。遵循这一运营规律，郭广昌带领复星人，在10年间使公司的业绩实现了几何级增长。

1993年，郭广昌抓住机会，为元祖公司做市场调研和咨询赚到了"第一桶金"，并在代理房地产业务中，再次积累了千万元财富。之后，郭广昌没有就此满足，而是将公司几乎所有的积累，都投入到了基因工程检测产品的开发上。那时，国家经济正处在一个复苏期，各行各业都在蓬勃发展。但谁都知道，万事开头难，谁也不知道选择什么项目有发展前景，选择什么项目会面临失败。

可在郭广昌的心里，项目方向已经非常清晰。他认为，现代医药一定是市场竞争的必争之地，现代高科技的主攻方向之一就是生物工程。在公司赚到1,000万元后，郭广昌果断决定把基因工程作为公司下一步的构建主体，将现代生物医药这个科技含量极高、风险也极大的高科产业方向，确定为公司的主攻方向。

其实，同是上海复旦大学遗传工程系毕业的范伟和汪群斌加入复星后，为郭广昌的战略选择提供了技术后台。范伟是典型的学者形象，专注于生物制品的研究，在复旦大学读书时，他就经常泡在实验室里做实验和研究，甚至达到了如痴如醉的程度。

在郭广昌的极力邀请之下，范伟带着自己对生物医药最新的研发技术来到了复星。他不仅给复星带来了技术，还带来了一大批相应的资源。在实验中碰到的一些技术难题，范伟通过学术关系网，群策群力加以解决，从而为复星创造了无形的价值。

郭广昌非常看重范伟的技术专长给公司带来的巨大帮助，他在进行市场推广的过程中，总是半开玩笑地说他自己"一无是处，干着剥削压榨他人的勾当"，以此来表达对范伟等人的一种由衷的敬重。实际上，做市场推广，一点也不比做药品研发轻松。在某种程度上来说，对市场的把握决定着药品研发的方向。

业内人士知道，郭广昌对市场的精确把握，来源于他事必躬亲的实干精神。"走到市场中去，体验鲜活的市场需求"，这是郭广昌拥有独到眼光的基石。中国现代伟大文学家鲁迅说过这样一句话："即使天才，在生下来的时候的第一声啼哭，也和平常的儿童一样，绝不会就是一首好诗。"而在郭广昌的心里，再独到的眼光，都不是一日之间练成的，而是需要经过长期市场的磨炼。

郭广昌对市场的研究把握，既来源于实践，又高于实践。他把高起点、高投入的开发基因工程新药，作为企业发展高科技产业和产品的追求。

除了范伟和汪群斌在生物制药方面具有高超的研发能力外，梁信军也是地地道道的行家里手。梁信军与范伟和汪群斌是同学，都是1987年进入复旦大学的，所学的专业都是遗传工程学，也都比郭广昌低了两届。梁信军与郭广昌作为复星最初的搭档，深知对市场的开拓是公司生存下去的重要基础，因此，梁信军一直在协助郭广昌开拓市场，自己所学的专业知识反而没派上用场。

当郭广昌决定复星向生物工程进军时，梁信军已经和郭广昌一起在市场上摸爬滚打了好多年，显然，丢掉市场去一心一意地做研发，绝不是明智之举。更何况此时郭广昌在市场的把握上，已经离不开梁信军这个如左膀右臂的搭档。

1995年，复星的几位研发人员在范伟和汪群斌的带领下，经过半年夜以继日的努力，把研究课题转化成了研究成果，研制出了成品。这一成品，就是后来在复星历史上大名鼎鼎的PCR乙型肝炎诊断试剂。

业内人士知道，乙肝的传染性很强，而且很难根治。传统的检测方法不仅程序繁杂，而且准确度也不够高，病人感到痛苦，医院感到头疼。如果有一种方便快捷的药具能够准确地检测出乙肝，那必将是应用医学的一大进步。

范伟和汪群斌的研究课题就是这种乙肝测试药具。他们在复旦大学学习期间苦练修行，刻苦钻研，反复实验，已经取得了一定的实验基础。但当时因为经费短缺，缺乏进一步的资金支持。正是因为梁信军相邀，促成了这一成果的诞生。在那次聚会之后，郭广昌经过深思熟虑，决定把生物制药作为复星的主攻方向。

随后，郭广昌与范伟进行了一次深谈，最终达成合作共识。范伟和汪群斌以技术入股，郭广昌则把之前公司积累的资金，全部投入乙肝试剂的研制实验。

其实,这无疑是一次超级赌博。如果实验成功了,所得的回报不可限量;如果失败了,所有投资都将付之东流,后果不堪设想。但郭广昌表现得非常淡定,在他看来,大不了重回无产阶级的原始身份,年轻人没有什么输不起的。

郭广昌一手抓 PCR 试剂的研制,一手抓销售网络的建设,做到两手抓,两促进。就这样,复星不惜投入巨资用于建立销售公司,从而确保了他们研制的 PCR 乙型肝炎诊断试剂,很快就在全国以压倒性优势形成销售网络。到 1995 年年底,复星凭借 PCR 试剂的销售,一举取得了 1 亿元的销售额,从而坐上同行业龙头老大的位置,而且为他们留下了一个价值不菲的全国销售网络。

后来,坊间对复星颇为顺利的"造富神话"有诸多猜测,对此,郭广昌回应说:"复星的第一个 100 万是靠咨询赚到的,靠知识赚钱;第一个 1,000 万是搞房地产营销做到的;第一个 1 亿是靠生物制药赚来的;而第一个 10 亿是通过资本与产业相结合达到的,复星发展的轨迹实际上非常清晰,怎么会是神话呢?我觉得,机遇便是你在正确的时间和地点,能够果断地做出决定。"

第四章

夯实基础，
审时度势抢抓机遇

发挥优势，拳头品牌保领先

1992 年，25 岁的郭广昌不仅放弃了出国的机会，而且毅然决然地辞去了在复旦大学任教的职务，拿着从亲戚朋友那里借来的 3.8 万元，开始了全新的创业历程。也许是"皇天不负有心人"，1995 年年底，郭广昌所创建的复星公司，营业收入超过了 1 亿元。

从此，郭广昌和复星的发展便一发而不可收。除了继续在生物制药行业进一步做大做强外，业务还逐步向房地产、钢铁、保险等领域扩展，经营业绩一片飘红，他也由此被外国媒体称为"中国巴菲特"。

在许多人看来，郭广昌具有鹰隼一样敏锐的眼光，具有虎狼一样拼搏求胜的精神，具有猎豹一样灵敏迅猛的执行力。而复星医药作为郭广昌和复星的拳头品牌，处处都体现着郭广昌身上所具有的超乎寻常的企业家精神。

复星医药自 1994 年创建以来，始终专注现代生物医药健康产业，抓住中国医药市场的快速成长、中国企业进军世界主流医药市场的巨大机遇，战略性地覆盖研发制造、分销及终端等医药健康产业链的多个重要环节，形成了以药品研发制造为核心；同时，在医药流通、医疗服务、医学诊断和医疗器械等领域拥有领先的市场地位，在研发创新、市场营销、并购整合、人才建设等方面形成竞争优势的大型专业医药健康产业集团。

1998 年 8 月，复星医药实现了第一次飞跃，在上海证券交易所挂牌上市。从此，复星医药凭借迅猛的发展态势和优异的财务业绩，成为医药领域的领军企业和 A 股市场的明星公司，也是第一批入选沪深 300 指数的公司之一。2017 年 12 月 20 日，复星医药的总市值，从年初的 551 亿元，猛增至 1,066 亿元，成为医药行业 4 家千亿元市值俱乐部成员之一。2018 年，复星医药实现营业收入 249.18 亿元，同比增长 34.45%。其中：药品制造与研发业务实现营业收入 186.81 亿元，同比增长 41.57%；医疗服务业务实现营业收入 25.63 亿元，同比增长 22.72%；医疗器械与医学诊断实现营业收入 36.39 亿元，同比增长 13.22%。

复星医药按照"创新、国际化、整合、智能化"的战略部署，秉承"内生式增长、外延式扩张、整合式发展"的发展模式，围绕未被满足的医疗需求，不断提升产品力、品牌力，持续提高创新能力、服务能力、整合能力以及国际化能力，高效运营，以此来实现长期且较快速度的业绩增长。

复星医药以创新研发为最核心的发展驱动因素，专注投资于疗效确切、符合现代医学发展导向的优势产品的研发领域，坚持提升自身全链条的研发和后期产业化开发能力。2018 年，复星医药研发投入 25.07 亿元，同比增长 63.92%，形成了国际化的研发布局和较强的研发能力，在中国、美国、印度等国家和地区建立了互动一体化的研发体系，并通过多元化合作方式，衔接全球前沿创新技术，推动前沿产品的全球开发和转化落地。公司持续加大包括单克隆抗体生物创新药、生物类似药、小分子创新药等在内的研发投入，积极推进仿制药一致性评价。2018 年，复星医药在制药业务的研发投入达 22.50 亿元，同比增长 76.49%，公司在研新药、仿制药、生物类似药及仿制药一致性评价等项目达 215 项。公司还通过产品合作、市场权益许可的方式，引入多项国内外先进、前沿的产品和技术。与全球领先的 T 细胞免疫治疗产品研发及制造企业——风筝制药（Kite Pharma），共同打造免疫治疗产业平台复星凯特首个产品——FKC876，并获得国家药监局临床试验批准启动临床研究。同时，作为公司科技创新孵化平台的复星领智，在包括创新药研发、可移动便携式医疗影像、基因治疗等多个具有发展潜力的领域，展开战略性布局。

2018年，复星医药在国内实现营业收入190.12亿元，同比增长25.22%；在海外实现营业收入59.06亿元，同比增长76.26%，海外收入占比为23.70%，同比提升5.62个百分点。公司于2017年并购的格兰制药公司（Gland Pharma）运营良好，受益于万古霉素、依诺肝素注射液以及卡泊芬净等核心产品的增长，营业收入同比增长26.62%、净利润同比增长39.92%。

复星医药通过战略性覆盖研发制造、分销及终端等医药健康产业链的多个重要环节，形成了以药品研发制造为核心，同时在医药流通、医疗服务、医学诊断和医疗器械等领域拥有领先的市场地位，在研发创新、市场营销、并购整合、人才建设等方面，形成了健康而强大的竞争优势。

由于复星医药建立了高效的国际化研发团队，从而确保了公司的主要产品在各自细分市场占据着领先地位。在国内市场，复星医药取得了肝病、糖尿病、结核病、临床诊断产品等细分市场的竞争优势；在全球市场，复星医药已成为抗疟药物的领先者。

参与混改，让国企焕发活力

2017年12月1日，郭广昌在出席"2017亚布力中国企业家论坛·天津峰会"发表演讲时说，在过去的20多年间，复星参与了35个国企混改项目，非常看好国企混改对经济发展的推动力，更希望把握住这个时代的机遇，积极参与国企混改。他表示，他们有信心通过这种灵活的机制，为企业深度赋能、价值创造。

郭广昌认为，改革开放的股份制改革，让像复星这样的民营企业如雨后春笋般涌现，而紧随其后的中国资本市场与混合所有制的兴起，则让复星有机会深度参与到改革的进程中，分享并成为中国高速成长的一部分。

郭广昌说："1986 年，改革开放的总设计师邓小平，将一张股票赠予来访的时任美国纽交所主席约翰·范尔霖先生，以表示要将上海打造为国际金融中心的决心。那个时候，我绝对想不到在 12 年后，我们复星会成为上海首家上市的民营企业。当时，IPO（首次公开募股）所实行的是总量控制的审批机制。当上海市政府以及计划委的领导听取了复星的汇报后，对我们这家由大学毕业生创业并进行医药自主开发的公司评价很高。为了支持上海本地科技民营企业的发展，也出于对大学生创业的扶持，上海市政府将一个 IPO（首次公开募股）的资格给了复星。就这样，1998 年 8 月，复星在上海证券交易所正式挂牌上市。在这里，我要再次感谢市政府能把这么好的发展机会留给了我们这几位初出茅庐、创业不过几年的大学生，我们还要感恩上海这座城市给予我们的包容，让我们有机会在这里闯出一片天地。"

复星的成功上市，为公司提供了推进产业高速发展的资本。当时，正逢国企处于大面积亏损、债务重组、去过剩产能的大背景之下，复星上市所融得的资金，让公司有能力参与到国企改制的历史进程中，从而让国企重新焕发活力。2003 年，复星与中国医药集团共同出资，设立了国药控股有限公司，其中，复星出资 5 亿元，占比 49%，中国医药集团总公司则以医药流通业务存量资产的方式出资，占比 51%。这是中国医药商业领域，第一家央企与民营企业联合成立的混合所有制企业。

当时,中国医药集团总公司的医药流通业务,正面临着艰难的运营困境,而复星所看好的,恰恰是全国跨省市的销售网络,与制药业务能够很好地协同起来。

随着复星的出资加入,还将决策机制、市场意识、管理方式、激励机制等更多市场化的管理理念引入到国药控股有限公司,并且成效显著。在随后的几年中,国药控股的销售额几乎年年激增。作为非控股股东,复星给自己的定位是负责任的长期战略股东,用郭广昌的话说,就是既不越位,也不缺位。

2009年,复星还帮助国药控股有限公司在香港成功上市,成为自2000年以来,全球医药行业最大规模的IPO。2018年,国药控股实现营销收入3,445.26亿元,同比增长11.73%。这一数字,对比国药控股成立第一年仅仅80亿元的营销收入,增长了43倍多,国药控股也因此成为中国最大、全球前三的医药分销与供应链服务提供商。

复星所参与的国企混改成功样本,在医药产业有许多,包括重庆药友制药有限公司、江苏万邦生化医药股份有限公司、桂林南药股份有限公司等,都已成为中国医药行业重要的创新引领企业。其中,桂林南药研发生产的青蒿琥酯注射剂是唯一通过世卫组织认证的重症疟疾治疗药物。2007年以来的10多年间,青蒿琥酯注射剂已在非洲挽救了超过2,000万患者的生命。

除了医药之外,复星还通过相似的方式,逐步进入其他产业,如南京南钢钢铁联合有限公司、豫园商城等。2016年,由复星牵头的民营联合体与浙江省人民政府签署协议,以PPP(政府和社会资本合作)方式,共同建造总投资达462亿元的杭绍台城际铁路项目,这是中国首条民营资本控股的城际铁路,让政府、国企和民营企业的资源和优势实现互补。2017年年底，这一项目全线开工建设，总工期4年。这一交通基础设施项目的建设，必将大大提升覆盖地区的城市功能和效率。

郭广昌说，通过紧跟国家产业发展和人民需求升级的脉搏，复星自上市以来，已参与了30多个国企混改项目，从公司治理、战略制定、资本对接、运营管理等多个层面，为合作的国企和央企注入活力，实现多方共赢。通过混合所有制，复星也受益于中国成长的动力，实现了自身产业的迅速扩张，从最初的医药、地产，发展到钢铁、零售、保险等诸多行业，成了一家多元化产业集团。通过对混合所有制企业的改善运营，复星的产业基础逐步夯实，战略眼界逐步放大，为复星的全球化战略打下了基础。

到2019年年初，郭广昌所领导的上海复星高科技（集团）有限公司，直接和间接控股的公司超过了100家，投资范围涉及信息产业、房地产、生物制药、商贸流通、金融、钢铁、证券、银行、汽车等多个领域。复星急剧膨胀的财富，大半来自所并购的企业。而郭广昌给复星的定位，就是要做产业整合者，他说："首先，中国的经济发展现状，使整合成为一种需要；其次，竞争壁垒在降低，中国社会正在走向工业化、城市化、民营化，这一过程，使整合成为一种可能。"

德隆崩塌，得到警示避覆辙

2004年，新疆德隆公司的崩塌给复星上了一堂极其深刻的投资和经营管理课，让复星得到警示，汲取了教训，及时对企业做出比较全面的"体检"，从而保证了企业肌体的健康茁壮。

1992年，唐万新在新疆注册成立了新疆德隆实业公司。随后，唐万新在深圳股市通过认股抽签表的方式发行 5 亿元新股时,花钱雇了几千人在深圳排队领取认购抽签表。三天后,抽签表变成了唐万新口袋里的现金。

1994 年,德隆公司在新疆进行农牧业开发。从此,投资农业成为德隆的一项长期稳定的资金源泉。

一年后,唐万新通过购买法人股的办法控制上市公司,一边在二级市场炒股获利,一边摸索着向实业运营转型。1996 年 10 月,德隆第一次在资本市场公开露面,受让了部分新疆屯河法人股。1997 年,成为屯河集团的第一大股东。

一时间,德隆在股市上可谓呼风唤雨,风光无限。尽管唐万新一直谋求以番茄酱加工生产为核心的"产业整合",并在水泥、汽车零配件、电动工具等领域取得一定成效,但实业始终未能成为德隆的主业。

于是,民间关于德隆是"庄家"的传言越来越热闹。无论是普通投资者,还是媒体都把德隆视为洪水猛兽,对其恨得咬牙切齿。在此期间,唐万新始终选择沉默,他的这种神秘,让德隆的负面影响不断放大,最终成为德隆危机爆发的导火索。

从 2003 年 7 月开始,中国证券市场频频爆出猛料:"啤酒花""南方证券""青海信托"等一连串危机事件接连爆发,德隆旗下的金融企业几乎没有收入。而"屋漏偏逢连夜雨",从 2003 年 8 月起,全国范围内的十几家银行突然宣布对德隆采取只收不贷的政策。

2004 年年初,德隆高层做出决定,抛售企业所持有的流通股套现,以求缓解眼前资金流短缺的窘境。由于德隆手中集中掌握了大多数筹码,抛售行为立即引起二级市场股价的持续下跌,从而引发了投资者和媒体的更大疑问与声讨。

2004 年 4 月中旬，德隆系股票跌入下降通道，上市公司的违规担保等不利情况显露无遗，金融机构的委托理财黑洞也全面暴露。由此，崩盘危机迅速击中了德隆。

4 个月之后，国务院向央行下达有关文件，正式批复了市场化解决德隆危机的整体方案：德隆将被一并交由华融资产管理公司进行整体托管。随即，德隆国际、新疆屯河集团与华融签订了《资产托管协议》，三家公司都将其拥有的全部资产不可撤回地全权托管给华融，由华融全权行使其全部资产的管理和处置权力。由此，唐万新彻底丧失了对德隆的控制力。

唐万新把金融看作博弈的平台，凭借自己过人的胆识和勇气，迅速积累了大量财富。但在实际操作中，他往往倾心于手段，而忘记了要达到的目的，使自己常常陷于资金窘境之中，然后不得不以曲线获取自己所需的资金资源。

业界人士分析指出，德隆是一个"货真价实"的家族企业，事无巨细都依靠唐万新定夺的模式，让德隆的决策明显带有浓重的个人色彩。缺乏进入行业需要的专业人才，最终导致德隆对所并购企业缺乏控制力，无法对目标企业进行实际运营管理。德隆依靠股市完成资本原始积累，但也因资金链断裂而寿终正寝。这是一个带有浓厚宿命意味的悲剧。

在德隆的崩塌中，媒体对德隆"庄家"恶名的肆意传播，极大地加快了德隆的覆灭。同样是多元化产业布局，同样是大刀阔斧并购扩张的复星开始受到牵连，更有甚者将复星视为"德隆第二"。有关复星资金链紧张的传闻开始在大街小巷流传。

危急时刻，郭广昌做出决定：请安永会计师事务所为公司做财务分析报告，并将这份报告公之于众。

这个决定无疑是明智的。此时,一切缺乏证据的解释都会被外界认为是掩饰,只会让猜疑越发严重,让形势变得更糟。

最终,这场主动的"体检"让复星脱离了危机。从那时起,复星加倍重视负债率,加倍重视稳健的运营。合规底线与严守纪律至今都是复星内部最重要的企业文化之一。

由于复星的适时转变,让郭广昌当选为"2004年CCTV中国经济年度人物"。"他用求实精神理性创新,率领企业阳光运营,一位知识经济时代的掘金人,一位资本投资的创造者,他的故事告诉我们:绿色财富更加健康。"这是中央电视台给郭广昌的颁奖词。在颁奖现场,郭广昌与多位专家进行了诙谐而意境深远的对话。

中银国际首席经济学家曹远征问:"据介绍,您是自费请审计师来审计,而且是非上市的部分,还把审计结果交给银行,那么一般的企业是怕审计的,更怕把审计出来的结果交给对手,您为什么这样做,原因是什么?"郭广昌说:"一个人得了感冒之后,最不希望的就是被别人怀疑成'非典',如果确信自己只是感冒,那么做体检是最好的证明。同理,如果企业遭遇的小问题给公众造成了一定的错觉,那么最好的解决方法就是出具一份审计报告。一个人不可能没有缺点,我们可以更好地发现自己的缺点在哪里,然后去改正它。另外,这种做法可以取得别人的信任,这种信任是非常宝贵的。"

一位经济学家问:"作为成功人士,您做了很多公益事业,我想问一下,您为什么要做这么多公益事业?"郭广昌回答:"我想这涉及我的人生规划,20岁以前我主要在学习,25岁以后主要在创造财富,而50岁以后把我主要的财富回馈给社会,去设立各种基金,去做各种有价值的事情。现在我回报给社会的还是很少很少，因为我现在的主要精力还是在创造价值，大家可以看看我 50 岁以后，我一定会实现我回报社会的承诺，我希望在 70 岁以后还能为社会做贡献。"

一位专家问："什么是关乎企业成长命脉的因素？"郭广昌说："市场。我觉得如果市场是对的，任何别的方面有点小问题都没有关系。但是一旦市场方向是错的，与市场背道而驰的时候，你会被别人抛弃，所以我会永远关注市场。"

主持人问："今天不光关注市场，还要关注财富。您今天多次提到了财富，我知道郭先生的父亲是一名石匠，您自己出生的家庭并不是非常富有，您能想到在今天您的父亲留给您的最大财富是什么吗？"郭广昌说："勤劳、善良，除了我父亲之外，我要说说我的妈妈。她非常善良，她是靠卖小菜让我读完大学的，但是卖小菜从来不去弄有毒的农药，她很反对农民种这个菜的时候了一些不该用的药，所以这份感恩和善良是我们复星集团团队的核心，也是我自己能走到今天最重要的动力，所以我感谢她。"

郭广昌的回答，引起了一阵热烈的掌声。

大刀阔斧，钢铁行业显身手

应该说，复星高科技（集团）有限公司在整个产业整合中，钢铁是公司涉足最晚的一个领域，但郭广昌对钢铁行业的了解却是比较早的。他在上海复旦大学哲学系读大三时，就开始涉猎钢铁冶金方面的知识，阅读过一些专业著作。当时他绝没想到，若干年后，他会在钢铁领域投资兴业。

2003 年，复星以 17 亿元的价格，一举收购重组南京钢铁集团。这一收购,成为中国历史上股市要约收购第一案。在此之前,中国还从来没有民营企业可以入主改造特大型国有钢铁企业。

2003 年 4 月 9 日,沪深股市有史以来首例要约收购横空出世,南钢集团公司与复星集团、复星产业投资有限公司和上海广信科技发展有限公司宣布,联合组建南京钢铁联合有限公司。复星向南钢联注入 3 亿元作为首期的注资,占该实体 30% 的股权,而国有企业南钢集团持有 40% 的股权。消息传开后,证券市场一片沸腾,"要约收购"也随即成为街头巷尾讨论的关键词。

郭广昌的投资哲学是,如果看好一个产业,复星便采取两种办法加以实施:一种办法是培养自己的管理团队,由这个团队来整合产业;另一种办法是考察这个产业中谁做得最好就投资谁,然后运用自身的产业资源帮助它做得更大、更好。

对钢铁行业的投资,郭广昌选择的是第二种办法。郭广昌之所以要选择投资钢铁行业,一是他在这一行业遇到了一批顶尖人才;二是他对钢铁产业一直比较看好。

2004 年 3 月,建龙集团、复星产业投资及吉林建龙以总价 4.63 亿元,分别向南京钢铁联合有限公司转让宁波建龙钢铁 5%、20% 及 10% 的股权,这样,建龙集团及南京钢铁联合有限公司所持有的宁波建龙钢铁股权,都变为了 35%,成为大股东,而复星产业投资和吉林建龙,都不再是宁波建龙钢铁的股东。

2005 年 1 月,南钢股份通过增发 1.2 亿股 A 股,筹资共计 7.86 亿元。此次发售,致使南钢联持有的南钢股份股权,由 71% 减至 60.6%。2006 年 5 ～ 7 月,南钢联以总代价 1.53 亿元,购入 4,064 万股南钢股份 A 股,所持有的南钢股份股权增至 64.9%。2006 年 10 月，南钢股份完成股权分置改革方案，南钢联持有的全部非流通股转为流通股。2006 年 10 ~ 12 月，南钢联以总代价 13 亿元，购入 6,403 万股南钢股份 A 股，使其持有的南钢股份股权增至 71.8%。

2007 年夏天，复星旗下的复星国际有限公司，与海南海钢集团有限公司决定，成立名为"海南矿业联合有限公司"的合营公司，从事开采及加工铁矿石业务，范围包括黑色金属、有色金属及非金属等。合营公司总投资额为 16 亿元。其中，复星国际的两家子公司——上海复星高科技有限公司和上海复星产业投资有限公司，共同注资 9 亿元，分别持有合营公司 20% 和 40% 的股权，海钢集团则以 6 亿元持有 40% 的股权。

就在复星入主海钢集团的第二天，有着"中国民营钢铁大王"之称沈文荣所执掌的江苏沙钢集团，成功地购得了澳大利亚的一处铁矿。作为中国最大的民营钢铁生产商的当家人，沈文荣早已注意到郭广昌。郭广昌这个和他相差了 20 岁的年轻人，只用了 7 年时间，就做到了中国民营钢铁行业榜眼的位置。这样的追赶速度，确实让沈文荣感到有些吃惊。

对于郭广昌来说，入主海钢集团无疑是一笔非常划算的生意。海钢集团希望通过此次合作，完成企业的股份制改造；同时，复星也希望借此机会，全面加大对海南的投入，以此来扩大企业的发展空间。

当时，"稀缺"是钢铁行业的一个关键词。在东亚和欧美，钢铁产业的走势表现为简单的量变。而在中国，一场革命性的转变正在悄然发生。

随着宝钢班师湛江、武钢进驻防城港、首钢看好曹妃甸，一批年产量超过千万吨的钢铁项目浮出水面。于是，曾有人预测，中国钢铁缺货的局面，将在几年后演变成钢铁大量过剩。然而，在短期内这样过剩的局面并未出现，中国钢铁集团在郭广昌等产业整合者的带领下,正在走向国际,并引发全球钢铁业的重新洗牌。

在郭广昌看来,企业有年轻,就有老化,任何工业的前景,都不可能是万世长青的。在中国钢铁产业积极推进整合时,世界钢铁行业便有权威人士预言:21世纪第一个10年结束时,欧美钢铁企业将全部退出历史舞台,日本劫后余生,但利润所剩无几。而在中国,将有一半的企业被清洗,剩下的将成为国际巨人,但为此所付出的代价非常巨大,将用上百亿的呆滞资产换来一个行将作古的夕阳产业。

面对世界权威人士的预言,以江苏沙钢集团为代表的一批大型钢铁企业,用实际行动诠释:只要有足够的原料,中国的钢铁企业就不会衰亡。事实上,中国钢铁企业巨头,已经完成或正在完成对原材料供应商的资本收购。沙钢、马钢、武钢和唐钢,都与必和必拓公司签署了金额巨大的合约,获得必和必拓转租的澳大利亚一家矿山近半数的股权。由此,在未来的20年内,每年都可从那里购买到1,200万吨铁矿石。而宝钢在里奥廷托公司的一家新矿山,已经拥有了一半的股份。

众所周知,复星做钢铁产业,依靠的是并购速度。复星雷厉风行的并购,加快了产业链的完善。复星在围绕主力板块做足文章的同时,通过并购"零件",使产业"机器"更快速、更稳定地健康运转。在众多国企力图通过合作和变通形成产业互补态势之时,复星钢铁板块则一直扮演着并购市场大买家的角色。

第五章

多业并举，
智慧成就商业传奇

上海复地,开拓地产新世界

1994 年,就在上海房地产业逐渐升温之时,郭广昌带领复星人抢抓机遇进军房地产业,最初从事房产销售,并很快赚到了第一个 1,000 万元。从此,在上海的黄浦江边,郭广昌与一批志同道合者,开创了房地产业的一个崭新世界。

作为从销售楼盘起家的中国房地产商,郭广昌无疑是中国房地产几十年发展历程的见证者。而复地(集团)股份有限公司能够从上海扬帆起航,是从公司开发了赫赫有名的"复星花园"开始的。

复地当初开发复星花园是一件很偶然的事情。当时,上海楼市虽然呈现出升温趋势,但还未形成规模,很多房地产公司并不清楚自己的开发方向。郭广昌和他的复星创业团队在做实医药产业的同时,已经洞察到房地产市场的巨大前景,当时他们也不太清楚盖好的房子怎么卖出去。就在此时,"小资"文化的出现和互联网的兴起给郭广昌和他的团队很大的启发与契机。

"小资"是 20 世纪 90 年代开始在中国流行的名词,本意是"小资产阶级"的简称,特指那些向往西方生活,追求内心体验、物质和精神享受的年轻人。小资一般为都市白领,在社会中有一定的地位和财富,但又与"中产阶级"在经济方面有一定的差距。

1995 年,中国互联网得到了迅猛的发展,出现了大批的网络用户,从而为奢侈品消费打开了便捷的大门。当互联网进入个人用户时代时,最有能力和机会使用互联网的人群,又是那些身份比较特殊的小资。

小资群体的形成壮大,意味着社会中产阶层的初步成熟。小资群体既有购买能力,又追求品位,在吃、穿、住、行上非常讲求独立性,尤其是对待住房上，有着非同一般的个性化需求。

为了摸准房地产市场的需求，郭广昌决定，复地通过互联网，开展一次针对小资阶层的地产市场调查。郭广昌带领复地人分四路，通过互联网对潜在的客户进行访谈。经过两个月的紧张工作，很快形成了调查结果。这个调查结果显示，被调查者都对拥有独特品位的公寓型住宅有着浓厚的兴趣，而对华丽的高档别墅并没有太大兴趣。

显然，小资所注重的是个性品位，而不是高档华丽。在小资的眼里，房屋只要品质优良，房间装饰设计能够突出主人对生活的态度，即使是公寓，心理也一定会得到很大的满足。这个结果虽然偏离了郭广昌最初建别墅房的构想，但在客观上，无形降低了复地对楼盘的开发难度，房屋的造价不会很高，他们要做的就是在房屋建造的细节上重点满足小资的品位追求。

这个调查结果就是复地的房产开发方向。于是，复地马上着手进行房地产开发规划。半年后，复地楼盘就全部到位。

接下来，应该给复地开发的楼盘起什么名字以吸引广大客户，扩大复地的知名度，这成为重要的环节。有人建议叫"白领公寓"，这个名字简洁又直切主题；有人建议叫"丽人之家"，这个名字温馨又富含深意；还有人建议干脆叫"富寓"，这个名字一语双关，既代表了入住者的身份，又揭示了楼盘的性质。

对于楼盘的名字，郭广昌有着自己独特的想法。他认为，"白领公寓"虽然切题，但没有诗意；"丽人之家"虽然温馨，但质感不足；而"富寓"虽然富有深意，但不直白。尤其是这些名字都没有包含开发商的字样。当时，复地还只是一个刚刚注册的新公司，品牌无法与已经小有名气的复星相比。郭广昌觉得，如果要涵盖企业特质，楼盘名字的前半部分应该是"复星"二字，而后半部分就应该是对小资楼盘品质定位的字样。

有一天,在一个花园中散步的郭广昌灵机一动,脑海中立刻出现了"花园"二字。他当机立断,将复地开发的楼盘取名为"复星花园"。

半年后,这个名字显现出强大的生命力。复地楼盘从开盘到售罄,只用了不到两个月的时间。一座针对上海小资阶层的"复星花园",让郭广昌和复地在上海地产界迅速崛起。

其实,复地是在1998年8月,以上海复星房地产开发有限公司的名义正式宣告成立的。2001年9月,复地改制为股份有限公司,并将公司名称由复地(集团)有限公司,改为复地(集团)股份有限公司。继开发建设"复星花园"后,复地又不失时机地投资了11个房地产项目。

2004年2月6日,复地在香港联交所H股主板上市,共发售6亿股,其中90%为国际配售,10%为公开发售,筹资合计港币17亿元。至此,复地经过10年的发展,让郭广昌初步实现了财富裂变的愿望,他的财富迅速增长了10,000倍,被媒体誉为"上海的盖茨"。经过10年的努力与积累,复地以准确的产品定位能力、成熟的多项目管理能力、周转快速的资金运作能力、完善的销售及服务体系,在中国的房地产业界逐步形成了自身独特的核心竞争力。

2004年12月,郭广昌当选"2004年CCTV中国经济年度人物"。在房地产业界打拼10年时间,曾经的书生意气,已经变得沉稳厚重,当郭广昌坐在位于黄浦江边的办公室里凭窗远眺时,复地已在不知不觉中成长为中国最出色的房地产公司之一。

2004年,在郭广昌与几位复地高管的共同努力下,复地全线飘红。毫无疑问,这一年属于复地,更属于郭广昌。就是这一年,郭广昌率领着梁信军、汪群斌、谈剑、范伟4位复星创业元老，一同登上了"福布斯中国富豪榜"，郭广昌并列富豪榜的第14位。

收购豫园，大举进军零售业

当初，郭广昌注册资金3.8万元成立广信科技发展有限公司，主打业务是市场调查和咨询。后来，公司经营走向了兼容并包，商业触角向房地产、生物制药和钢铁等行业延伸，进而又大举进军零售业。

复星大举进入零售业的征程，是从收购豫园商城开始的。豫园商城位于豫园商业旅游区这个上海著名的旅游区域，是A股上市公司。豫园商城的业务范围，主要包括黄金珠宝等贵重首饰零售、餐饮业和商用物业租赁。豫园商城的旗下，拥有"老庙黄金"和"亚一金店"这样的全国黄金珠宝零售招牌店，还拥有400多家商铺、500多个零售网点。

豫园商城是上海国资委的下属企业，也是不多见的股权相对分散的上市公司。当时，豫园商城第一大股东所持的股权份额仅占13%，两个最大的股东所持的股权份额，加起来也只有25%。豫园商城所具有的相对稳定的现金流、充裕的土地资产、比较分散的股权构成等基本条件，使其成为一个非常好的收购对象。

应该说，豫园商城是一个身处闹市、品牌悠久，具备区位优势和700年文化沉积，而且每日拥有10万人次以上、年均拥有4,500万人次以上客流量的大型商业零售企业。豫园商城每年有数亿元的纯经营现金流，而投资于主营业务上的现金支出，不过只有两三千万元。同时，企业还有大批未开发的商业土地权益，这些土地资源，潜藏着不可限量的现金流价值。

面对国外零售业对国内零售业的冲击，郭广昌看在眼里急在心上，并因此产生了要做中国老牌零售业新时代复兴者的念头。他觉得，复星是在上海起家的，而上海又是中国经济最发达的城市之一，如果能够整合上海的一批老字号零售企业，加以现代化的经营管理和运营，必将可以对抗国外零售业巨头。

经过几番周折，复星最终于 2001 年和 2002 年，以每股 4 元的价格，分别买断了豫园旅游服务公司 14% 和上海豫园集团 7% 的豫园商城股权。复星以 21% 的股权，一举成为豫园商城的第一大股东，郭广昌也同时入主了豫园商城董事会。

2002 年，豫园商城实现纯经营收入 5 亿元，而投资现金支出却不到 7,000 万元，巨大的赢利空间和丰厚的经营现金，为复星借助豫园商城进行多渠道战略投资，打下了非常坚实的基础。

就在复星准备依托豫园商城大施拳脚之时，一场意外却悄然来袭。

2003 年，"非典"暴发期间，豫园商城的经营虽然受到了巨大的影响，但在郭广昌的主持下，豫园商城出资 3 亿元参股德邦证券，一举购得 30% 的股权；同时，复星旗下的产业投资公司出资 2 亿元，获得 20% 的股权。同年，豫园商城还配合复星的金融战略，再次出资 2,300 万元，认购上海银行股权。

"非典"结束后，豫园商城的现金流一跃暴涨到 2 亿元。2004 年，豫园商城同复星共同参股招金矿业，出资 1.687 亿元，获得 21% 的股权；同时，复星旗下的另一个投资公司出资 1.607 亿元，获得 20% 的股权。

自从复星成为豫园商城的第一大股东后，豫园商城在巩固零售业地位的同时，自身角色渐渐发生了变化。郭广昌通过掌控豫园商城，更方便对零售行业进行产业并购。

除了进军零售行业外，豫园商城还将触角延伸至金融投资和产业置地，与复星商业公司、豫园房地产开发公司共同收购的上海城隍庙广场。

豫园商城收购的脚步一旦迈开，就不会轻易停止。2005年，豫园商城的现金流已经达到了3.4亿元。这一年，豫园商城再次出资3,000万元认购德邦证券股份，加上额外购置部分土地，净投资现金支出达6,000万元。这些投资在2006年得到了回报，豫园商城的年纯收入高达9,500万元，并将前期收购的上海城隍庙广场卖出，一次性收回投资现金6亿元。

在收购豫园商城的同时，郭广昌还酝酿并完成了对友谊股份的收购。郭广昌先与友谊股份的大股东——友谊集团共同出资4亿元，组建了上海友谊复星控股有限公司，其中，友谊集团占新公司股份的52%，复星占新公司股份的48%。紧接着，友谊复星与友谊集团共同签署了股权转让协议，转让了友谊集团部分股份，从而使友谊复星成了友谊股份的大股东。

其实，在郭广昌看来，有时收购比战胜对手更具可行性。像豫园商城这样的老字号零售企业，其生命力依然强劲，而且赢利空间巨大，股权又相对分散，收购起来更容易一些。另外，与国外零售巨头相比，中国零售企业整体不成规模，显得势单力薄。因此，只有通过整合，才会有能力抗衡国外零售企业的巨大冲击。

郭广昌认为，随着零售业竞争的更加激烈，必然会出现这样一个趋势：仅仅依靠开新店，已经跟不上企业壮大发展的速度，而通过并购扩大市场份额，则是企业参与扁平化世界竞争合作的唯一途径。郭广昌说："商业的本质是一种规模经济，如果没有规模，就没有竞争力。有规模，才能形成货源和渠道优势、形成强大的竞争力。针对外资企业的规模优势，国内企业选择连锁经营的方式，快速做大企业，提高自己抵御市场风险的能力，是必由之路。"

多元经营，壮大综合性实力

始创于1992年的复星，最初单一开展社会调查和咨询业务。后进军房地产业、生物制药业、钢铁业和零售业，强力推进多元化经营战略，不断壮大公司的综合实力。

事实证明，复星所实施的多元化经营战略是成功的，多元化业务的经营指标是健康的。即使是这样，郭广昌总是提醒自己，眼下的成功并不意味着多元化经营就是企业的必经之途，作为一家成熟的企业，应该在深耕自己的核心产业上做足功课，来培养企业的核心竞争力。对于企业来说，专业化经营才是根本道路，而多元化经营更像是一个甜美的陷阱。

意识到这一点，郭广昌在实施多元化经营战略的过程中，总能小心谨慎地绕过陷阱阔步前行。

在郭广昌看来，随着城市化和工业化进程的加快，必将为综合类公司的成长壮大提供相应的机会，而复星的多元化经营必将重新塑造多元化企业的面貌和内核，使之发展成为受到社会尊敬的企业。

一直以来，郭广昌从不刻意回避外界对复星实施多元化经营战略的质疑。这些质疑曾在2004年一度达到最高潮。当时，以多元化经营著称，与复星同于1992年创立的新疆德隆帝国轰然倒地，公司总裁唐万新因涉嫌变相吸收公众存款和操纵证券交易价格非法获利，被警方逮捕。由此，国内众多快速扩张的多元化经营企业，都面临宏观调控的重压，而将专业化经营做到极致的如家、百度等企业则快速崛起。

对于多元化经营，郭广昌是这样理解的："多元化对应的并不是专业化，而是专一化。并不是只做一件事情就叫专业化，做一件事情也可以做得很业余。一家公司同时涉足多个领域，也可以在每个领域都做得很专业。"

其实，复星的多元化经营有着非常独特的运营特点，所追求的是投资上的多元化和经营上的专业化。对于复星来说，在多元化经营上体现了明确的行业选择。在公司已经进入并长期投资的领域，都是立足于中国巨大的市场需求，而且具有比较优势和高成长性。

在多元化经营的行业选择上，郭广昌带领复星人总是善于先人一步逢低进入，而且几乎没有犯过致命的错误。1994年，进入房地产业、生物制药业；2002年，进军商业零售业；2003年，进军钢铁业、证券业；2004年，屯兵黄金产业；2007年，投资矿业……后来，随着这些行业接连进入上升期，复星的投资收益格外丰厚。

如果说复星早期的多元化经营所取得的成功带有一些偶然性，那么，2004年后经历了外界质疑和宏观调控两道关卡，进而通过复地在香港联交所上市获得资本市场认可，显然是综合实力的增强才能做到的。

2007年，复星正式确定了建设"专业的多元化产业集团"的发展战略。

在复星召开的2008年度大会上，郭广昌首次提出了复星独创的持续融资、持续发现投资机会、持续优化管理"三大价值链"，并总结归纳了"锻造三大价值链"的复星模式。他所归纳出的复星模式，就是以认同复星文化的企业家、团队为核心，以持续融资、持续发现投资机会、持续优化管理为圆周的正循环运营模式。

毫无疑问，正是"三大价值链"的正循环成就了复星的成功。郭广昌表示，在布局复星的未来发展时一定会遵循已经形成的复星模式。他说,复星面向未来的发展战略就是以成为中国特色、复星特点、国际一流的综合类公司为目标。

郭广昌认为,与持续融资、持续发现投资机会、持续优化管理"三大价值链"相对应的,就是三个企业家团队:一是融资的专业团队;二是投资的专业团队;三是持续管理、运营的专业团队。他说,人才缺乏的问题已在复星显现,复星的首要任务就是要多花一些时间培养和引进人才。显然,在郭广昌的心目中,当公司具备了资金、框架和战略等要素,最重要的就是人的问题。

作为一名杰出的商人,郭广昌总是谦虚地说自己的商业智慧不高,而当他投资德邦证券,大举进军金融领域后,人们都被他无所不通的商业智慧所折服。

德邦证券的全称是德邦证券股份有限公司,成立于2003年5月,是一家经营规范的全国性综合证券公司,也是中国净资本最大的民营证券公司。显然,投资德邦证券成为复星进军金融领域的试金石。郭广昌进军金融领域的目的是与世界上最好的证券公司展开合作,从而降低企业的经营风险,增加企业的经济效益。

最初,复星注入资金5.01亿元,持有德邦证券20%的股权。2010年4月,复星旗下的兴业投资以5.5061亿元的价格,收购了德邦证券32.73%的股权。郭广昌投资德邦证券,目标是推动德邦证券增资、上市,快速发展证券业务。

从郭广昌的投资行为可以看出,无论是进军房地产业,还是进军钢铁业,复星都是在产业处于低谷时期选择进入,而选择进入证券行业,也是因为当时证券行业处于低迷时期。显然,郭广昌选择在一个行业处于低谷时期适时进入，都是基于企业发展的长远战略考虑的。郭广昌认为，国内证券行业还处于起步阶段，未来的发展空间，远远超过商业银行等其他金融投资形态。

入主德邦证券后，郭广昌积极与排名世界前 10 位的证券公司进行接触，寻求合作，更好地推进证券业务。

在郭广昌看来，复星实施"多元化产业集团"的发展战略，必须有金融产业的支撑，而德邦证券就可以为整个复星积累大量的金融资源。复星投身证券行业，始终强调专业化操作和市场细分，进而形成核心竞争优势。投资证券公司，复星就可以参与基金发行，可以做投资银行合资。

由于扎扎实实地推进多元化经营战略，复星的万亿帝国梦成为现实，形成了强大的"复星系"。到 2017 年年底，复星旗下共有 142 家公司，其中拥有豫园股份、复星医药、南钢股份、招金矿业、上海钢联、海南矿业 6 家上市公司。

招金矿业，该出手时就出手

优秀的商人有许许多多，但杰出的商人不是很多，郭广昌就是一个称得上"杰出"的商人。在他的身上，无疑兼具了杰出商人所具备的"三大超常"：超常的胆量、超常的大脑、超常的直觉。作为杰出的商人，郭广昌有着对商机的灵敏嗅觉和迅捷反应，正因为如此，他所带领的复星团队，总能出其不意地取得辉煌的发展业绩。

由于郭广昌一直遵循多元化经营的企业发展战略，当某一个产业渐渐出现升温的迹象时，就会看到复星团队的出现。

2004 年,当黄金产业在低谷中徘徊了很长一段时间,黄金价格出现大幅飙升的势头时,复星再次果断出手。这一年的 4 月,复星旗下的豫园商城和复星产业投资有限公司共同出资 4 亿元,与山东招金集团有限公司合作,发起创建了招金矿业股份有限公司。新组建的招金矿业,山东招金集团控股比例为 55%,复星系控股比例为 45%,主要经营黄金矿产。

郭广昌认为,复星旗下的豫园商城是全国最大的黄金及珠宝零售企业,参股招金矿业后,可进一步增强商城黄金产业的整体实力,健全黄金饰品营销的产业链。

豫园商城 2005 年度经营业绩表单显示,商城实现净利润 1 亿元,到 2006 年商城的净利润超过了 1.5 亿元,增长幅度超过了 50%。显然,复星投资入股招金矿业,获得了比较丰厚的回报。

除了投资招金矿业外,郭广昌还与国外贵金属企业进行合作洽谈,其中包括南美、南非地区的大型黄金加工企业。显然,郭广昌的目的是力求进入黄金初加工这一黄金产业链条的重要节点,进而形成覆盖上、中、下游的一条完善而有效的黄金产业链条。

在郭广昌的主导下,豫园商城投资招金矿业的同时,还在向其他产业进行拓展。豫园商城旗下的上海豫园商城房地产发展有限公司,出资 36 亿元,通过竞拍获得了武重机械厂 800 亩地块的使用权。以黄金促进地产,这是郭广昌的又一记奇招。

郭广昌选择豫园商城出资竞标武重机械厂地块,而不是让复地出资,其目的在于,豫园商城参股招金矿业后,必然要对黄金市场作一个全面解码。而武重机械厂地块,恰恰位于武昌东湖和沙湖之间,紧邻湖北省行政中心,是繁华的武汉市中心不可多得的宝地。复星收购豫园商城后,"老庙黄金"

和"亚一金店"以及豫园老街等大量商铺和地产项目的结合，已经成为复星提升黄金招牌的一个连锁策略。不难看出，豫园商城竞拍武重机械厂地块是为了更好地走"以金促地、互相补充"的发展道路。

2006 年 12 月，招金矿业在香港联交所成功挂牌上市，开盘发售价为13 港元，豫园商城的身价随即激增。豫园商城扣除对招金矿业的投资成本外，投资收益甚至超过 20 亿元。

招金矿业上市后，大力实施收购、兼并和扩张战略，不断增加黄金资源的储备。2007 年，招金矿业在山东招远以外的地区，共收购了 16 个项目，使业务扩张到全国 12 个主要产金的省、市、自治区。到 2008 年年末，招金矿业在全国各地已拥有 58 个探矿权，21 个采矿权，黄金资源总量达253.06 吨，可采黄金储量达 165.29 吨。

复星竞标武重机械厂地块，必将成为豫园商城的主要利润增长点，也必将带来新的融资渠道，为商城的持续发展奠定坚实基础。

"弱时看强，衰中见盛"这 8 个字，是郭广昌和复星人一直坚守的信念。郭广昌认为，一个高速成长的新兴经济体，必将托起一些多元化的产业投资企业，因此，他一直强调要打造一家多产业控股型公司。面对来自方方面面的种种嘲笑，郭广昌始终坚信，这个世界并不是掌握在那些嘲笑者的手中，而是掌握在能够经受得住嘲笑并不断前行的人手中。

业界知道，管理好一个多元化产业公司，是全球商业界的一个重大课题，也是一大难题。面对这一难题，郭广昌表现出超常的胆略，带领着复星人用超常的商业智慧，去挑战，去破解。郭广昌心中有一个信念：那些尝试去做某事却失败的人，比那些什么也不尝试做却侥幸成功的人不知要好上多少倍。

后来的实践证明,郭广昌凭借逆潮流而动的勇气和敏锐的商业洞察力一路打拼过来,逐步建立了庞大的"复星企业王国",一步步缔造了一个千亿级年销售收入的多元化控股集团。

2007年6月,在复星国际首次公开募股路演期间,一些海外投行针对招股价位于6.48港元至8.68港元这一标准提出:就一个多元的综合类企业而言,招股价有些高。面对这一质疑,郭广昌毫不让步,在路演大会上慷慨陈词:"看看你眼中的中国,你就不会质疑复星的定价了。中国的生产力经过了30年的高速发展,相信还会有更多个30年的蓬勃势头。如果你不相信,我跟你谈了也白搭。另外一点,相信复星的团队,相信这个创造了民营企业神话的公司,相信这个团队对投资的判断力、决策力和提升企业管理的实力。如果不相信,那也不要投。如果相信这两点,就没理由在乎价格多加5%,一个企业的价值并不是由这小小的5%决定的。"结果,复星国际的国际发售部分,一举获得超过上百倍的超额认购,香港公开发售更是获得高额的散户超额认购。2007年7月16日,复星国际在这种强势狂潮的助推下,成功在香港联交所上市,融资额高达132亿港元,新股占复星国际扩大后总股本的22%。

复星国际的上市,无疑让人们重新认识了复星这个横跨多种产业、拥有更大发展前景的企业帝国。

第六章

科技创新，
长线投资大获全胜

瞄准时机，科大讯飞显身手

在复星，几乎所有的人都知道，对于郭广昌来说，一旦机会来临，就会牢牢抓住，绝不会让机会轻易错过。

2000 年 11 月 30 日，正当全球互联网泡沫集中爆发之时，在郭广昌的主导下，复星旗下的复星高科向科大讯飞一次性注资 1,677 万元，得到了科大讯飞 21.5% 的股份，成为该公司的第一大股东。这笔投资，标志着复星正式进军人工智能技术，准确地说，是进军人工智能中的语音技术。

说起科大讯飞，业界首先想到的就是刘庆峰。1999 年，在中国科技大学读博士的刘庆峰，带领着 18 名同学，创立了科大讯飞，满怀激情地投身到创业大潮之中。

科大讯飞成立不久就经历了世界互联网泡沫的高涨和破灭，公司很快陷入了资金短缺的窘境。就在刘庆峰感觉走投无路之时，公司幸运地得到了复星高科的投资。

提起郭广昌对科大讯飞的投资，还有一个非常有意思的故事。当时，刘庆峰和江涛一起，带着一个厚重的东芝笔记本电脑去见郭广昌，想用他们刚刚开发的软件"畅言 2000"，来演示使用语音实现在电脑上听音乐、上网、打开浏览器等功能。但他们的演示还没开始时，笔记本电脑却突然自己开始不停地说话，场面让双方都觉得非常尴尬。江涛后来回忆说："当时，我们真的不知道应该怎么跟郭广昌解释，只能灰溜溜地离开了。"

这次失败的演示让郭广昌差点就放弃投资科大讯飞。但最终，郭广昌还是看好科大讯飞的发展前景，义无反顾地给予投资，并成为科大讯飞的第一大股东。

后来，科大讯飞又幸运地得到了联想投资的 300 万美元资金。先后得到这两笔资金，谋求上市便成了科大讯飞的一个奋斗目标。

为了实现尽早上市，科大讯飞经过认真的分析研究，很快调整了公司的发展战略。公司决定，不再自己开发新的产品，而是向联想、华为、中兴等客户提供语音核心技术模块，将自身技术应用于 PC、呼叫中心、智能网等领域。就这样，科大讯飞于 2002 年和 2003 年，陆续推出了一系列面向电信级、桌面级、嵌入式芯片级的解决方案，从而找到了适合自己的发展模式，并取得了初步成功。随后的 2004 年，科大讯飞一举实现扭亏为盈，并从 2005 年起进入了业绩快速提升期，上市也因此被提上公司的议事日程。

在科大讯飞紧锣密鼓地筹划上市时，复星内部实施了科大讯飞的股份转让。2005 年 6 月 10 日，复星高科与上海广信签订股权转让合同，复星高科将所持科大讯飞 1,290 万元股权转让给上海广信，转让价格为 2,060.85 万元。

谋划上市初期，科大讯飞一度首选在纳斯达克上市。但考虑到追求高风险、高增长的纳斯达克，并不适合科大讯飞，公司最终选择了境内 A 股上市，并于 2008 年 5 月 12 日登陆中小板。上市当天，科大讯飞以 28.21 元/股的价格开盘，比发行价上涨了 122.83%，最后以 30.31 元/股的价格收盘。通过登陆 A 股，科大讯飞不但让上海广信和联想投资获得了丰厚的回报，也让公司本身在业绩和市值方面获得了长足发展。

2010 年 8 月，郭广昌在提起投资科大讯飞时，非常骄傲地说："创新、创业是企业家精神的基本组成部分。我们投资的安徽科大讯飞，脱胎于中国科技大学的国家语音实验室，一群年轻博士组成的创业团队带着成果离开校园，在复星、联想为大股东的市场资金的支持下，只花了 6,000 多万元、用了 6 年时间，就将中文语音技术做到了世界领先，并从国外公司手中，一举夺回了中文语音产业80%的市场份额。他们又以市场机制,把中国科大、中科院、清华大学等多个国家级语音研究机构有效整合在一起,从源头技术上聚拢国家语音研究资源。同时,科大讯飞还代表国家牵头制定语音技术标准。研发团队长期只拿极少的工资,忘情投入智能语音技术的持续提升和应用推广,创业6年终于成长为年利润3,000万元、年增长超过60%的全球中文语音合成的龙头老大,使中国人自己成就、垄断了中文语音产业。在全球英文语音合成大赛中,科大讯飞还取得第一名的好成绩,标志着我国多语种智能语音技术研究,已经达到了世界领先水平。"郭广昌还说:"尽管复星在科大讯飞的投资不是最高的,可科大讯飞的产出和效益却是最高的,原因就在于它是民营企业,有很好的机制,有很好的团队。在这个团队中,始终贯穿着企业家精神,始终追求每一分投入都有最大的产出。"

在郭广昌的主导下,复星注重长线投资,对大势判断准确,整体节奏把握得非常好。从2011年6月24日~2012年5月17日,上海广信通过深圳证券交易所累计出售所持有的科大讯飞股份约1,208.19万股,占总股本的4.79%;从2012年6月1~4日,又通过竞价交易系统累计出售约74.52万股,占总股本的0.2%。就这样,上海广信在两个集中时期累计减持数额占科大讯飞股份总额的4.99%,累计收回资金约4.74亿元,获得了巨大的投资收益。

在2012年7月之后的一系列减持中,复星早期投资的1,677万元,在2013年年底全部退出后,共计退出金额约17亿元,回报超过了100倍。复星能够获得这么高的回报,一是因为复星的投资都是自有资金;二是因为在投资战略上,复星看重长线投资的价值。

2013年4月23日,全球最大移动通信商——中国移动公司宣布,向安徽科大讯飞投资 13.63 亿元，获得了科大讯飞 15% 的股份，成为单一最大股东。未来，两家公司将在智能语音门户、智能语音技术和产品等领域展开合作。而当初，复星得到科大讯飞 21.5% 的股份时，才仅仅投资了 1,677 万元，可见郭广昌眼光之长远。

作为国内智能语音技术翘楚，科大讯飞一直在人工智能领域不断发展，相比之下，在人工智能技术领域影响巨大的百度和搜狗，都是后来者。郭广昌认为，人工智能商业落地较为艰难、新技术还未能创造巨大收益、创新项目变现进展缓慢等都亟待解决。但是，人工智能必将颠覆所有行业，行业的竞争会越来越激烈。

科大讯飞推出的语音技术，实现了人机语音交互，使人与机器之间的沟通变得像人与人沟通一样简单。语音技术主要包括语音合成和语音识别两项关键技术。让机器说话，用的是语音合成技术；让机器听懂人说话，用的是语音识别技术。此外，语音技术还包括语音编码、音色转换、口语评测、语音消噪和增强等技术，有着广阔应用空间。

2017 年 6 月，在美国《麻省理工科技评论》杂志推出的"2017 年全球 50 大最聪明公司榜单"中，科大讯飞超越百度、阿里巴巴和腾讯的 BAT 组合，成为中国最聪明企业。

2017 年 8 月 10 日，科大讯飞中报投资者交流会在安徽合肥举行，会议吸引了 300 多名投资者和 200 多位机构投资者参会。科大讯飞董事长刘庆峰在交流会中表示，要用未来的梦想看待科大讯飞和人工智能的发展，更大的梦想和发展空间在后面。

交流会期间，刘庆峰骄傲地宣称，科大讯飞有两个独一无二：一是上市 9 年，董事长没卖过一股股票；二是从 2008 年上市以来，公司 30 个核心成员没有一个离职。

交流会上,刘庆峰不止一次提到全球人工智能正面临前所未有的窗口期机遇。他表示,科大讯飞在教育、医疗、客服、车载上都有很高的护城河,挑战在于怎么才能把握好机遇。他说:"我们不止是想做中国的BAT。未来3~5年,人工智能格局将定,5~10年,现在大量的工作都会被人工智能所替代,科大讯飞会不断突破。"

2008年科大讯飞上市之初,市值只有32亿元,而到了2017年8月下旬,最高达到了886亿元,增加了多达26.69倍。

2017年11月9日,科大讯飞年度发布会在北京召开,从教育到医疗,从客服到智能家居,再到移动手机端和车载环境,科大讯飞一口气发布了多个领域10款以上的人工智能产品,令业界刮目相看。

2018年3月15日,作为2018年度"3·15诚信企业纳斯达克联展"中国企业中唯一的人工智能领域代表,科大讯飞旗下的"讯飞开放平台"出现在了纽约时代广场的著名地标——纳斯达克广告大屏上,再次成为业界的翘楚。

股价冲天,上海钢联创奇迹

郭广昌的投资决定,总给人以果断而英明的感觉,总是让投资业界一次次地感叹不已。投资科大讯飞是大手笔,投资上海钢联同样是大手笔。

2007年1月,复星旗下的兴业投资出资3,690万元,得到上海钢联这家钢铁电商60%的股份。

上海钢联的全称是上海钢联电子商务股份有限公司,成立于2000年4

月30日，是集钢铁资讯、电子商务、网络技术服务为一体的全国性大型综合信息技术产业服务企业，主要提供专业的钢铁资讯交互平台、一站式钢铁电子商务服务。上海钢联通过旗下的"我的钢铁网"，开设了钢材、炉料、特钢、有色、国际五大资讯频道，提供综合资讯、产经纵横、统计资料、钢厂资讯、下游动态等资讯内容。公司借助旗下的英文网站，与世界知名钢厂和交易商展开合作。公司还凭借旗下的研究中心，编印《钢市动态与分析》周刊、《我的钢铁网研究报告》月刊、*Mysteel Weekly*，*Mysteel Daily*，*Mysteel Monthly* 等系列研究刊物，供企业和政府做决策时参考。

2005 年，上海钢联荣获了上海名牌称号，并通过了 ISO9000 管理体系认证。2005 ～ 2008 年，上海钢联连续四年入选"中国行业电子商务网站100 强"榜单。

2008 年 8 月，上海钢联旗下的"我的钢铁网"的收入规模，一举超过了中国化工网，排名占中国行业垂直类 B2B 网站中的第一位。同时，网站页面访问量、网站用户量、网站访问时间、网站流量等主要指标，连续三个月在国内同行业排名榜单中稳居第一位。

2010 年，"我的钢铁网"收入再创历史新高，达到了 1.228 亿元。网站的增收，直接助推上海钢联实现营业收入 1.607 亿元，扣除非经常性损益后的净利润达 2,367.89 万元。

2011 年 6 月 8 日，上海钢联于深圳创业板上市。这一年，公司营业收入创纪录地实现 3.5 亿元，扣除非经常性损益后的净利润为 3,237.15 万元。

上海钢联上市后，兴业投资对其持股比例降至 39.69%。当时，郭广昌的目标是把上海钢联打造成我国最具国际影响力的大宗商品生产、交易、需求数据等市场信息供应商和电子商务服务商。但让郭广昌感到有些失望的是，上海钢联在致力于抢占市场份额营收猛增的同时，2012年，公司的净利润开始出现迅速下滑的迹象。在营收猛增172.66%，达到9.54亿元的情况下，扣除非经常性损益后的净利润却下降14.36%，仅有2,772.23万元。

2013年7月，上海钢联的上半年财报显示，公司当时经营情况仍旧没有改善，扣除非经常性损益后的净利润为1,065.26万元，同比下降了38.762%。但同时，公司搭上"互联网""电商"概念，股价却一飞冲天。7月1日，上海钢联收盘于8.59元。在7月2日和7月9日实现两天涨停后，上海钢联从7月11日开始，连续4天实现涨停。7月24日，上海钢联盘中最高上涨至21.25元，成为当时最耀眼的明星股票。2013年9月，上海钢联的股价一度突破了30元大关。2014年1月30日，公司股价达到了55.83元。一个月后的2月24日，股价再创60.94元新高。

在郭广昌的主导下，上海钢联将2014年称为公司发展大宗商品电子商务的关键一年。公司宣称，基于前期对钢铁电商的持续探索及取得的成果，提出了建设线上线下一体化的电商生态体系，致力于打造交易闭环。除了继续大力发展钢铁在线交易平台——钢银平台，还开始建设集合支付结算、仓储、物流、数据、金融服务的服务体系，并致力于推动各个平台的无缝对接、通融发展，形成完整的电商生态体系。

在上海钢联股价一浪高过一浪的上涨中，旗下的钢银平台起到了重要的助推作用。这个集合了电商、互联网、金融等多个热门概念的平台，给予资本市场无限的想象空间。

2014年7月，上海钢联更是推出"要将上海钢联打造成为大宗商品交易市场的'阿里巴巴'"的口号，再次让资本市场群情振奋。

一面是股价的节节攀升，一面却是业绩的不断下滑。上海钢联2013年财报显示，公司营收实现 15.53 亿元，同比增长 62.73%，但扣除非经常性损益后的净利润为 1,393.95 万元，同比下降了 49.72%。2014 年，公司扣除非经常性损益后的净利润为 1,067.24 万元，再次下降了 23.44%。2015 年，公司扣除非经常性损益后的净利润出现了负数，竟然亏损了 2.55 亿元。

针对业绩连续下滑的状况，上海钢联与港股上市公司慧聪网展开合作。双方表示，继续在 B2B 领域寻求突破，以期尽早实现公司业绩的回暖。

在深圳创业板上市伊始，上海钢联以运营"我的钢铁网"著称，是国内最大的以钢铁及相关行业信息服务为基础的电子商务运营商。当时，上海钢联是郭广昌投资涉及科技、媒体和通信产业的唯一绝对控股企业。为此，郭广昌将上海钢联未来的发展定位为：我国最具国际影响力的大宗商品生产、交易、需求数据等市场信息供应商和电子商务服务商，公司将打造三大平台，即大宗商品资讯平台、大宗商品交易平台和大宗商品研究平台。

让郭广昌颇为苦恼的是，上海钢联在股票价格连连上涨的同时，业绩上却出现了连续下滑，离他投资之初为公司设计的宏大目标越来越远。糟糕的业绩表现，让上海钢联的中小股东们感到无可奈何，甚至有些心寒。

垂直整合，打造万亿大平台

面对股价上涨和业绩下滑的不正常状况，郭广昌开始对上海钢联实施新的一轮整合。上海钢联决定，以发行股份及支付现金相结合的方式，从慧聪网手中收购中关村在线，以此来开创公司转向 B2B2.0 的美好前景。

上海钢联是中国钢铁行业最大的资讯＋电商平台，中关村在线是中国信息技术产业领域最大的资讯＋电商平台。郭广昌认为，在上海钢联内生性增长缺乏根基之际，外延式并购成为必然选择。

2014年12月，上海钢联股价再次一路上涨，最高一度涨至85.46元。2015年5月，在"创业板牛市""互联网+"热潮的裹挟下，上海钢联的股价达到了157.95元，再次成为不折不扣的明星股。

2017年5月15日，在原湖畔大学给学员授课时，郭广昌所提频率较多的两家企业，一个是国药集团药业股份有限公司，另一个就是上海钢联。郭广昌说："我十分看好这两家企业的前景：三五年内，它们的年销售收入可以超过一万亿人民币。"

郭广昌认为，一个好的企业，必须具备这样的条件：有积累、有产业深度、有着绝佳的产品力。他说："国药和上海钢联，正是符合这几个条件的好企业。"

在授课中，郭广昌对上海钢联的商业模式和战略进化，进行了细致入微的讲解，对于成功的经验和下一步的战略方向，也做了详细的说明。

郭广昌在讲课中指出："很多人总喜欢风头上的企业，我是比较喜欢不在风头上、看上去不是很潮流的企业。其实，钢铁过去风潮过，也很赚钱。没有电商大家都活得下去，但没有钢铁大家真的没法活。我们现在出的任何东西，没有钢铁行吗？不行！制造业是核心，是基础。本来，我们觉得钢铁是不是就放弃了，但事实上，钢铁业利用移动互联网进行改造，是有大量机会的。我说这些有一个目的，大家多关注传统行业，多关注那些不被重视的行业，多关注产业深度，不要人云亦云。"

郭广昌说："我最不喜欢的模式，就是那种谁都看得懂的、谁都在抢的模式。我喜欢的模式，是需要积累、一般人看不懂的模式。上海钢联一步一步走来非常有趣，其实整个钢联的发展几乎就是淘宝、阿里走过的路。它最先做什么呢？咨询数据，到钢厂去把数据收集起来，然后卖给客户。然后研究咨询，就相当于当时阿里的黄页。前几年它开始做电子交易，包括开展现货交易平台。现在进一步怎么发展？上海钢联会成为大宗商品的交易平台，现在电子商务基本都是在 C 端的电子商务，大宗商品交易量非常大，但缺少一个大宗商品交易服务闭环的企业。"

郭广昌在讲课时说："上海钢联今年会做到一千亿元左右，我们希望打造大宗商品的高效生态系统，发展下去也可以成为万亿元级的产业平台。钢铁贸易里面大家很不喜欢的是骗贷，为什么会形成骗贷？因为交易过程不是闭环，存储是第三方提供的，第三方诚信又不行，所以容易导致骗贷。我们下一步做什么呢？要进入供应链的金融服务里面，在一个万亿元大宗商品平台里面提供金融服务，相当于现在的支付宝、蚂蚁金服。所以复星非常看重大宗商品，非常看重产业深度，产业深度里非常看重 C2M，C2M里面很重要的一点是供应链改造。所有的供应链改造里，很重要的一块是大宗商品供应链改造，这里有巨大空间。"

业界知道，上海钢联并购中关村在线，主要是为了打通产业链上下游，而中关村在线及商城，则属于钢铁的下游用户。上海钢联和中关村在线都是资讯＋交易，并将由交易延伸到仓储、物流和金融服务。媒体资讯是导流口，交易信息是核心，金融服务是利润。上海钢联、聪慧网和中关村在线的三方合作，有利于实现三方的互惠互利。对上海钢联来说，可实现互联网业务的延伸，从而改变多年来依赖大宗商品业务的局面，提高公司的抗风险能力；对慧聪网来说，将逐步改变由媒体属性转型升级为交易属性，从而依靠上海钢联强大的交易量，有助于构建慧聪网的"交易闭环"；对中关村在线来说，本身在电商行业内知名度不高，也急需拓展业务板块及寻求更长足发展。

投资上海钢联只是开始，而打通整条大宗商品产业链，以实现 C2M 才是终极目标。

十年磨剑，复宏汉霖科创梦

2019 年 9 月 25 日，复星医药子公司复宏汉霖在香港联交所敲钟上市。复宏汉霖本次上市发行定价为每股 49.6 港元，总计发行 6,469.54 万股，募集资金约 32 亿港元，约合人民币 29 亿元。当日，复宏汉霖的开盘价为每股 47.45 港元，报收于每股 49.45 港元，市值最终定格于 267 亿港元。

复宏汉霖有着"中国生物医药独角兽"之称，它在香港的成功上市，是复星十几年来深耕医药科技创新所达成的重要里程碑。对于十几年来的无悔投入，郭广昌常常自嘲复星是屡败屡战、屡战屡败。然而正是这种"傻傻"的坚持，让复宏汉霖一举打破国外原研药在中国的垄断，从而大幅降低了药价，让更多的患者能够用上价格更合理的抗癌药物。

作为国内首个获批上市的生物类似药"汉利康"的创造者，复宏汉霖在生物类似药、创新药及联合疗法上的研究、开发与商业化进度，均为业内领先，故而它的上市被业界与资本市场寄予厚望。

十年磨一剑，复宏汉霖从酝酿创建到最终上市，走过了整整 10 年的发展历程。当年，进入 21 世纪，中国本土医药企业因产品同质化严重，不得不为价格拼得头破血流，互相伤害。而由仿制药起家的复星，为了尽快摆脱国内医药企业残酷的同质化竞争，决定沉下心来专注研发创新，同时到海外寻找机会。一度，复星试图通过海外并购的方式，来获取创新研发技术，但始终未能如愿。这也让复星更加坚定了要从头做起，走自主研发的创新道路。

复宏汉霖的诞生，始于 2009 年，源于与刘世高、姜伟东两位科学家的合作。

刘世高祖籍江苏徐州，出生于台湾，台湾东吴大学微生物系第一届学生，获得了美国普渡大学博士学位。后来在生物医药领域从事一线的研发和管理工作，积累了丰富的行业经验，成为一名生物医药领域的资深专家。

姜伟东毕业于杭州大学生物系，毕业后考入了中科院细胞生物学研究所，之后在公费留学选拔考试中，一举获得学院全科第二，并选择远赴德国攻读博士学位。在德国吉森大学获得微生物与分子生物学博士学位后，前往美国加州做博士后，并选择进入波士顿的一家制药公司。

刘世高的父亲和姜伟东的妹妹都因为身患癌症去世，这让两个人在精神上受到了极大的打击。2008 年 10 月，刘世高与姜伟东在浙江大学美国加州湾区校友会上相识。交谈中，两个人都感觉非常投机，相见恨晚。很快，他们就达成了创业共识，并认定对方作为自己创业路上的合作伙伴，从此一同拼搏，同甘共苦。

2009 年 2 月，刘世高与姜伟东正式注册成立美国汉霖。当时，正好赶上百年不遇的金融风暴，美国经济不景气，两个人的创业很快陷入困境。

就是在这个时候，复星医药出现在了两个人面前。复星医药与美国汉霖在理念、价值观和目标上，都体现出高度的一致。于是，2009 年 12 月，复星医药与刘世高、姜伟东为代表的美国汉霖，签署了合作协议。2010 年 2 月，复星医药出资 2,500 万美元，与美国汉霖共同组建复宏汉霖。

复宏汉霖组建伊始就下定决心要做世界最好的医药企业，要把自己的产品销往全世界。从此，复星除了持续的资金投入外，还在企业管理、研发战略、市场准入、商业化等方面，对复宏汉霖投入大量的人力、物力和财力支持，为打造全球领先的生物制药企业倾尽全力。

在战略制定上，复宏汉霖结合国内外不同的比较优势，确立了"患者可负担的创新"这一市场定位，研发质高价优的生物药，服务更多病患。公司在研究中国每年患者的人数和患者使用生物药比重中发现，大量病患的需求未被满足，其中不少是因为费用过高。

为此，复宏汉霖采取自主试验、多品种研发的经济规模化效应，以及包括一次性生产系统在内的一连串技术创新等多种途径，大幅降低研发及生产成本。

2019年2月25日，复宏汉霖生物类似药"汉利康"，获得了国家药品监督管理局批准上市注册申请。"汉利康"是国内获批的首个生物类似药，主要用于非霍奇金淋巴瘤的治疗。所谓"生物类似药"，是指在质量、安全性和有效性方面，与已获批准注册的参照药具有相似性的治疗用生物制品。"汉利康"的获批上市，实现了中国国产生物类似药的零突破，为国内患者带来了高达40%的降价，为许多原本因价格问题而无法接受治疗的患者带来福音，更为国家医保节省下了大量经费来支持其他好的药物。

复宏汉霖组建以来，已逐步建立了高效的一体化全球研发平台，分布于中国上海、中国台北及美国加州等地，复宏汉霖积极开展全球商业化布局，与 Accord、Cipla、Biosidus 及 Jacobson 签订了商业合作协议，对外授权覆盖全球82个国家和地区。到2019年3月底，公司已经拥有一支多达239名资深研发雇员的研发团队。拥有强大自主研发能力及全流程开发能力的全球研发平台，使复宏汉霖完全掌控了从发现、产程开发、生产至产品上市后的临床研究等药物开发的全过程。同时，复宏汉霖已在中国大陆、中国台湾、菲律宾、乌克兰、波兰及澳大利亚6个国家和地区，进行处于多个临床试验阶段的8种候选产品及两个肿瘤免疫联合疗法的11项临床试验。

复宏汉霖始终将质量放在产品标准第一位，无论是产品质量，还是生产质量，公司都按照国际化的高标准进行。

复宏汉霖另一核心产品——曲妥珠单抗HLX02，在完成中国、乌克兰、波兰和菲律宾等国际多中心三期临床试验后，2019年6月24日，成为中国第一个本土研发生产、获得欧盟上市申请受理的生物类似药。公司已经建立了一套全面质量管理体系，完全符合美国、欧盟及中国的质量标准，为公司产品在多个国家及地区的商业化奠定基础。公司的上海徐汇生产基地，已通过欧盟质量受权人QP检查，并具备了GMP认证的生产能力。复宏汉霖还以国际标准的质量体系，积极参与到中国生物类似药法规体系的建立中，帮助国内监管机构建立了一个与国际接轨的生物医药法规体系。

复宏汉霖的科创团队，包含了大量的海归人才，其中大部分都曾在国际知名药厂工作过。80名医药行业专家，60%都有海外工作经验。这些人才，一方面能将领先企业的一些最先进的技术引进来，另一方面也将这些企业的经营理念和管理经验引进来，从而加速企业的健康发展。

在"汉利康"研发的背后，是一系列数字的支撑：超过10,000项监测，耗时60万余小时，生产20余个批次，花费整整10年时间……而"汉利康"，只是复宏汉霖深耕科技创新的一个缩影。

复宏汉霖的成功，正是凭借在人才、研发、市场等多个维度的全球化运营获得了成功。生物医药是一项较为新兴的技术，而领先的技术基本都在海外。在郭广昌看来,如果不在全球广纳优秀人才,不在全球建立研发机构,动悉最前沿的科技水平,单靠闭门造车,是无法追赶国际领先技术的。在自主孵化和研发方面,复宏汉霖专注大分子生物药,并在小分子化学药物的创新上,携手海外科学家孵化了复创医药,所研制的抗肿瘤新药 FCN-437,已获得美国 FDA 临床试验批准。

　　未来企业的竞争必定是科技创新的竞争,也是全球化的竞争。复星全球化的科技创新平台,未来将诞生多少个复宏汉霖,令人期待。

第七章

海外发展，
深度推进全球布局

中国动力，嫁接好全球资源

2014 年 11 月 14 日，复星发布公告，旗下的全资附属公司超越能源出价 4.39 亿澳元（约合 23.6 亿人民币），收购澳大利亚领先的石油和天然气上游公司——洛克石油有限公司 92.6% 的股份，成为该公司的第一大股东。

郭广昌拍板收购洛克石油是基于复星在矿业和能源领域拥有强大的产业运作经验考虑的。复星将洛克石油纳入麾下，将充分利用复星在产业运营方面的专业知识，将上游石油生产资源，充分整合到公司整体能源的产业链中，助推洛克石油最大限度地发挥其在整个价值链中的协同效应。

洛克石油公司首席执行官 Alan Linn 说："收购洛克石油是复星战略性进入石油和天然气行业的重要而令人振奋的一步。在来自复星的石油和天然气行业专家的支持下，洛克石油期待未来建立起一个领先的石油和天然气业务平台。"

收购完成后，复星根据洛克石油运营状况的战略评估结果，全面保留了洛克石油的现有管理团队，并继续沿用洛克石油的品牌名称进行运营。

收购洛克石油公司，只是复星推行全球化布局的一个缩影。复星全球化布局的核心是"中国动力嫁接全球资源"。

2015 年 4 月 25 ～ 26 日，"2015 杜克国际金融论坛"在昆山杜克大学校园举行，论坛的主题是"跨境并购"，来自世界各地的商业领袖与知名学者齐聚论坛，共同探讨如何在中国成功进行战略投资、如何帮助中国企业成功开展海外并购、在"新常态"下企业成功因素会发生哪些变化等话题。

论坛期间，郭广昌发表主题致辞：

"过去，我们看到全球大的基金在投资中国企业时，他们讲得最多的一句话，就是我不是来挣钱的，我来是要把你带到全球去，来把国际经验教给你。这样一说，我们中国投资者还怎么跟他竞争？所以，复星在做投资时碰到的一个关键问题，就是在没有一个全球能力但又必须面对全球竞争的时候，就会有弱势。那怎么办？兵法说，以长攻短。所以，我们2007年时在想，跟这些跨国的投资企业比，我们的优势、弱势在哪里？简单地说，我们的优势就是我们知道中国，我们深耕中国，我们有中国深刻的产业基础。所以，当时我们提出一个口号，就是'中国动力嫁接全球资源'。

"什么叫'中国动力'？大家可能没有意识到一个数字，现在全球的GDP一半增长量是来自中国。中国的GDP虽然在全球还是第二名，但是全球经济一半的增长量来自中国。增长量才是动力，其他都是存量。所谓动力，就是增长量，就是你植根于中国，也是各位坐在这片土地上的优势所在。可以说，现在全球增长的第一动力、第一发动机，就是大家所在的这片土地。所以，我们觉得，怎么样把这个动力跟全球好的资源相结合？就是复星进行全球化发展最好的一个途径。找谁呢？我们的想法是去找那些要在中国发展的企业，复星是可以帮你的。但是，一开始很多人都不相信。所以，我们前三年只投了一个项目，叫法国地中海俱乐部。当时，我们做这些投资时，确实很艰难。

"现在出现了很好的转变。我们基本每一两个月都会有一个国际性的跨国并购能够做成，其原因是什么？为什么大家认可了我们？我觉得，其中的主要原因，就是我们提出的'中国动力嫁接全球资源'打动了人家的心坎。如法国地中海俱乐部等，我们投资之后，加快了企业在中国的发展；同时，也加快了企业在全球的发展。所以，现在很多企业说要到中国来发展，希望找一家企业能在中国帮助他们，他们觉得这样的企业就是复星。由此，我们现在至少解决了一个关键问题，就是将以前你找他变成了现在别人来找你，而且他还相信你的故事。一句口号是解决不了问题的，我感觉更重要的是你要帮他做事。这样的话，我们后面的投资速度就大大加快了。

"我们希望自己是一个价值创造者，是在产业里面的一个价值创造者。所以，复星非常清楚，我们希望在产业这一块能够站在中国这片土地上，并在全球范围之内做一个产业的整合者。而在这个产业整合里面，我们最想做的是三块：第一块，就是大健康产业。现在中国医药行业市值前五名的上市公司，我们深入参与了两家——复星医药、国药。所以我们会投资在养老、医院、健康保险这块上，而且会加大投资。第二块，就是快乐时尚产业。我们投资了地中海俱乐部、亚特兰蒂斯，最近投了太阳马戏，投了 Studio 8，投了博纳等。我觉得，这块产业，我们会逐渐把它做起来。第三块，大家耐得住寂寞的话，现在多看看大宗商品，因为大宗商品已经血流成河。也许我是错的，但是我觉得至少投这个的话，你不会睡不着觉，还是可以放心回家睡觉的。还有一个，'互联网＋'，我感觉所有的传统产业，都要跟互联网相结合，逐渐做一个改造。所以，我们要做这些产业的整合者。"

郭广昌的这篇主题致辞，主要分享了怎样把中国动力与全球好的资源结合起来，怎样嫁接好全球资源。"中国动力嫁接全球资源"是复星进行全球化发展最好的重要途径。郭广昌还分享了如何打造一个全球性投资集团的经验，提出了企业发展要坚持"站在价值的地板上与周期共舞"，坚持资本应该老老实实为产业服务，在论坛期间引起了广泛关注。

走出国门，是为更好地回来

2016 年 9 月 11 日，郭广昌携手三一重工总裁向文波和新希望集团董事长刘永好，在中央电视台财经频道"2016 国际投资论坛专题节目"中，共同讲述了各自企业国际化投资背后的思考，深度解读了中国企业全球化过程中面临的机遇和挑战。

在节目中，郭广昌主要回答了主持人提出的 11 个问题。

如何看待"中国制造"到"中国拥有"？

郭广昌：中国以前所谓的全球化是被动式的，更多是别人来整合我们。而现在看到的，是我们的反向全球化，我们的企业有这个实力，让全球资源为我所用，这个阶段刚刚开始。

复星在 7 月一个月内宣布 4 起收购，是疯狂购物吗？

郭广昌：其实，复星的每个收购都历时一两年之久，完全是一个深思熟虑的结果。所以，看上去它们都发生在 7 月份，但这纯属于一种巧合。这 4 起收购的总金额加起来，还没有达到 20 亿美元，和之前的收购账单相比，数额不算大。

缺少"外国亲戚"，会不会阻碍企业海外投资发展？

郭广昌：你讲的亲戚，就是外部的咨询机构、投行团队和律师团队，这的确是非常重要的。当然，这些服务也很贵，所以，如何节省为"亲戚"付费，也是学问之一。同时，我们一定要有自己的判断力，千万不能只听他们的。对复星来说，我们觉得现在处于一个深度全球化阶段，所以不能只靠这些机构，还是更多地依靠当地团队，比如说日本、巴西、印度，我们都是找到了当地已经做了 10 年、20 年的团队，以此来实现控股。这些当地的团队，有非常成熟的经验，这就不再仅仅是依靠别人，而是深度本土化，只有你拥有了自己的队伍，才能扎根下去。

复星投资领域众多，复星投资的逻辑是什么？

郭广昌：复星的投资逻辑其实是非常清楚的，就是两条主线：第一条主线从全球角度来看，复星坚持"保险＋投资"。我们要在全球打造一个以保险为核心的具有综合金融能力和有产业深度的投资集团，尤其强调这两者之间的配合。一个是能够取得更好的长远的资金，另一个是能够找到长期的回报率。第二条主线也非常简单，就是围绕"中国动力嫁接全球资源"，打造一个能够满足全球家庭"富足、健康、快乐"需求的解决方案。所以，复星的投资是形散而神不散，不能用一种粗浅的武功来理解复星，复星是练太极神功的。

有人说复星投资就是为了赚钱，您怎么看？

郭广昌：我一直认为复星是一家很有情怀的企业。投资是我们运营企业的一个方式，我们的目标不在于投了这个投了那个。我们的目标是通过这些投资，为家庭生活的"富足、健康、快乐"提供一个闭环的解决方案。我们是为所有人的健康快乐生活，提供一个全方位的保障，这多有情怀啊。

怎样看待王健林在《对话》节目中提到的"空手套白狼"？

郭广昌：我不相信天下有免费的午餐。所谓"人家的空手"一定是有你看不到的手，比如说迪士尼，千万不要觉得只有拿钱或者拿房子过来才是手里有东西，其实这些东西是第二位的，最最重要的是迪士尼的 IP（知识产权）。对医药企业来说，厂房和资金是第二位的，第一位的是药品研发能力和专利认证。这个是看不到的东西，但是这个东西最值钱。我觉得最重要的还是那份韧性，那份努力，那份耐心。你打造出来别人没有的东西，这份东西你可以去撬动别人的钱、别人的资产,如果是这种空手套白狼的话,我佩服。

现在前往美国投资越来越多,在你看来最该注意什么?

郭广昌:最重要的还是选择合作伙伴。美国的整体规则还是比较透明的,但问题是你的合作伙伴如果不好的话,他会利用这些规则阻碍你,这是最可怕的。所以,我觉得选择最好的合作伙伴,就跟女孩子嫁对人一样重要,尤其在美国。

怎么看待"抄底"?

郭广昌:对于投资,每个人都是说反着来。巴菲特说得最经典的一句话,就是"别人贪婪的时候你要恐惧,别人恐惧的时候你要贪婪",这不就是抄底吗?所以,对于一个投资来说,当然希望买到相对底部,这是很正常的。我们出去投资,都是自己的真金白银,每一分钱,我们真的是想了又想,这方面绝对不会乱做决定。我们是要做一个审慎的、长期的投资者,而且更在乎投资以后,如何把每个企业都管理好,创造价值,而且要每个企业都为员工负责,要为当地社区负责。我相信企业越大,这份责任心也会越大。

你有没有想"买",没"买"成的企业?

郭广昌:我们有几个想做没做成的案例:比如 Prada,那是我们刚开始做时尚产业的时候;另外,还有一个品牌叫 Moncler,我们也很喜欢;还有一家我们谈了很久的保险公司叫 AIA,非常好的保险企业,但当时因为各种原因没有买。没有买 AIA 的主要原因是:第一,那时候复星的资本结构也没那么充分;第二,复星在面对这么大的收购时,自身的国际化也没准备好;第三,是时机不一定很好,最后他们选择了直接上市。我觉得,去投一个企业,做成与不做成都是很正常的。

中国企业的海外"出征"和"回归"，意义是什么？

郭广昌：我觉得复星全球化的基本逻辑，就是"中国动力嫁接全球资源"。所以，我们出去的目的，从某种角度上是想更好地回来。比如说我们投资了地中海俱乐部、太阳马戏、印度的格兰制药公司，同时，复星在美国硅谷投资了三个研发中心，在葡萄牙投资了葡萄牙保险公司 Fidelidade 和最好的医院。我们投资很重要的一个因素，就是可以将这些技术和品牌带回中国，能够让中国的家庭生活更丰富多彩，这是我们一个基本的投资逻辑。所以，中国是我们的起点，也是我们的终点。

复星的海外投资锦囊是什么？

郭广昌：我觉得两个字吧——用心。无论是全球化，还是在中国做生意，你都要用心去听、去学。去听你客户的声音，去听你合作伙伴的声音，去听方方面面传来的声音。所以，我觉得一切东西要想轻易获得都很难，但用心了之后，再难也就不难了。

投资哲学，强调深度全球化

2016 年 9 月 8 ～ 11 日，郭广昌作为嘉宾，出席了在福建厦门举行的第 19 届中国国际投资贸易洽谈会开幕式，并在发表"复星投资哲学"的主旨演讲时表示，复星下一阶段的发展要追求多赢全球化和深度全球化。郭广昌的演讲既充满激情，又富有理性，简明扼要，干净利落：

"今天，想跟大家交流关于全球化的个人思考。中国是全球化的受益者，现在也面临很多的挑战。而且，当今有一股反全球化的浪潮也非常的强劲。我们该怎么做？我们又能做什么？

"在全球化的过程中，中国在之前快速发展的三十多年中，有很多优势，比如成本优势、强有力的政府招商引资的能力。现在，我发现这两点都面临着很大的挑战。中国目前的劳动力成本和印度相比已经偏高，印度的劳动力成本可能只有中国的三分之一或者是四分之一。同样，美国的部分招商引资能力比中国还厉害。比如，我们的一个兄弟企业，去美国做项目，州政府提供免费的土地，水电网络也都铺设好，配套铁路设施，税收上也十分优惠，支持力度非常大。面对这种情况，中国企业在全球化的过程中，如何继续保持竞争力，是我们要面对的问题。

"因为复星投资了加拿大'国宝'太阳马戏，加拿大总理来到复星时，一同探讨全球化这个问题，对全球化有一个共识，就是全球化肯定是对全球经济有利的。但是，这个有利并不是能够惠及所有人，我们能不能做出更多的范例让大家相信？全球化可以让更多的人受惠，而不仅仅是一个工作的转移，或者一个污染的转移，这是复星在思考和努力的方向。在全球化的过程中，复星践行'中国动力嫁接全球资源'的发展模式。中国动力依然强劲，全国工商联副主席林毅夫教授刚刚提到的中国这么多数字，都说明我们还有巨大的空间，我们可以通过创新，通过科技投入等，找到我们的比较竞争优势。

"我觉得不要认为我们全球化的道路已经走得很好，其实我们才刚刚开始。虽然中国现在每年非金融类对外投资超过一千亿美元，但是总存量还不到一万亿美元。所以，对很多企业来说，全球化的进程才刚刚开始，还没有进入到深度全球化阶段。以前，我们更多的是被全球化，现在我们更多的企业，在政府的主导和引导下，是积极正向的、主动的全球化，这条深度、主动的全球化道路,才刚刚开始。

"我们不是为了对外投资而投资,我们的目的是想通过全球投资、全球化布局,能够整合世界上各个国家不同的禀赋和不同资源,并为我所用,提升企业的创造力和竞争力。复星最近在印度投资的医药企业 Gland Pharma,在 7 年之前就开始设立位于美国的医药研发创新基地,有大量的创新研发成果将会在这几年出来。Gland Pharma 在中国和以色列的创新投入,这几年也非常大,基本上形成了 24 小时的医药研发体系。所以,复星通过投资 Gland Pharma,把印度低成本高质量的医药制造、全球两个最大的消费市场美国和中国,与全世界最有研发能力的以色列、美国串联协同起来,形成医药行业中最强有力的互赢综合体。

"再比如复星投资的太阳马戏,并没有因为复星的投资而减少加拿大的艺术元素,衣服道具的一针一线都是加拿大匠人手工制造。但我们投资后,正在帮助它加快在中国的发展,分享中国市场的成长。同时,太阳马戏已经与复星投资的法国全球度假品牌——地中海俱乐部合作,将独特的文化艺术体验和法式度假服务融合在一起。我也相信,就像王健林兄所说的那样,中国的太阳马戏表演,也会带动更多的海外游客来中国旅游。

"复星会更加注重对发展中国家的投资。我自己的体会是,以前,我们在发达国家投资比较多。去发达国家投资意味着什么?意味着我们要知道我们未来要走向哪里去。现在,我们更多去发展中国家投资,其实代表着你可以看到他们会往哪里去。对发展中国家的投资,中国的企业是有优势的。因为我们面对和处理过怎样从一个相对落后、到逐渐往中等发达国家走的道路上会碰到的问题,无论是企业的做法,还是政府的很多做法,都值得被发展中国家所学习。

"发展中国家也面临很多问题，新兴市场也是如此。但是，很多类似于高通胀的发展难题中国都面对过，并不可怕。所以，我们看到巴西、印度、俄罗斯以及东南亚地区的投资机会，认为现在是一个好的时机。"

郭广昌的演讲不仅是一场国际投资领域智慧分享的饕餮盛宴，也是当前全球投资促进趋势的一个全面展望，更是复星参与深度全球化的一种诠释。

同时拥有，中国和全球动力

在郭广昌的心里，对复星为什么要全球化这一问题，自始至终都有着非常深刻的认识。2018 年 6 月，郭广昌在纪念中国改革开放 40 周年前夕谈到："如果你想在全球发展，一定要了解中国，因为中国已是全球第二大经济体；如果你想在中国发展，一定要了解全球，因为中国此时已非常国际化。这是我对未来商业的一个最基本看法，同时拥有了中国和全球的动力，将是未来我们最强大的竞争力之一。"

郭广昌说："2007 年是复星全球化的元年，也是接近改革开放的第 30 个年头。随着成功在香港上市，我们首次踏入了一个国际资本市场，采纳国际标准的财务和会计制度，接受全球投资者的检验，也将自己的视野放眼到了全球。那时候我觉得，中国经济已经发展到了一个阶段，就是世界上最好的企业都来中国了，如果中国企业不能'走出去'，没有整合全球资源的能力，就没办法跟别人竞争。所以复星在那时提出了全球化战略，而且我们相信全球化是中国经济和企业发展到一定阶段的必然选择。

"2008 年，美国爆发次贷危机，全球经济在接下去的数年陷入衰退。由于当时中国全球化的步伐还较为谨慎，真正'走出去'的企业还不多，故而受到的冲击也比较有限。反倒是大量海外资产出现估值深度回调，由此产生了大量价值错配的投资机会。然而，即使机会不少，海外投资依然风险重重，尤其是当时复星在海外投资领域还是一名'新学生'，不仅找标的不易，评估标的价值更不易。所以我们初期只是在海外二级市场上试水一些价值被严重低估的中国优秀企业，因为至少在评估中国企业时，我们是有底的。此时，复星急需一位领路人把自己'领进门'，帮助自己在海外尽可能地多'排雷'。同时，在战略层面，我们'走出去'并不是为了低买高卖，而是希望借力中国消费市场的崛起，把海外优质的品牌和产品'引回来'。当时我觉得，30 年的改革开放使中国政府积累了较为丰富的市场经济的运作和管理经验，中国多年来持续的工业化和城市化进程，以及国内逐步释放的巨大消费和投资需求都将为复星未来的发展提供强劲且持久的动能。作为'中国专家'，我们要善用'中国动力嫁接全球资源'。

"2010 年年初，美国前财长约翰·斯诺首先加入复星担任董事会顾问，分享他在世界 500 强企业和政府部门高级行政工作的经验。然后，复星与全球最大的私募股权基金——凯雷投资集团宣布在全球展开战略合作，共同聚焦中国经济高速增长所带来的机会，并成立了中国首只外商投资的合伙制基金。通过和国际领先的个人、团队合作，复星开始在全球化投资、融资、运营管理、人力资源等各方面向国际一流企业对标、学习，逐步向成为一家全球化企业迈进。很快，我们也迎来了复星有史以来第一笔重大的海外投资——法国旅游度假连锁集团地中海俱乐部。在这之前，复星从未正式涉足旅游业。为了这笔投资，我们做了大量研究，发现全球旅游产业非常庞大，尤其是休闲度假这一旅游产业的大头，在中国几乎为零。于是，我们决定把国外的品牌和经验引进来，帮助中国在旅游供给侧方面做一些事。

"当时的地中海俱乐部已经连续 5 年亏损，对于来自中国的我们，陷入困境中的董事会同意让我们以小股比参股，但要帮助他们进入中国市场。因为说起旅游产业，当时的我们不及他们专业，但要说中国市场，我们多年产业运营所积累下的知识和资源，对他们来说简直就是无价之宝。2010 年，仅仅在入股后六个月，我们就成功帮助地中海俱乐部在中国黑龙江的亚布力开出第一家度假村。这次高效的合作让高傲的法国人对我们刮目相看，信任也在彼此间建立起来。之后我们再接再厉，继续帮助他们在中国扩张，中国游客数高速增长，很快中国便成了继法国之后的全球第二大市场。与此同时，对旅游产业已有相当深度的理解和认识后，我们于 2013 年对地中海俱乐部提出私有化控股，并于 2015 年私有化完成。通过我们的管理输出与资源赋能，地中海俱乐部在私有化后成功扭亏为盈，近三年度假村经营利润的年复合增长率达到 26%。

"在整个地中海俱乐部项目中，从接触到参股再到私有化，通过与全世界最好的投资机构和个人合作，我们一直在了解、学习和钻研，探索全球化的路径和方法，积累人才，并逐渐形成了复星出海模式的雏形。而这个项目则是我们模式得到验证并走向成熟的过程，之后通过不断地复制这一模式，我们的全球化战略也得以全面铺开。今天我们已经在 17 个国家深度开展业务，产业也越做越广，已拥有在医疗、旅游、时尚、保险等多领域下的数十个国际品牌。复星自己已变身为一个全球赋能平台，凭借自己多年积累的产业运营能力对旗下企业的协同整合来创造价值。

"回望过去的 10 多年，复星的全球化可能不是最快的，但一直很稳。

它的成功基于我们对中国未来经济发展趋势的准确判断，也基于我们步步为营、行稳致远的产业发展理念。此外，随着中国产业今天的不断进步升级，我们也已经在不少领域有能力向全球输出产品、技术和模式，尤其是非洲、印度等新兴市场。所以，我们今天的全球化战略不再只是'中国动力嫁接全球资源'，而是中国—全球双向驱动。"

第八章

足球为媒，
欧洲战略稳扎稳打

进军体育，联系市场联资源

2016 年 1 月 18 日，由郭广昌控股的上海复娱文化传播股份有限公司高调宣布，公司与欧洲知名体育经纪公司——葡萄牙 Gestifute 公司达成战略合作，携手进军足球产业。

关于复娱文化与 Gestifute 双方合作的内容，郭广昌说，一是充分利用 Gestifute 旗下顶级球星及教练资源，全权代理其中国商业代言，承办球星见面会等各类商业活动以及公益活动；二是引进国外优秀球员进入中国市场；三是帮助中国国内优秀球员转会至欧洲俱乐部；四是建立青少年足球培训机构，培养有潜力的球员到海外深造；五是围绕球星 IP 进行衍生品业务运营，如网游开发 IP 授权、专属品牌销售经营等。

继复星在国际上先后向旅游、健康和时尚等产业大举进军后，这一次，郭广昌的商业帝国又通过与 Gestifute 达成战略合作，开始进军体育产业，准确来说是进军足球产业。这一举措，郭广昌再一次将复星与葡萄牙的市场和资源联系在了一起。

Gestifute 是整个欧洲最负盛名的体育经纪公司之一，旗下拥有穆里尼奥、C 罗、J 罗、德赫亚、迭戈·科斯塔等顶级教练和球星。公司的创始人就是大名鼎鼎的豪尔赫·门德斯，被公认为能够影响整个欧洲转会市场的人。

作为一家在全球资本市场上富有影响力的金融投资公司，复星感兴趣的领域从来就不止一个。郭广昌说，只要任何有可能投资的机会，复星都不会放过。从 2014 年年初开始，复星的投资方向逐渐转向海外市场，其中，葡萄牙是复星大力投资的市场，这也使复星成为在葡萄牙最为活跃的公司。郭广昌认为，葡萄牙是一个充满吸引力的重要市场，完全符合复星的全球化战略和布局。葡萄牙是全欧洲最适宜投资的国家之一，复星非常关注葡萄牙各个领域的投资机会，包括地产、旅游及品牌产品等行业。一旦投资机会出现，郭广昌和他的复星就会果断出手。

2014年1月，复星以10亿欧元的价格，在竞标中击败了强大对手——美国投资基金阿波罗全球管理公司，一举收购了葡萄牙保险公司Caixa Seguros的控股权；2014年6月，复星以5,680万欧元的价格，收购了葡萄牙电网公司REN的3.9%国有股份；2014年10月，在连续两次提高收购报价后，复星最终击败全球500强企业——美国联合健康，以每股5.01欧元、总计4.6亿欧元的价格，收购了葡萄牙医疗保健服务商ESS 96.07%的股权。在收购这些葡萄牙企业的过程中，复星均得到国家的大力支持。

在葡萄牙一系列大动作投资过程中，郭广昌凭借追随巴菲特的伯克希尔哈撒韦公司的投资模式，并关注中国消费者需求的战略思维，与葡萄牙政、商两界的杰出人物，一同入选了"葡萄牙2015年度TOP影响力物"榜单，排名第30位。

郭广昌高调宣布复星选择与Gestifute展开合作，毫不掩饰复星进军体育行业的野心。郭广昌说："我们正面临着一个拥有巨大发展潜力，并富有激情和创造力的体育市场。与门德斯这样经验丰富的世界级大师合作，借由他在世界体坛所拥有的丰沛资源和影响力，一定能为中国体育产业尤其是足球产业的发展带来更多积极变化。"

实践证明，从进军保险、电网和医疗，再到进军足球，郭广昌的确没有放过葡萄牙任何一个值得投资的机会，一直都在努力地关注一切投资的可能，而且投资力度非常强大。郭广昌表示，复星未来还将拓展至演出、影视等多个领域。

随着葡萄牙经济利好的消息频频传出,以及李嘉诚、王健林等成功企业家纷纷愿意将资金落地葡萄牙,也极大地增强了中国国内投资者投资移民葡萄牙的信心。葡萄牙的招商引资政策非常优惠,只要将 50 万欧元投资葡萄牙房产,仅需 3 个月的时间,一家三代就可以快速移民葡萄牙,并享受葡萄牙福利待遇,从而实现"投资 + 移民"的双赢局面。有了众多的中国投资者投资葡萄牙,更加坚定了郭广昌加速推进复星的"葡国战略"。

入主狼队,扩大经营产业链

2016 年 1 月,复星与葡萄牙 Gestifute 公司达成战略合作后,郭广昌就开始紧锣密鼓地筹划收购欧洲的顶级球队。经过多次谈判,2016 年 7 月,复星国际以 4,500 万英镑的代价,从斯蒂夫·摩根手中如愿地收购了英格兰足球英冠联赛球队——狼队 100% 的股权,向进军足球产业迈出了实质性的一步。

而就在半年前的 2015 年 12 月,英国媒体曾传出中国网易公司董事局主席兼首席执行官丁磊有意收购狼队的消息,声称相关的收购谈判已持续数月,急欲出手球队的狼队老板斯蒂夫·摩根态度积极,有意促成俱乐部股权的尽快转让。

丁磊是中国互联网上市公司中持有股份比例最多的创始人,手中持有近 45% 的网易股份。当时,网易市值为 237 亿美元,由此计算,丁磊身价应为 106.65 亿美元,相当于 690 亿人民币。

狼队足球俱乐部是英格兰的一支职业足球队,成立于 1877 年,是英格兰足球联盟创始成员。在 2009 ~ 2010 赛季,这支球队曾在英超征战,但在 2012 年 5 月,因球队战绩不佳而降级到英冠。

最终，丁磊因故未能完成对狼队的收购。这一结果，无形给郭广昌留下了机会。

复星收购狼队100%的股权后，球队老板摩根在写给狼队球迷、员工及媒体的告别信中说："现在，是时候让后来者接过俱乐部的接力棒了，我很高兴复星与我们达成协议，未来的两年时间，他们许诺投资给俱乐部2,000万～3,000万英镑，而在至少一年内，他们也依然会延续狼队的社区公益计划，以及其他慈善项目。我预祝复星一切顺利，无论现在还是未来，我依然与狼队的一切紧密相连。"

接手狼队后，复星许诺在两年内投资2,000万～3,000万英镑，对比于摩根每年不到400万英镑的投资，翻了一番甚至翻了两番，这足以让狼队球迷满怀期待。这个数字，虽不及英超各大豪门，但在英冠联赛队伍中位列前茅。

在复星收购狼队的过程中，葡萄牙Gestifute公司老板豪尔赫·门德斯无疑扮演了中间人的角色。

对复星以4,500万英镑的代价收购狼队，英国《金融时报》刊文指出："对于以投资地中海俱乐部和太阳马戏这些著名品牌为荣的复星来说，收购一家36年没有赢得重要奖项的中部二流球队，着实有点出人意料。"

而随着时间推移，已属于复星旗下的狼队，一度被英国《卫报》《泰晤士报》和《独立报》推上风口浪尖，称葡萄牙人豪尔赫·门德斯介入了对狼队俱乐部的管理，并引起了英冠联赛球队的不满。

媒体的推测和联盟的不满，主要来自两个方面：一是狼队在最近4个转会窗，接连引进门德斯麾下Gestifute的签约球员：2016年8月，伊万卡瓦列罗，700万英镑；2017年1月，赫尔德·科斯塔，1,300万英镑；2017年6月，米兰达，270 万英镑；2017 年 7 月，鲁本·内维斯，1,580 万英镑；迪奥戈·若塔，租借加盟；2018 年 1 月，托马斯·雷芒，自由加盟。这样，狼队一线队已经拥有 7 名葡萄牙球员，几乎占到名单的三分之一。二是 2017 年 5 月出任狼队主帅的努诺·埃斯皮里托·桑托是葡萄牙人，更是门德斯的老熟人。1997 年，当时还是夜店老板的门德斯，就是通过受雇于桑托而进军职业足坛。十多年间，为了报恩的门德斯，一直是桑托的义务代理人，双方的情义非同一般。

在英国媒体看来，从球员、教练到转会市场，门德斯俨然代替复星成了狼队的实际掌控者。

对此，狼队在一份官方声明中表示："复星确实与门德斯的 Gestifute 存在着股权合作关系，门德斯也是郭广昌的圈内顾问，但这样的关系，是足坛的普遍现象，并无任何特别之处。"而有关经济事务和代理费的问题，狼队没有在声明中加以回应。

即使狼队被众多媒体推到了风口浪尖上，但郭广昌始终没有停止与门德斯的合作。郭广昌认为，门德斯是 C 罗等大腕球星的经纪人，在足坛有着较高的人脉，这正是复星所看重的。其实，复星联合 Gestifute，本身就是郭广昌"葡国战略"中的重要一步。早在 2015 年 6 月，郭广昌就宣称葡萄牙是"全欧洲最适宜投资的国家之一"，复星也将欧洲投资的重点首先放在了葡萄牙。

在收购狼队前后，复星一直在稳步推进集团在葡萄牙的投资，先后赢得了葡萄牙保险公司 Caixa Seguradora 的控股权、收购了陷入困境的 Espírito Santo 集团的医院业务、收购了千禧银行近 17% 的股份。

对于复星的大动作收购，葡萄牙《贸易周刊》指出，2015 年，郭广昌便竭尽全力扩大复星在葡萄牙的产业链，尤其在时尚和传媒行业等方面目标非常明确，就是将中国动力嫁接上全球资源。

在郭广昌看来，由于门德斯在葡萄牙拥有极高的人脉，复星没有理由放弃这一资源。复星必须充分利用好门德斯这一资源，从而搭上"葡国攻略"的"顺风车"。

随着时间的推移，郭广昌和门德斯逐渐为狼队进入世界顶级舞台做好了准备。在2017～2018赛季的英冠联赛中，狼队提前3轮锁定英冠冠军，从而在时隔6年后，再次重返英超联赛。

经过两个赛季的磨合，狼队的葡萄牙籍主帅努诺把狼队打造成了一支非常具有拉丁派风格的球队，来自葡萄牙的鲁本·内维斯、若塔和卡巴莱罗等球员，都在联赛中有出色的表现，成为球队冲上英超的功臣之一。在2018～2019赛季，狼队更是以57个积分，排列积分榜的第7位，将参加欧洲联盟杯的赛事，改写了球队的历史。2018年9月，狼队主教练努诺还当选了英超联赛当月最佳主教练。不仅如此，球队甚至喊出了7年之内拿英超冠军的口号。

下一个赛季，狼队令人期待。

心中有数，葡国经济有前景

2017年，葡萄牙《检视杂志》4月号的"封面故事"栏目中，用横跨10个版面的篇幅，刊发了郭广昌和复星在葡萄牙投资发展的专题报道。作为葡萄牙的主流财经杂志，用这样大的篇幅来介绍中国的企业家和企业还是第一次。

这个专题报道指出，复星在葡萄牙已是声名斐然。近三年来，复星入股了银行、保险和医疗等领域的龙头企业，成为 Fidelidade，Luz Saúde 和葡萄牙商业银行 BCP 的大股东。复星在房地产和能源领域也有涉足，下一步将向旅游市场进军。

杂志在报道中说，2014 年，复星刚刚收购 Fidelidade 时，人们可能不会想到，复星在不久的将来会成为在葡投资最多的外商之一。今天，复星在葡萄牙的投资，已经超过了 23 亿欧元，并且还在继续寻找合适的标的。对于复星来说，葡萄牙是一个进入欧洲市场的门户，有助于复星加强在葡语国家的布局，比如巴西、安哥拉和莫桑比克等。郭广昌在访谈中表示，他对葡萄牙的经济形势充满信心，对葡萄牙人民也赞不绝口，称这是一个勤劳的民族。

《检视杂志》甚至将郭广昌定位为中国民营资本在葡萄牙的"最佳代言人"。

在接受《检视杂志》采访时，郭广昌表示，健康、快乐、富足是复星的投资重点，其中也包括体育、娱乐业务。近些年来，除了足球运动吸引了众多来自中国投资者的关注外，旅游业更是吸引了许多企业慕名而来。

在谈到复星在葡萄牙怎样操作投资这个问题时，郭广昌表示："在投资之初，我们非常谨慎，因为当时刚经历欧洲经济危机，葡萄牙也处于经济低迷时期。随着对葡萄牙人民和经济的了解逐渐加深，我们的信心越来越充足。葡萄牙社会非常稳定，对外来投资也很友好，而且是一个非常勤劳的民族。因此，我对葡萄牙的经济前景非常乐观。"

事实证明，复星在葡萄牙的投资都取得了让郭广昌十分满意的结果。2016 年，Fidelidade 和 Luz Saude 合计取得了 2.29 亿欧元的净利润，其中，2.11 亿欧元来自 Fidelidade。而 Luz Saude 年报显示，安哥拉健康医疗机构已获得审批将实施推进，拟于 2018 年开业。Fidelidade 的 CEO 若热·马加良斯·科雷亚先生曾在公开场合表示，Fidelidade 的发展战略是"海外扩张"，目标是"实现公司的数字化并建立保险领域的领先地位"。

在郭广昌看来，复星的全球化战略在持续稳步推进，而葡萄牙则是复星打开葡语国家市场的钥匙。他说："我们在巴西有投资，如 Rio Bravo。希望未来 Luz Saude 和 Fidelidade 也可以加大在巴西市场的发展。此外，我们正在非洲寻求更多机遇。复星医药是非洲疟疾治疗药物的最大供应商，同时，我们在大健康领域，也有很多创新业务。"

显然，复星把葡萄牙作为进军欧洲市场的大门，在金融等多个领域拥有充足的运作资产。复星持有葡萄牙商业银行 BCP 23.9% 的股份，持有葡萄牙电网公司 REN5.3% 的股份。郭广昌说："葡萄牙是我们投资欧洲的门户，同时，它也是我们投资其他葡语国家的门户。我们在欧洲投资的国家除葡萄牙外，还包括德国、英国和法国。"他还说："复星很愿意帮助 BCP 进入中国澳门和中国内地市场。"

早在 2013 年，复星就来到了葡萄牙首都里斯本。当时，葡萄牙本土面临严重的资金缺乏，失业率达到 17% 的历史高位。就是在这一年，密切关注海外投资机会的郭广昌，在葡萄牙私有化改革中寻找到了合适机会，一次又一次地展开了项目布局。到 2015 年夏天，复星已经成为在葡萄牙投资最多的一家中国民营企业，同时也成为中国在葡萄牙最杰出的投资集团之一，从而傲视群雄。

2016 年 11 月 21 日，复星通过增资，以 1.746 亿欧元一举收购了葡萄牙商业银行 BCP 16.7% 的股权，并成为大股东。这家由 Jardim Gonçalves 创立的银行，从此成为复星旗下企业中的一员。

而在此之前的 2014 年，复星收购了葡萄牙保险公司 Fidelidade，获得 80% 的股权。几个月后，复星和 Fidelidade 合作，一举进军医疗业务领域，收购了 Espírito Santo 家族的医疗业务 Luz Saude。郭广昌并不是随意选择投资项目，他寻找的是具有强大品牌和增长潜力的优质企业。Fidelidade 是葡萄牙保险行业的市场领导者，而 Luz Saude 也是葡萄牙医疗行业数一数二的企业。

算起来，复星是在 2010 年拉开公司国际化序幕的。当年，复星收购了法国旅游业的标志品牌——地中海俱乐部的 7.1% 股权。

2013 年 12 月，复星在纽约买下了由大卫·洛克菲勒所建的第一大通——曼哈顿广场。这栋名满华尔街的大楼，是摩根大通的总部。2014 年，葡萄牙进入了郭广昌和复星的投资视线。

到 2015 年，复星已经投资了 12 个海外项目。就在这一年，复星收购了加拿大太阳马戏 25% 的股份。

2016 年上半年复星财报显示，复星的总资产超过 590 亿美元，实现了每年以 7.4% 的速度增长。在此期间，公司的收益达到 43 亿欧元，同比增长 9.3%。利润达到了 5.9 亿欧元，实现了以 21.4% 的速度增长。公司所发布财报显示，复星资产负债比率取得了改善，债务结构进一步优化。郭广昌在接受 Expresso 采访时表示："我们的负债保持在适当水平，但是我们还想也应该进一步降低负债水平，缩减成本。"

总统称赞，中法合作的典范

2018 年 1 月 9 日，法国总统马克龙在访华期间，专门在北京举行了中国企业家座谈会，复星董事长郭广昌受邀参加了这次座谈会。在座谈中，马克龙将复星投资的地中海俱乐部称为中法合作中"教科书"一般的成功案例。

法国地中海俱乐部（CLUB MED）成立于 1950 年，是全球一站式旅游度假村概念的创始者，并于 1966 年在巴黎上市，是全球最大的旅游度假连锁集团。该集团总共拥有 80 多座度假村，遍布全球 5 大洲 30 多个国家和地区，每年向全球超过 120 万人提供高品质的一站式度假体验，集团年收入 13 亿多欧元。地中海俱乐部醒目的海神戟标志几乎遍布全世界所有最美丽的角落。

复星是在 2010 年首次完成了对地中海俱乐部的收购。2010 年 6 月 13 日，法国地中海俱乐部集团与复星联合发布公告宣称，中国最大的综合类民营企业复星，以 2.1 亿元人民币的价格，收购地中海俱乐部 7.1% 的股权，从而成为该企业最大的战略投资者之一。

随后，双方签署了关于建立战略伙伴关系的合作备忘录，将在中国高端度假村建设运营及全球业务协同方面展开深入合作。

郭广昌表示："与地中海俱乐部的合作，不仅为中国消费者带来更高品质的旅游度假体验，也将为利益相关方提供分享中国成长的机会。多项数据表明，中国旅游业正在经历快速增长并带来了巨大商机。随着全球经济进入调整期，中国经济增长方式的转变正引起全球的关注，以中国国内消费升级为重要动力的经济增长，将为世界带来新一轮的商机。"

2015 年 3 月，复星以每股 24.6 欧元的报价、总计超过 9 亿欧元的收购金额，完成了对地中海俱乐部的全资收购。从 2010 年 6 月的第一次收购，到完成全资收购，历时近 5 年时间。

就在 2018 年 1 月法国总统马克龙访华的前一天，复星被英国《全球银行与金融评论》杂志授予了"亚洲最佳投资管理公司"荣誉。这一奖项，无疑彰显了复星国际一直致力于追求提供优质的产品和服务,并专注于投后管理和增值,以及着重于提升产业运营能力和持续创新,从而为复星投资的成员企业带来赋能增值效益。

郭广昌心里明白,为地中海俱乐部开拓中国乃至亚洲市场,是复星2007年明确全球化征程以来最核心的战略,其背后是中国经济的迅猛发展、中国快速融入世界的现实。借助中国快速发展的强大动力,复星希望抓住机遇,在全球聚集优质资源,并将这些资源与中国动力紧密结合起来,服务于中国人日益增长的消费升级需求。对复星实施全球化战略,郭广昌始终有着非常明确的目标:一是成为股东;二是帮助企业在中国拓展市场;三是与被投企业一起发掘世界市场。而复星投资地中海俱乐部,三方面的目标都达到了。

复星实施国际化战略,拥有强大的产业和资本基础。到2018年年初,复星的总资产已经超过了5,000亿元,自身就是一个巨大的生态系统。复星旗下丰富的资源,可与被投企业进行充分的对接,庞大的用户数据库,必将在"C2M"战略中打通旗下各产业板块。

在投资后管理地中海俱乐部的过程中,复星在国内、海外同步推动集团体系内资源与地中海俱乐部对接,如加拿大蒙特利尔的太阳马戏深度合作地中海俱乐部,一些项目迅速在法国、多米尼加等国家的地中海俱乐部度假村落地。这些太阳马戏主题体验项目,可以让游客在G.O[1]指导下,亲身体验吊绳、吊环项目的感觉。这种沉浸式的体验,无疑丰富了地中海俱乐部活动主题,也打通了两大IP的流量。

地中海俱乐部被马克龙称赞为中法合作中"教科书"一般的典范,充

1　Gentle Organizer(亲切的组织者)

分验证了复星实施全球化战略的可行性，复星的管理模式也越来越成熟。

从 2010 年 6 月入股地中海俱乐部开始，复星在法国先后投资了女装品牌 IRO SAS、资管平台 PERAF、植物黄油生产商 St Hubert 以及医药分销公司 Tridem Pharma，投资总额达 25 亿欧元，产业遍及健康、富足、快乐等多个领域，成为在法国和欧盟投资产业最多、最具影响力的中国民营企业之一。仅在法国，复星旗下就管理资产近 100 亿欧元，占复星海外管理资产的四分之一。

马克龙在座谈会讲话时说，复星收购地中海俱乐部时，曾一度引起法国各界的担忧。但经过反复协商，双方扩大了合作，实现了互利共赢，渐渐平复了法国社会的焦虑。这一投资案例说明，中法两国贸易不平衡的解决办法不是"塞"，而是"疏"，进一步扩大贸易与交往，在了解分歧中增进沟通，才会取得意想不到的效果。最后，马克龙将复星称作是"走出去"的中国企业榜样。

面对马克龙的高度评价，郭广昌满怀希望地表示，2017 年年底，地中海俱乐部在华度假村达到 6 家，而到 2020 年，在华度假村预计将超过 20 家，客户人数也将从每年 2 万人次，增长到每年 25 万人次，人数将增长 10 多倍。

毫无疑问，复星已经成为地中海俱乐部全球业务复苏的核心动力，也成了地中海俱乐部冲击休闲度假领域新的"世界第一"的强劲动力。

法国总统马克龙一直是全球化的积极倡导者，他说：对于中法合作，可以盖墙，也可以建风车。墙用来挡风，但风车是利用风的，会创造更大价值。马克龙积极鼓励中资企业联手法国企业，在人工智能、大数据交流和能源转型等方面加强合作。

座谈会结束时，马克龙主动走到郭广昌的身边，与郭广昌握手致意。

第九章

做好产品，
企业发展灵魂所在

产业投资，坚持做好四件事

我们一定要有产业深度、产业背景，一定要通过投资，打穿我们的一些核心痛点，并在之后形成闭环，然后逐步培养、壮大它。这就是我们要做的事。

——郭广昌

每周一，复星员工都会参加例行的晨会，聆听投资团队分享最新投资热点、复盘投资案例。

2016 年 8 月 15 日，跑遍美国、俄罗斯、巴西等国，刚刚回到上海的郭广昌，为复星员工带来了对投资的最新感悟，就是复星要在投资中坚持做好四件事：

"第一，必须强调到现场亲自去看、去发掘价值。过去两个月里，我去了三次美国、一次巴西、一次印度、一次俄罗斯、一次英国和一次葡萄牙，这还不包括国内的出差。为什么要说这个？因为我感觉现在信息太发达了，我看大家的眼睛，绝大多数时间都盯在移动互联网上，信息获取也变得太容易。但我认为，再多的信息都比不上面对面的交流。所以，提醒各位复星同学，千万不能只是坐在办公室里，仅限于分析别人给你的信息。你需要自己去发现、去面对面地谈。复星的投资哲学，一直在强调要有深刻的产业理解和深入当地的本土化能力，所以，复星的同学在做项目时，一定要到当地、要深入市场、要找到合适的关键人，亲自去听、去看和去交流。而且，这不仅仅是对投资团队的要求，包括我们的中后台，比如 HR，也不能单纯的信息来、信息去，没有面对面的交流。很多时候，你靠公开信息或者只是打个电话，永远不如你真的跟别人喝杯咖啡效果好。到现场，这一点太重要了。而且从我的感受里，到了俄罗斯和巴西看到的，和我从新闻上获得的信息是不一样的。这很正常。如果我们得到的信息跟别的投资者得到的都一样、做的判断是一样的、投资方式也是一样的话，那要复星干什么呢？所以，我们必须能够深入一线，自己去看、去听、去交流、去发掘价值。这是对复星所有同学一个基本的要求，就是要去现场，去发掘别人没有看到的价值。

"第二，坚持做对的事情、重要的事情、难的事情。企业发展就像逆水行舟，坚持做对的事情、重要的事情和难的事情，往往会感觉到不顺。但如果你觉得很顺时，那可能你是在坐享其成，可能是在退步，往往是一天不如一天。我觉得，复星现在面临的情况，就像逆水行舟，的确有很多东西需要突破。因为我们在选择做对的事情、重要的事情和难的事情，这是与别人不一样的事情。比如我们对足球的投资。我觉得我们就是在做一个不一样的途径，当然这会比较难。我们要做的事情，是用比较少的价钱，买一个有潜力的球队，然后利用我们的优势、我们在足球上的布局，迅速提升球队的水平。这是一个不容易的事情，但是做成了，带来的价值、品牌溢价等都会很大。所以说，复星要走的道路，就是要做出别人没有做的事情，做跟别人不一样的事情。如果都是做一样的事，我们还有什么价值？

"第三，要在重要的地方有突破。今年以来，复星在核心战略上有两个比较明显的突破。首先是复星的大健康战略。我们重金收购了印度的Gland Pharma，加大了复星在印度的投资布局。Gland Pharma绝大多数产品都是卖到美国的，它是印度制药企业中向美国出口最强的企业之一。我有时候跟团队说，其实，我们应该反思一下，为什么我们感觉各方面都很强，但在医药产品向美国出口方面，还是不如人家？这些方面，印度有很多值得我们学习的地方。而投资这个企业，我们既可以很好地借鉴印度的经验，又能很好地把美国市场打开。这样，复星在未来就可以将中国、美国和印度这三个全球最大的医药市场和各自的资源禀赋链接起来。当然，这是一个不容易的事情，也是一个需要重金投入的事情。现在，复星就是要着眼于做这种对的、重要的事。因为大，所以我们必须要全神贯注地把它做好。还有，最近复星联合健康保险获得了保监会的批筹。这对整个复星来说，是非常重要的。但拿到批筹只是第一步，我们还要不断思考如何把健康保险与我们的医疗、健康服务打通，形成闭环。这是一个对的事情、重要的事情，我们就是要着力去打穿它。的确，有时会觉得做这种事情是很累的，总觉得不顺。你做投资，其实绝大部分人家有资金需求，更多是在求你。但你去做那种人家不需要钱的项目，你要说服他要你的投资，因为你能给他带来价值，这才是我们投资哲学的关键。我们一定要在重要的地方有突破。

"第四，我们不仅注重投资，更注重投资后管理。大多数时候，我们做了一些投资，这些投资好与不好，可能很多方面是靠投后管理。很多人就是投的时候很开心，积极性很高，投完以后就不管了。这就像你对待自己的小孩，只管生、不管养。其实，小孩好不好关键在于培养、发现，天才都是被挖掘出来的。那你投了一个有天才基因的项目，投资之后能不能为它创造价值、帮它做上去？所以，投后管理很重要。好与不好不只在于投资这一头，更在于投以后你怎么培养它、挖掘它、浇灌它。该给阳光的时候给它阳光，该给水的时候给它水。这两年，复星也有了不少耐心培养的项目。比如，今年我们获得了支付牌照，但是支付怎么发展？怎么整个打开？我们获得健康保险牌照，怎么壮大和发展？这是很大的问题，要一步步去做。我们有投资基因的企业，最容易犯的一个错误，就是走捷径，总觉得只要买对了就行。其实，投资只是刚刚开始。除了投资之外，更重要的还是要花精力、心思，能有耐心做产业的事情，做一步步培养人的事情。这是别的投资企业没有的气质，而复星一定要有这样的气质。我们一定要有产业深度、产业背景，一定要通过投资，打穿我们的一些核心痛点，并在之后形成闭环，然后逐步培养、壮大它。这就是我们要做的事。"

集团发展，进入深度全球化

复星的投资，是深度全球化，并遵循两个原则：一是在全球建立起深度本土化的投资团队；二是放眼全球投资，深度产业化发展。

——郭广昌

2016 年 8 月 25 日，"亚布力论坛第十三届夏季高峰会"在西安锦江国际酒店正式开幕，郭广昌出席并发表演讲。

郭广昌在演讲中说，复星的投资，是深度全球化，并遵循两个原则：一是在全球建立起深度本土化的投资团队；二是放眼全球投资，深度产业化发展。

"复星下一步要做的是深度全球化。我要讲一下历史，关于复星现在在海外的投资企业的历史。复星投资的 H&A 德国私人银行于 1797 年成立，有 219 年历史，复星全资控股；复星投资的葡萄牙保险公司 Fidelidade 1808 年成立，有 208 年历史；复星投资的英国著名婴童车品牌 Silver Cross 1877 年成立，有 139 年历史，复星全资控股；最近刚刚宣布投资的英冠俱乐部狼队，是英国足球联盟的创始成员球队，1877 年成立，有 139 年历史；复星投资的印度 Gland Pharma 医药公司，1978 年成立，有 37 年历史；复星投资的加拿大太阳马戏，1984 年成立，有 32 年历史；复星投资的以色列护肤品牌 AHAVA，有 28 年历史。而复星，有着 25 年历史。

"这些复星投资企业的历史与古都西安相比，无疑显得很短。但是，和我们在座的各位企业家所领导的企业，包括和复星相比都要长。我觉得，伟大的企业都是'熬'出来的。全球化也是一样的，也是一步步脚踏实地走出来的，从血与泪的教训中闯出来的。复星从 2007 年开始全球化，现在提出来的是深度全球化。对复星来说，全球化与深度全球化是两个概念。

"第一，深度全球化的一个方面是完全本土化，复星要在全球建立起完全本土化的投资团队。所谓'完全本土化'，并非将中国员工派驻到我们全球的办公室，而是在全球寻找独立的本土投资团队。这些团队，已经在当地积累了 10 年以上的地区经验，并且认同复星的文化和投资逻辑。这两年，我们在俄罗斯和巴西找到了这样的团队，之前是在英国伦敦和日本东京找到的，他们的投资成绩十分优异。复星会继续在全球进行这样的本土化团队建设。之前所提到的复星在巴西的 Rio Bravo 团队，其中成员之一就是前巴西中央银行的行长，经验非常资深。也只有拥有这样优秀人才的团队，才能说是真正的深度本土化团队。

"第二，深度全球化的另一个方面是深度产业化。深度全球化，以前提出来是全球投资，但各个地方的禀赋是不一样的。比如医药行业，科研创新最前沿的地区肯定是在美国，所以复星 7 年前在硅谷设立三个研发实验室。但最近，复星又投资了印度的 Gland Pharma。为什么投资 Gland Pharma？就是因为印度在创新药上比中国做得好。25 年前，Gland Pharma

就已经获得 FDA 认证，而且 25 年来没有任何不良记录。包括最近美国监管机构对印度企业进行了大量的审查与处罚，但这家企业表现得非常好。通过对 Gland Pharma 的投资，复星在医药领域更加深度产业化，把美国的科研优势、印度的低成本高质量制造和中国的巨大市场需求结合起来，使三个市场的各自优势得以充分发挥出来。正是这条路，让我对复星医药的未来发展充满信心，我们可以成为全世界最有竞争力的企业。我们用美国优势，用印度优势，同时深耕中国本土优势。复星下一步要做的，是深度全球化，而不是简单地做一个投资。

"复星要踏踏实实地做负责任的全球化企业。在全球化的过程中，一定会有文化等相关差异表现出来。而有些所谓的企业间、国家间在文化上、利益上的差异，其实是好企业和坏企业的差别。全世界的好企业文化都是差不多的，都是企业家导向，注重效率，强调产品力，关爱员工，这都是一样的，这是普遍原则。而不好的企业，也都是差不多的，官商勾结，不注意效率，官僚主义。美国和中国有什么区别吗？所以，一定有一些文化上的区别，但是不要把好企业和坏企业的区别误解为国与国之间的区别，这是我的第一个观点。

"我的第二个观点，就是将心比心。如果 20 年前，一个美国或者欧洲的企业把中国最大的保险公司，那时候是中国人寿，85% 的股权一下子买走了，中国人会有何感想？复星花了 10 亿欧元，在 2014 年把葡萄牙最大的保险公司 85% 左右的股权购买下来，它在葡萄牙的市场占有率约为30%，包括寿险、财产险等。尽管政府批准这个交易，但是难免老百姓和其他机构有些想法，这很正常。将心比心，你要理解，要理解当地民众的想法。所以，我觉得我们要主动地遵守规则，主动地去做一个合格的公民，主动地为当地社会多做一些事情。所以，当复星了解到葡萄牙的青年人存在就业问题时，我们就去更多地支持青年创业，开启青年创业计划，多做社会公益。有一段时间，我们在葡萄牙受到很多的舆论压力，但现在情况好多了。所以，遇到问题，是企业全球化过程中很普遍的，不要怨天尤人，也不要自卑，更不要有大国主义。我们不卑不亢地做事情，用行动得到更多的理解与认同。

"保险，是属于复星要走的最独特的路。复星没有某些企业那么勇敢、生猛。没有泰康的 20 年积累。复星一开始对保险业不懂，连年亏损，投资几年之后才加速发展。复星在保险行业没有这么长的历史与积累，要跟上发展就要收购兼并，寻找人才，同时不断地学习，不断地提高。复星保险更要走自己的有特色的道路。所以，复星刚刚取得了健康险的牌照，在健康保险上一定会发力。另外，全球布局意味着国外发展的机会比较多，我们要通过国外的保险公司加快自身的发展。"

好的产品，是好企业的灵魂

好产品，是一个企业特别是好企业的灵魂，比如阿里巴巴，虽然做电商，但最了不起的产品其实是支付宝；比如腾讯，如果没有微信，也不会远远超过其他竞争对手；还有像陈东升董事长带领的泰康，核心也是靠好产品一步步发展起来。

——郭广昌

2018 年 8 月 24 ～ 26 日，以"中国经济：初心与再出发"为主题的"亚布力中国企业家论坛夏季高峰会"在江西南昌举行。这次峰会，600 多位知名企业家、学者和政府官员相聚在一起，共同探讨中国经济改革的初心与再出发。

郭广昌在峰会发表讲话时说："大抵所有人都想知道商业的秘诀，也希望获得别人所不知的捷径。但创立复星 26 年来，我越发觉得商业实在没有什么秘诀可言，如果非要归纳出一点，那一定就是'产品'和'产品力'。好产品，是一个企业特别是好企业的灵魂，比如阿里巴巴，虽然做电商，但最了不起的产品其实是支付宝；比如腾讯，如果没有微信，也不会远远超过其他竞争对手；还有像陈东升董事长带领的泰康，核心也是靠好产品一步步发展起来。有些企业家朋友遇到了各种不顺、问题，会抱怨电商冲击、会抱怨渠道不顺、会抱怨市场不好。但让我说，其实就是你的产品出问题了。没有好产品，怎么做一个好企业？对复星来说也是这样的，想要持续发展、想要让全球每个家庭生活更幸福，靠的就是产品。

"好产品怎么来做？好产品，首先，一定是靠时间积累出来的。所以做好产品，就是要耐得住寂寞，并不断进行创新研发。比如 9 年前我们成立了生物创新药物企业复宏汉霖，十年磨一剑，已经发展成为全球生物医药行业的独角兽。而且复宏汉霖有一个核心目标，就是要让癌症成为慢性病，而且老百姓还能消费得起。还有复星支持内部创业的杏脉科技，用人工智能和大数据，帮助医生更好地读片、判断病情。当把读片的任务交给人工智能的时候，全社会的医疗诊断的准确性和水平都将大大提升。复星与 Kite Pharma 共同在上海成立了复星凯特，专注 Car-T（嵌合抗原受体 T 细胞免疫）技术在癌症治疗中的应用。通过 Car-T 技术，我们预计未来 5～10 年，癌症将变成慢性病。其次，做好产品，还要精益求精，用匠心打磨全球好产品，好产品自己会说话。复星在内部有个明确的要求,就是'复星出品,必属精品'。地球的负担已经很重了,如果不是精品,你在地球造那么多垃圾干什么呢?我们宁愿不做。所以要精益求精,一定要做好产品。

"有一个好产品,是位于纽约的 Liberty 28 大楼。这幢楼的前身,是摩根大通银行总部,由洛克菲勒先生悉心打造。而他用了同样精力打造的另一幢建筑,是纽约洛克菲勒中心,这幢楼有 60 多年历史了,但现在看仍然非常经典,这种产品力、对精致的追求让我震撼。这也是我下定决心要做好产品的原因之一。最近,我们在这幢楼的 60 层做了一个全纽约风景最好的餐厅,要提前三个月排队预订,这就是好产品的力量。因为地产可以很直观地体现对产品的打磨,所以,另外一个我想说的好产品,就是我们在上海的办公室——BFC 外滩金融中心。只要大家去外滩看过,都给了我们很高的评价。

"做好产品,要敢为人所不为,创造独特的幸福生活。好产品不一定是一个建筑、一个实物,好产品也可能是做好服务,是一种生活体验,是一种生活方式。所以,做好产品,作为服务的提供者一定要敢为人所不为,能够为我们的客户创造独特的幸福生活新模式。比如我们的地中海俱乐部,虽然房间不是特别漂亮更别提奢华,但是,小朋友在那里会特别开心,去了还想再去。小朋友开心了,家长也一定会开心,所以,家庭客户就会在地中海俱乐部享受难忘的假期。这是别人所不具备的,这就是敢为人所不为。今年年初,复星用了五年时间打造的三亚亚特兰蒂斯正式开业。这不是酒店,而是包括水族馆、水上乐园、海豚剧场等在内的旅游目的地。哪怕在三亚旅游相对淡季的夏天,亚特兰蒂斯入住率也非常高。所以我深深感到,只要我们真正做出来好的、有特色的产品,一定会有好的反响。

"做好产品，Be Smart！踢球如此，做商业更如此。因为世界杯，大家都在讨论足球。对我来说，足球之所以迷人，是因为它太像商业了。比如一脚任意球，非常漂亮的弧线世界波，踢的球员叫鲁本·内维斯，英超狼队的当家球星。我相信，他在踢这个球之前，一定有着充分的观察、思考和判断，才能像手术刀那样精准，一击命中。这就是 Be Smart，聪明！所以我们要做好产品，也是一样。傻大粗地去买或者是砸钱，这是不行的。包括研发，我们做好产品当然要研发，但是，研发也要聪明的投入。公司越大，研发的投入越大。为什么很多人买技术，而不仅仅是自己去做？大企业以并购、以买为主？因为投入的成本非常低。所以，我们做好产品，还是要做聪明的投入。无论局势再复杂，解决焦虑，一定得回归初心，做好产品。

"最近和很多企业家朋友聊天，大家都感觉心情不是很好、比较焦虑，经济状况也不是最好，还有中美贸易等问题。但是我觉得，无论局势怎么复杂，无论碰到什么问题，对一个企业工作者来说，最好的解决焦虑的方法，就是找到乐趣。我个人的乐趣现在是什么？我越来越对产品有乐趣，越来越喜欢琢磨产品，琢磨产品和产品的链接，琢磨如何创造更好的生活方式等。所以，我觉得解决焦虑的方法，就是找到好的方式。作为企业工作者，最好的方式就是产品本身。我非常高兴经过一千多天的打磨，复星旗下的 Studio 8 的第一部电影《阿尔法：狼伴归途》终于全球上映，9 月 7 日将来到中国。我已经看了 4 遍。说实话，试映的时候我是有点失望的。可那次放映之后，我们团队总结了大家的各种意见，又打磨、调整了 20 多个版本。用他们的话说，突然之间就感觉电影升华了。所以，他们又满怀信心地邀请了不少观众看了好几遍，我也都在。现在最终放映的电影，史前、史诗级别的画面加上能够打动内心的关于爱、温暖和勇气的故事，百看不腻。

"打磨好产品，不容易，但成就感非凡。我乐在其中。"

复星产品，要是全球的精品

复星产品，一定要是全球的精品。精品不仅仅是产品好，更应该有号召力，我相信好产品本身就会说话，好产品本身就是一个号召力。

——郭广昌

2018 年 9 月 14 日，复星携手天津捷威动力工业有限公司，在上海复星艺术中心联合主办了"绿色中国星行动·新能源汽车产业论坛暨复星投资捷威战略发布会"，复星正式宣布投资捷威动力，并全面赋能捷威，打造中国乃至全球新能源动力电池行业的领导者。

发布会上，郭广昌在发表对新能源汽车产业的看法时，发表了这样一些观点。

"第一，我们在做一个伟大的事业。新能源汽车是中国的一个机会，也是中国必须走的一个战略。因为我们缺少石油，环境已经非常脆弱，新能源汽车这块，我们已经有比较好的技术积累。这的确会成为中国下一张名片，蕴含着巨大的机会。

"第二，靠补贴的产业，都是不长远的。前几年，捷威和复星没有享受到新能源大补贴。但是我个人有个基本的观念，就是只有在市场上获胜的企业，才是真正能长远发展的。像太阳能，到现在还是靠补贴，即使在欧洲，太阳能也是靠补贴。一旦欧洲减少补贴，对于我们整个太阳能产业，就是一个灾难。复星既然投入一个产业，肯定不是着眼于短期。为什么我们对这个产业有这么大的兴趣？根本来说，现在到了一个靠市场拼搏的时候。

"第三，复星为什么投资捷威？因为我们是高度吻合的。复星的战略是一步步在升华的。这几年我们提出，要深耕产业，要围绕家庭消费的'健康、快乐、富足'布局，要全球化的布局，要科技创新，要加大技术投入，等等。任何家庭的幸福，离不开整体的环境。我们投资捷威，助力中国电动汽车产业的发展，也跟我们这样的战略是分不开的。

"我相信任何伟大都是熬出来的。就像杉杉集团董事长郑永刚前面提到，他投资电池上游19年了，捷威了不起的地方也恰恰在于这一点。我跟捷威的郭董事长（郭春泰）、王总经理（王驰伟）团队沟通时，非常尊敬他们，因为这10年很不容易。虽然走过了很多弯路，但一直在坚持，这种工匠精神，让我非常感动。捷威已经有很好的产品和技术基础。从复星角度来看，如果产品不好，光靠复星投资、放大、产业运营，是做不好的。团队不好，再有钱，也没有用。但捷威已经有了一个团队的基础、产品的基础，复星能帮助捷威更好地发展。

"我理解，捷威在未来一定会在几个方面做得更好：一是加大技术研发，继续加大创新投入。二是相信我们会跟上下游有更多的合作。刚才奇瑞的高总（高新华）提到电动汽车不赚钱，但电池厂赚钱。高总可以投资我们电池厂，我们一起赚钱。我们会跟更多的上下游企业，尤其是好的汽车厂，建设更多的合资公司。三是规模。规模还是很重要，郭董（郭春泰）提出做五看三，我们目标可以更高一点，规模还是要做上去，未来会更快的发展。要达到这个目标，我最看重的还是人才。我们很高兴，不仅原来团队不错，最近捷威在整个行业里也在招兵买马。我们有院士带队的名誉研究院院长，相信我们的技术团队、开发团队、运营团队会越来越强。另外，钱也是不会缺的。复星会作为捷威的坚强后盾，绝对不让捷威因为资金不足而放慢了发展速度。四是全球化布局。包括人才的全球化布局，生态系统的全球化布局。这一块，我们的团队已经在对接了，就像南钢现在在英国、日本都合作建立了研发中心，捷威的技术方面我们也要全球布局。捷威也会融入复星生态系统，复星跟汽车相关的产业里，已经投了德国的轻量化材料厂Koller，未来在这个大生态里，捷威跟他们都有很多可以协同的方向。在人才投入、全球化布局、融入复星生态系统方面，我们会给捷威高度的支持。"

郭广昌说："复星的确是一个有投资基因的企业，但我们绝对不满足于自己是一个投资者，我们要深耕产业。对这方面，我们非常有耐心。大家很羡慕复星现在持有南钢，但在2015年前，南钢每年要亏二三十亿。产业总要起起伏伏，我们有耐心。既然我们选择了这个产业，选择了捷威，复星和我们的团队会非常有耐心地深耕产业。无论这个产业在顺的时候还是不顺的时候，相信那些能坚持的人，那些坚持创新、坚持一直走下去、有团队精神的人，那些有全球眼光、有足够资金的人，一定能做出一个强大的企业，一个伟大的企业。我们都会为此而努力。"

就在刚刚宣布投资捷威动力后的9月20日，复星旅文的FOLIDAY阿尔卑斯度假小镇项目，又在江苏太仓市正式开工。

在项目开工仪式上，郭广昌高度评价了复星旅文的产品力，他说："复星的使命愿景，是为世界十亿家庭智造幸福生活，我们通过健康、快乐、富足这三大板块实现这个愿景。特别是我们这几年在快乐板块增长十分快，为众多的家庭带来了更多的欢声笑语。这其中，复星旅文做出了巨大的贡献。我们复星旅文已经在全球20个国家和地区建立了69个度假村地中海俱乐部，尤其今年 4 月，我们在海南三亚的亚特兰蒂斯盛大开业，成为海南乃至中国旅游 3.0 的标杆。更重要的是，复星旅文也正在打造一个生态系统，为全球家庭的休闲度假提供一站式的解决方案。

"从亚特兰蒂斯开始，我们对团队，包括复星本身都提了一个要求，复星出品，一定要是全球的精品。精品不仅仅是产品好，更应该有号召力，我相信好产品本身就会说话，好产品本身就是一个号召力。就像我们的亚特兰蒂斯一样，今年 7 月份一建成就爆满，无论是口碑，还是在实际效果上，都取得了双丰收。亚特兰蒂斯的成功，复星旅文的产品力得到了全球家庭的认可，复星的同学们将会继续打造精品产品。回到创业的心态，我们不断地打造产品，无论是在医药上，还是在体育运动上，还是在其他领域上，我们都在为全球贡献好的产品。尤其是今天正式开工的 FOLIDAY 阿尔卑斯度假小镇，也会按照这样一种思维和模式去打造，打造全球精品。"

第十章

回报社会，
热心做好公益事业

支持医疗，复星的健康梦想

业界知道，在大健康领域，复星是一个有着长期积累和竞争优势的民营企业。当国家提出"精准扶贫，精准脱贫，打赢脱贫攻坚战"基本方略后，复星能够做点什么？曾经在儿时目睹过农村"赤脚医生"送医送药到家的郭广昌，做出了这样一个姿态："要像支持教育一样支持医疗，像支持乡村教师一样支持乡村医生，让广大的农村老百姓不再为看不上病、看不好病而发愁。到了脱困攻坚的关键时刻，复星人不能落后。"

根据全国因病致贫、返贫率不降反升的现实状况，尤其是乡村医生队伍面临的"进不来、用不上、留不住"三大难题。2017 年年底，复星基金会联合健康报社、中国人口福利基金会等相关部门，联合启动了声势浩大的"乡村医生健康扶贫项目"，旨在赋能乡村医生群体，完善基层健康管理与医疗服务体系，贡献于"两不愁、三保障"中的"就医保障"。这一项目通过 3 ~ 10 年分阶段、分目标的实施，切实提升国家级贫困县乡村医生的社会保障、技术能力及行医条件，有效降低贫困地区重点疾病的发病率，乡村医生将在全国 100 个贫困县得以巩固和覆盖，使当地受惠居民总数超过 1,500 万人。

为了落实好"乡村医生健康扶贫项目"，复星从成员企业内部精选了 38 名优秀员工组成扶贫工作队，奔赴一线驻村驻点开展工作。复星扶贫队员所到达的区域，覆盖了四川、山西、甘肃、云南等中西部地区的 37 个国家级贫困县。到 2019 年 1 月，复星扶贫队员共走访了 485 家乡镇卫生院、4,083 个村卫生室，在调研走访的基础上，建立 5,082 份乡村医生帮扶档案。扶贫队员的工作，为"乡村医生健康扶贫项目"接入"中国大病社会救助服务平台"

积累了极为宝贵的原始材料。

根据"乡村医生健康扶贫项目"在实施过程中遇到的实际情况，在涉及社会保障、大病救助、智慧卫生室改造、公共服务签约奖励包、荣誉激励等多个层面采取了措施，重点辅助开展了"五个一"工程：一个乡村医生保障工程、一个健康扶贫慢病签约服务奖励包、一个大病社会救助服务平台、一个暖心乡村医生评选、一批乡村卫生室智慧升级。

在复星以及相关部门的共同努力下，"乡村医生健康扶贫项目"已发放意外险保单 10,659 份，承保重疾险 1,326 份，总保额近 2.8 亿元；已组织村医培训超过 49 场，4,476 名村医参加；已建设智慧卫生室 276 间，总投资 80 余万元；已上线大病救助 52 例，总筹款近 33 万元；赠送各类医疗办公设备合计 652 万元；设立乡村医生慢病签约管理奖励基金 500 万元……所有这些，让复星喊出的"我们守护乡村医生，乡村医生守护大家"的口号显得无比响亮。

2019 年 2 月 16 日，一年一度的中国经济界盛事——2019 亚布力中国企业家论坛第十九届年会，在黑龙江亚布力隆重启幕。一年一度的"亚布力中国企业家论坛"，已成为中国最具影响力的思想交流平台，吸引着无数商界精英及行业翘楚们齐聚论道，共襄盛举。

令人感到意外但又温暖的是，一场别开生面的"2018 十大暖心乡村医生及乡镇卫生院院长"颁奖仪式，成为这场颇具影响力的企业家论坛的重要议程。当晚，走到聚光灯下的是杨天奎、张瑞廷、白俊美、马金花等 10 位乡村医生和 10 位乡镇卫生院院长，他们成为亚布力中国企业家论坛上的焦点人物与光荣代表。他们来自中西部地区的四川、山西、甘肃、云南等偏远乡村，代表着全国 150 万乡村医生这样一个庞大的队伍，他们也逐步由"乡村医生健康扶贫项目"的受益对象，蜕变为健康扶贫的助力使者。

受到表彰的 20 位乡村医生和乡镇卫生院院长，都长期扎根在乡村、奔波和服务在乡村，每个人的背后，都有说不完道不尽的故事，故事里也都充满着无数的艰难与辛酸。

四川省阿坝州壤塘县上杜柯乡卫生院院长杨天奎，在青藏高原服务藏区农村已经超过了 30 年。因为常年在缺氧地区超负荷工作，他患上了肺水肿，但仍坚持超负荷地工作在基层第一线。漂亮时髦的 80 后院长白俊美，2010 年妇幼专业毕业后，就来到了云南省蒙自州屏边县白云乡卫生院工作，任副院长一年多，2014 年任院长。她土法上马，一步步地建立了妇产科。她找县上的疾控中心要来一辆破旧的皮卡车当"救护车"救急、出诊。

这些乡村村医和乡镇卫生院院长的事迹，无不体现了他们的奉献精神，绽放了他们的精神光辉。

颁奖礼上来自甘肃省临夏州东乡县果园村从医 7 年的村医马金花异常激动。她 26 岁，被村民亲切地称为"孖大夫"。2018 年，一场山洪将"孖大夫"的村卫生室和出诊用的三轮摩托车冲走。"乡村医生健康扶贫项目"工作组向全社会发起慈善募捐号召，24 小时内募得善款 467,686.65 元，资助果园村 1,300 名村民所依赖的卫生室完成重建。"孖大夫"卫生室完成重建，只是"乡村医生健康扶贫项目"实施过程中的一个缩影。

"乡村医生健康扶贫项目"实施一年多来，复星及有关部门为中西部地区的贫困乡村送医送药送温暖，努力践行了"乡村不病，中国健康"的活动宗旨。

颁奖典礼当晚，还在现场举行了"乡村医生守护联盟"启动仪式，"乡村医生健康扶贫项目"发起人、复星国际董事长郭广昌，亚布力中国企业家论坛理事长、泰康保险集团股份有限公司董事长兼 CEO 陈东升等企业家一起拉动丝带，共同启动了"乡村医生守护联盟"。参与"乡村医生守护联盟"的多位企业家表示，将尽最大可能动员社会资源，推动更多机构、企业和个人参与乡村医生健康扶贫行动，为乡村医疗找到可持续解决方案。

其实，从某种意义上说，郭广昌推动越来越多的企业家参与"乡村医生健康扶贫项目"，成为中国企业家倾注力量改善中国基础医疗的一个重要标志。

走出国门，主动担当助天下

2018 年 6 月 21 ~ 22 日，"中国与葡语国家企业经贸合作洽谈会—里斯本—2018"主题活动在葡萄牙首都里斯本举行，400 多位来自中国内地、澳门和葡语国家的工商界代表出席了活动。

长期以来，复星将自身的发展战略与中国互利共赢的对外开放战略及"一带一路"倡议有机地结合起来，积极在葡萄牙、巴西和非洲葡语国家拓展业务。自 2014 年起，复星先后投资了葡萄牙最大的保险公司 Fidelidade、葡萄牙最大的医疗集团 Luz Saude、葡萄牙最大商业银行 BCP 等项目，在葡投资总额达 21.5 亿欧元，成为在葡萄牙投资规模最大的国际投资者之一。在充分尊重葡萄牙法律和企业文化的基础上，复星不断加大与这些企业的融合力度，取得了非常好的业绩表现，为葡萄牙经济发展提供了强有力的支持。

复星于 2016 年下半年进入巴西市场，投资了当地数一数二的资产管理公司 Rio Bravo。除此以外，复星一直在积极寻找健康、能源矿产、特色产业等领域的投资机遇。在非洲葡语国家，复星通过葡萄牙的保险和银行企业，积极在非洲开展相关业务。同时，复星旗下作为中国最大的青蒿素类抗疟疾药品生产企业的桂林南药，相关产品在包括非洲葡语国家在内的近 40 个国家得以注册并销售。业界知道，桂林南药的抗疟药，让全球近 2,000 万重症疟疾患者获益，挽救了约 10 万人的生命，其中大部分是非洲儿童。

令人感到欣慰的是，复星在向葡语国家"走出去"的过程中，时刻不忘企业所肩负的社会责任和国际担当。多年来，复星以葡萄牙为基地，先后举办了两届全球创新创业大赛 Protechting，通过与葡萄牙本土创业孵化器合作，帮助当地青年人进行创新开发并扶持相关初创企业成长。种种迹象表明，复星还将利用自身独特优势，在非洲葡语国家抗疟疾方面，做更多的公益活动。

到 2018 年，中国与葡语国家企业经贸合作洽谈会成功举办了十三届，影响力不断扩大，已成为中国与葡语国家经贸交流、合作的重要平台，起到了巩固及深化葡语国家经贸关系、提升中葡经贸合作水平的积极作用。

郭广昌曾经说过这样一段话："如果你想在全球发展，一定要了解中国，因为中国已是全球第二大经济体；如果你想在中国发展，一定要了解全球，因为中国此时已非常国际化。这是我对未来商业的一个最基本看法，同时拥有了中国和全球的动力，将是未来我们最强大的竞争力之一。"

虽然复星已经成为一家大型跨国企业，但在郭广昌的眼里，不管在国内，还是在国外，身边依然还有许许多多的人未能安居乐业，需要复星通过"立业"去"助天下"，帮助他们过上幸福的生活。为此，郭广昌将《大学》中那句"修身，齐家，治国，平天下"的哲言，改为"修身、齐家、立业、助天下"，以此作为复星的使命和价值观。

在"助天下"的指引下，郭广昌逐渐确立了一个非常宏大的使命愿景——让全球每个家庭生活更幸福，并用毕生的努力去实现这一目标。

2018年6月，郭广昌在发表《我与复星走到今天的"6个为什么"》专题演讲时说："当我看着大都市里那些为了美好生活而深夜加班的年轻人，公园里与家人一同快乐奔跑着的孩子们，医院里由儿女陪伴守护着的老人，还有贫困山区里为自己孩子的温饱、健康、教育而烦恼着的父母，我知道这世上还有太多的事需要复星和我去做。把以上这些事归纳起来，就是复星的使命——让全球每个家庭生活更幸福。这绝不是空口而谈，在复星眼中，因为改革开放40周年、因为中国与世界的融合、因为全球技术的创新，我们正处在一个最好的时代。同时，站在最好的时代潮头，我和复星对未来也充满了憧憬。

"我们看到，消费者的时间越来越宝贵；技术转化为产品和产业的速度越来越快；商业环节的各个参与者的边界更加模糊；柔性化的工业智造已经实现；因为移动互联网等新技术，组织内部管理更有效率、更到边到底，将让复星全球跨界的融合大而不钝。

"基于此，复星将业务重新划分为健康、快乐、富足三大板块，并以'植根中国，服务全球十亿家庭客户，智造健康、快乐、富足的幸福生态系统'作为我们新的企业愿景。

"之所以不是个人，而是家庭客户，是因为家庭是我们这个世界最小的幸福单位，无论你处于生命的哪个阶段，家人的相伴都是你幸福不可或缺的一部分。之所以是健康、快乐和富足，是因为这三者基本涵盖了一个幸福家庭的全部需求，而这三个需求所对应的产业也是复星深耕运营多年的领域。之所以要植根中国，服务全球，是因为复星始终坚信中国发展动力，坚信中国市场水大鱼大,中国的未来一定会更美好;同时,伴随着中国产业的全球化,复星也要承担起越来越多的全球责任。之所以是幸福生态系统,是因为一个家庭的健康、快乐、富足需求是相互关联的,复星为家庭客户提供的产品和服务也不是单一的,而是一个有机的生态系统,一个客户与智造者无缝链接的C2M生态系统,它提供的是一整套以客户需求为中心的定制化解决方案。

"复星将牢记'助天下'的初心,实实在在去帮助更多的人。无论是'乡村医生健康扶贫项目',让中国150万乡村医生活得更有尊严、更好地去服务当地村民;还是以青蒿琥酯为基础,助力全球彻底消灭疟疾……复星已经在路上。我们要做对的事、难的事、需要时间积累的事,并将坚持走下去。我将用我毕生的努力,去实现复星的使命、践行复星的责任。因为复星,全球每个家庭的生活将更幸福。"

近年来,复星积极拓展海外公益事业,先后在葡萄牙里斯本、德国柏林、美国纽约等地成功开展各种公益活动,造福当地家庭。

用爱守护,更多回馈给社会

郭广昌深知,对于一个企业家来说要懂得感恩社会,回馈社会,因为一个企业的成长离不开社会的支持。为此,创业以来,郭广昌带领复星人用爱守护,力所能及地给予社会更多的回馈,在社会公益方面的捐助数不胜数。

2007年7月25日,郭广昌向中国光彩事业基金会捐赠了1,300万元支票,全国工商联主席黄孟复接受了郭广昌的捐助。

2008 年 5 月 12 日，四川汶川发生强烈地震，损失严重。复星得知灾情发生后，立即伸出援助之手，第一时间对外宣布向灾区捐助 1,000 万元。同时，还紧急自辟航空运输渠道，将救灾药品及时送往灾区。那一次，复星捐赠的物资超过 4,000 万元，员工个人捐款超过 360 万元。

2010 年 4 月 17 日，青海玉树发生强烈地震。郭广昌携复星医药向灾区先期紧急捐赠价值 100 万元的救灾药品，并通过海南航空的专机火速运往灾区。同时，复星医药在成都和重庆的制药、销售网点，也紧急组织救灾药品货源支援灾区。

一个优秀的企业，注定是一个懂得感恩的企业，复星能有今天的成就，离不开全社会的支持，因此，在公益路上，复星不设终点。郭广昌说："人的生命是有限的，但是传承却能将精神一直延续下去。就像巴菲特创造了投资界的神话，我领悟到了，并为己所用。现在，我也必将不断精进，让更多的后来者来传承。"

2018 年 11 月 26 日~12 月 8 日，在复星基金会成立 6 周年之际，复星基金会联合复星一家，隆重推出了以"FOSUN FOR LOVE 星·爱"为主题的公益周活动，并号召全球复星员工参与活动。

这次主题公益周活动，复星内部 40 余家成员企业，围绕"对人感恩，对己克制，对事尽力，对物珍惜"四大主题，跨越 8 个国家的 50 余个城市，举办了 60 余场活动，吸引了超过 3 万名复星员工参与其中。

为表彰复星员工在公益周活动中的善举，由复星基金会公益周组委会评选出的"十大明星公益项目""五大爱心公益团体"及"五大公益启明星"等奖项，在 12 月 8 日庆祝复星基金会成立 6 周年晚上会揭晓，并给予表彰。

受到表彰的"十大明星公益项目"是：公益赋能奖——"康养有

爱,相伴有怡"——鲜蜂社区公益行;益动 Fosun 奖——"FOSUN FOR LOVE"复星全球公益跑;朝花夕拾奖——星堡圆梦婚纱摄影展;扶助青苗奖——藏区"暖冬"小太阳;启明星奖——星太极"抗帕"公益;公益时光奖——一笼爱·公益聚南翔;绿色出行奖——"益"骑星绿动;守望相助奖——守护马塔,让爱回家;雪中送炭奖——香港邻舍冬日送暖;爱心帮扶奖——三亚·亚特兰蒂斯关爱福利院儿童。

受到表彰的"五大爱心公益团体":来自 Protechting 项目组的"公益科创链接中外青年创客"团队;来自 Club Med 的"Apples of Madaifu"团队;来自 Millennium BCP 的"Food Bank Against Hunger"团队;来自复星北京区域总部的"京益求精与爱同行"团队;来自智能科技创新部的"0.01 秒——智能科技赋能公益"团队。

受到表彰的"五大公益启明星":来自豫园黄金珠宝集团的"星志愿"志愿者侯毅;来自中国动力基金的"星志愿"志愿者余慧艳;来自复星金服的"星志愿"志愿者周继猛;来自葡萄牙办的海外公益人 Rita Delgado;来自江苏万邦医药的"益起跑"达人崔洪广。

除此之外,晚会上还为 37 位"健康暖心——乡村医生健康扶贫项目全体驻点队员"颁发了一项"公益年度特别奖",以表彰这些基层乡村专职扶贫工作队员,在实施"乡村医生健康扶贫项目"中的坚守。

晚会上,复星基金会理事长、复星国际高级副总裁李海峰表示:"今年的'复星公益周'只是一个开始,这一活动将成为复星一家的公益传统,在每年 11 月的最后一周如期举行。"他说:"公益之路没有终点,复星一家员工将因善而聚,向善而行,不忘初心,将爱心和公益的善举一年年坚持、传递下去。为爱奔跑的脚步从来不会停止,每一个爱心传递的故事,都是下一次善心善行的动力。我们相信,未来复星的公益事业,一定会向更加伟大的方向前进。让我们向每一位永存爱心的公益人士致敬!让复星的公益之光,点亮更多幸福。让所有意义,因为爱而更有意义。"

努力创业,终极目标助天下

从2001年开始,复星每年出资50万元,在上海久隆模范中学设立了"复星尊师奖",专门用于奖励久隆模范中学在教育教学、管理服务中表现优异的教职工。每逢教师节,郭广昌都要带领复星高管到学校,为"复星尊师奖"获奖者颁奖,郭广昌更是抽出时间为师生们作"成长·理想"的报告,给师生们带去无尽的精神力量,复星"修身、齐家、立业、助天下"的企业理念深深地影响着久隆师生。

作为大学生成功创业的典范,郭广昌从来不忘对母校的感恩和回报。从2006年起,复星设立"复旦大学生命科学学院复星医药奖学金、奖教金",支持该院教学、科研、人才队伍建设等各项事业。总额100万元的奖学金、奖教金,专门用于奖励家庭贫困的优秀学子以及取得科研创新成果的青年教师,帮助获奖教师和学生在研究道路上取得更大成就。

2017年6月,复星与香港科技大学智造幸福生活创业计划正式启动。按照计划,复星与香港科技大学合作,培养香港学生的创业精神,鼓励大学生创业,并借助复星丰富的网络、资源,在金融、科技、健康、旅游、保险等方面,共同设计优秀的创业计划。

从2013年开始,复星在江苏每年都要举行一次"复星保德信青少年社区志愿奖"颁奖典礼。保德信青少年社区志愿奖是美国最大的、授予青少年的、完全基于自愿性社区义工服务的奖项,旨在通过寻找并认可为社区做出杰出贡献的青少年志愿者,吸引和鼓励更多的青少年投身公益。复星将这一奖项带入江苏后,5年来共收到近2,800份有效申请案例,表彰了225名为公益事业做出杰出贡献的中学生。

2018年1月21日,在温暖如春的三亚地中海俱乐部度假村,一群青春洋溢的00后高中生们,与郭广昌进行了一场别开生面的"我与海南的未来"座谈会。

这10多名高中生,是来自海南热带海洋学院附中的学生,也都是获得了复星光彩教育奖助金资助的学生。为推动海南省教育事业发展,解决部分品学兼优且家庭经济困难的普通高中学生上学问题,复星自2007年起,设立海南省复星光彩事业教育奖励基金,每年资助部分海南普通高中学校的优秀学生完成学业。

郭广昌与同学们回忆起自己小时候的生活时说:"我小时候的家庭状况不比你们好。生活的艰难,的确不是我们所追求的,但是,你要把它看成你这辈子最好的安排之一。小时候的艰难也是一种财富,对你的意志品质都是很好的锻炼。"他说:"我和复星对教育一直有着深厚的感情。我们应该给大家更多机会的平等,尤其是教育机会的平等。现在贫穷是两个因素带来的,一是没有教育,跟不上知识的更新;二是生病,没有能力去改善生活。教育和医疗是复星公益事业应该努力解决的问题。"

郭广昌建议同学们"一定要养成阅读和运动的习惯",他说:"大学生活要好好读书,游戏少玩一点,多参加一些体育运动,一定要养成运动和阅读的习惯,它会让你终身受用的。总之,大学生活可以丰富多彩一点,自我学习的能力很重要。"

在海南，复星 11 年时间累计资助学生多达 4,840 人次，资助资金 726 万元，海南中学、海南华侨中学、文昌中学、嘉积中学、海南师范大学附属中学、琼州学院附属中学、国兴中学、昌江中学、万宁中学九所普通高中学校的学生受助。

郭广昌表示，复星将进一步扩充在海南的教育奖励基金，充分开展助学活动，结合复星在海南的项目团队，在提供助学金之外开展更多的教学拓展体验。

2019 年 1 月 19 日晚，复星一年一度全球经理人会议期间，由复星基金会主办的"围炉夜话 CSR"火热进行。来自全球复星一家 100 多位员工济济一堂，脑力激荡，共同畅谈关于爱和公益的话题。

业界知道，一年一度的全球经理人年会是复星大家庭成员明确愿景、集中智慧、头脑风暴的黄金时刻。会议期间，复星总共将举办三场"围炉夜话"，而复星基金会所主办的"围炉夜话 CSR"是其中的一场。

从活动主持人精彩的主持词中，就可以感受到复星人参与公益事业的精神风采："这个夜晚，注定着它的不平凡。在这里，我们聆听温情的故事；在这里，我们碰撞对人人公益的解读；在这里，我们思考公益项目如何可持续发展。爱心传递，各显神通！一场以'改变'为主题的公益脱口秀，各路大咖尽显风采，将自己与公益之间的故事娓娓道来。用爱守望，用心相助，点点滴滴，涓涓细流，汇成了一片爱的海洋，只愿更多有心人加入这个大家庭，一起把这份温暖传递下去。"

活动中，复星员工可谓大咖云集，各显风采。

星堡总经理陈煜宇：我们从哪一刻开始变老？机体上来说，从出生开始！精神上来说，永不！

阳光印网首席运营官杨斌:阳光印网的环保型包装箱,阳光宝盒既支持环保,又提高生产效率。

复星保德信青社奖慈善大使姚紫馨:我们也许不能通过公益去改变全世界,但我们依然能够奉献出自己应尽的一份力量!

东仑传媒董事长乔柏华:东仑传媒专门派出了采风小组深入乡村医生健康扶贫的第一线,将会开拍一部关于乡村医生的电视剧,让更多的人了解他们。

活动现场,复星国际首席执行官汪群斌在致辞中说:"复星一切努力的终极目标,就是为社会创造价值。当然贡献的形式多种多样,包括全球化、科技创新、产品创新、公益模式创新,等等。我们要向全球优秀的公益基金会对标、学习、合作、推进。复星人一直在公益的路上,我们希望大家能多参与,多提宝贵建议,共同成长。"

郭广昌也参加了"围炉夜话 CSR"活动,并呼吁鼓励更多的复星同学加入公益的事业中来。他说:"你有爱,为社会去创造,整个社会是积极向上的,这样的生活才会更美好。"

附录

郭广昌经典演讲

我的四个扪心自问和四个自信

2018 年 12 月的第一天，浙江商会总会年会在杭州召开。会上，郭广昌作为浙江商会总会副会长发表演讲。以下是演讲的内容：

今年是改革开放 40 周年。在过去 40 年里，我们浙商靠着"四千"精神，吃苦耐劳、不懈努力，应该说一直走得比较顺。前几年，虽然我们每年都说困难、"年年难过"，但实际上还是"年年过"。但这个冬天，我感觉有些不一样。尤其今年很多企业家朋友都出了问题，他们的企业之前发展得都很好。

我就在想，到底怎么了？刚才陈龙教授也给大家详细说了外部环境的变化，那我们自己呢？这么多年来，我们一直说我们要改变自己，那我们改变了多少呢？

所以我对现在经济的看法是：

经济的确会很困难，这个冬天会非常冷。

世界上要有一个救世主，就是市场；而在市场里，能救你的只有你自己。

所幸，党和国家已经很清楚地看到了这些问题和困难，也出台了一系列针对民营企业发展的政策和举措。所以，我判断未来的形势会好一些。但能否度过这个冬天，根本点还在于自己。

作为我们自己，现在必须要做的一件事，是反省、是扪心自问。我觉得现在我们必须认真想想我们遇到的问题是什么？前五年我们又做了些什么？

以下这四个问题，是这几年我自己一直在扪心自问的。

我们要扪心自问，我们到底花了多少时间在客户身上？花了多少时间

161

在了解自己的产品上？花了多少时间在提升产品服务上？

每个董事长，首先应该是自己公司的首席产品体验官。产品好不好，客户满意不满意，我们自己应该是最了解的。但这种了解绝不能依靠你的喜好和直觉，你需要花更多的时间跟客户去沟通。尤其产品销量不好，市场上又有很多竞争，你就特别需要更用心地体会产品。

现在，我花时间最多的就是研究产品。经过这段时间的研究，我基本认为要造好产品，方法大致有两种：第一种是做平台，但是能做成像阿里、腾讯这样大平台的企业毕竟是少数。第二种就是花更多的时间去琢磨怎么做好产品。

但如果做产品，我必须要强调一点：我们一定要做精品，一定要千锤百炼，一定要为客户创造价值。

我们经常要扪心自问，我们花了多少钱在研发上？花了多少时间在学习新的业态上？花了多少时间在感受新的趋势和方向上？

我相信，现在大家都很重视移动互联网。但我想问：我们的制造企业，有多少人真正懂得了移动互联网吗？移动互联网只是在淘宝上卖东西吗？马校长已经把阿里这家互联网企业做得这么好，但他还是会花大量的时间在研究线下商业、实体制造。

所以说，我们千万不能因为取得了成绩，就不学习了。永远只有比别人学得更快，我们才能比别人走得更好、更远。现在客户的需求变化非常快，我们也进入了一个科技研发能快速转化为成果的时代。在这样的时代，技术的进步、产业的进步、市场逻辑的进步，逼着我们要不断学习。

另外，一定要重视科技研发和创新。我们很多出问题的企业，虽然他们的公司已经很大，但总体感觉他们生产的大部分产品还是有同质化、低科技的问题，而且他们以前一直是靠低毛利来不断扩大销量。但这个时代变化太快了，很可能你生产出来的不是产品，直接就是库存。所以，现在尤其要用科技创新来引领。

我们要扪心自问，我们花了多少精力在组织升级和人才培养上？我们花了多少精力在引进高级人才上？花了多少精力在年轻人身上？我们有没有在90后、00后身上学到了什么？

组织、人才，绝对是一家企业最核心的资产。因为所有的事都需要对的人去实现。而且根据市场的发展和变化，我们的组织需要不断升级，企业的人才要不断换仓。我们一定要吸收具备高能级、更在状态、更渴望成功的人。大家都有自己的团队，但我们花了多少精力在团队的升级上？

我举个例子。复星的狼队这个赛季从英冠踢到了英超。但我突然发觉，英冠虽然踢得好，但是到英超以后，却碰到了很多的问题。为什么？因为英超要求我们球员的素质和英冠是不一样的。现在中国经济不管跟美国发生什么，都是一个比较长期且难以解决的问题。但不管怎么解决，中国经济已经在参与全球竞争了，客观上我们已经在踢"世界杯"了。这个时候，你的人才还是停留在原来的状态，不出问题不是很奇怪吗？

我们还要扪心自问：我们到底愿不愿意慢下来，去做点慢的事情？

改革开放40年，中国速度是大家津津乐道的，什么都发展得很快。这让我们已经习惯了快。比如我们看到马校长用十几年打造了一个世界级的巨无霸企业，大家都很想去复制他成功的路径。

但全世界只有一个马云，谁都像他一样，这个世界还了得？所以你要知道，你自己该做什么，你有没有沉下心来做你该做的事？我们很多企业，我对他们做事的风格有一种感觉，就是All in（全押），就是"赌"。这个"赌"

不是说去赌场，而是说做企业很有"赌"性。之前的40年，因为整个市场在发展，一俊遮百丑，你很大概率赌成功了。但你千万不能把经济的大势当作你自己的能力，如果市场不好了，会怎么样？All in一下会很爽，但之后呢？

我相信我们真的要沉下心，做对的事情，做难的事情，做需要时间积累的事情。

当然，讲了这么多困难和问题之后，我还是对未来始终充满信心：

我坚定地相信，中国的市场化程度一定会越来越高，我们民营企业的营商环境会越来越好。包括我相信，不久的将来一定会减税，以降低企业的成本、激发企业活力。

我坚定地相信，中国的企业家，尤其浙商，都非常能吃苦，只要我们加大创新，我们在未来会得到更多的发展。

我坚定地相信，我们一定会融入全球。对于我们来说，尤其浙商，这是未来我们重要的方向。我们浙商不害怕去全球竞争，在越来越开放、越规范的市场，在全球化的融合中，全球浙商只会越来越好。

这就像中国足球一样。中国足球要踢世界杯，只有让我们球员去全球踢球，才能得到真正的锻炼，而不只是在中超拿高工资。

我坚定地相信，我们浙商有这份期望，我们浙商有这份能力，让我们一起努力。

商业的常识，知否？知否？

2019年4月25日，郭广昌在甘肃敦煌举办的2019年中国绿公司年会上，发表了《商业的常识，知否？知否？》的主旨演讲，以下是演讲内容：

最近一直在思考一个问题：为什么我们的很多行为会违反商业的常识？坦白说，做企业的人往往都很聪明，尤其企业做得越大，越不可能在技巧性的事上犯错。可为什么还是每年都有企业出现问题？我发现，大多数的错误是因为违反了商业的常识。

商业的常识有哪些？

商业的常识，是每一个做企业的人都应当理解和具备的基本知识，这一切都基于最基本的商业规律。

比如做企业肯定要盈利。但有些人总觉得：盈利不重要，要先烧钱；当把所有的竞争对手都"烧死"之后，市场就全是我的了，自然能赚钱。大家想想，现在还可能有垄断吗？

再比如做企业是要控制负债的。但有些企业就是觉得要多点负债，负债越多人家越怕我，信奉所谓的"大而不倒"。

还有，我们说要以客户为中心，这也是商业的常识。但永远有不少人热衷于各种开会、聚会，却很少把时间花在客户身上。

我们还说好产品是造出来的。可有些人这几年销售不行，总觉得是电商的原因让渠道的竞争变激烈了，都是别人的问题，可从没想过是不是自己的产品不好、过时了。

还有一点非常重要的商业常识：我们要有未来，就要对未来投资。所以，我们除了当期的利润，科研投入、人才培养，也非常重要。

为什么我们很难去坚持常识？

看起来非常清楚、非常简单的事，为什么我们很难去坚持呢？我一直在思考这个问题，感觉的确有一些非常清楚的原因：

人性永远存在着弱点。

比如说投资，当股市到五六千点的时候，按理说应该更谨慎一些，但我们往往会特别贪婪，觉得还能到一万点。但当股市在两三千点的时候，虽然我们可能还在亏钱，但其实投资的价值已经出现了，我们该勇敢一点，可往往大家反而非常恐惧。

我们身边总是有太多的诱惑，让我们贪婪；也有太多负面的事，让我们过分恐惧。这些都是人性的弱点，而我们总是要和这些弱点做斗争。

还有一种因素，每个人对自我的判断、预期。

有时候我们会对自己过分的自信，因为改革开放 40 年，有些人每次都在"赌"，还每次都"赌"对了。所以他就会觉得，凭什么这次我会错？但是这个世界已经变化了，原先的那套已经不灵了，如果还继续"赌"下去，每次都 All in（全押），你能不输光吗？

还有一些人截然相反，是过度不自信。本来他们是那种过度自信的人，但互联网一来，马上被打趴下了，就觉得马云说的每一句话都是对的，也不知道自己到底要信什么。这样就会违反常识去做很多事。

当然还有些情况，就是单纯觉得累了。

有些人干了 20 年、30 年已经累了，开始懈怠、懒惰了，就开始找一批很有经验或者学历很高的人，所谓的接班人或者空降部队。其实，这只是为自己的不作为、想偷懒找了一个借口而已。

怎么避免这些人性的弱点？避免犯常识的错误？

往往商业的成功，在找到对的方向之后，我们只要坚持紧紧围绕商业的常识去做该做的事情，每天一点点地去努力就可以了，其实并没有什么特别高深的东西。但具体到怎么避免这些人性的弱点？避免犯常识的错误？在这方面，我也有些想法：

一个是思考问题的方法论。

我相信，任何一个取得商业成功的人，都有很好的商业直觉，能敏锐地感觉到客户的需求是什么、商业的模式应该往哪里走。但是，我们的直觉也会因为各种原因而失真。所以光有直觉是不够的，直觉的背后应该有一套完善的商业逻辑。很多时候，我们会重直觉而轻商业逻辑，这是一个非常不好的弱点。

但是，当我们获得了直觉和逻辑的统一、平衡，还要知道此时此刻的给定条件是什么？因为任何一个人都是在给定条件下来实现目标的。这包括我们自己有什么禀赋，以及外界又是一个什么样的环境。

所以，商业的直觉、逻辑和外部的给定条件，是我们缺一不可的增长因子。在这个基础上，我们就可以制订出属于自己的战略规划。

但我们也要知道，战略规划不是越多越好、越强越好、越快越好、越漂亮越好，还要符合自己的定位，你要把它落实到组织、人才、文化，等等，一步一步地做，这样才不会偏离你的常识，才能把你带上一条正确的道路。

还有一些技巧性的手段，尽量避免违反常识的发生：

第一，我们应该设立更合适的绩效指标。曾经有一家海外企业的业务发展得一直不好，经过我们复盘，发现其中很大一个原因就是企业的主要考核指标只有"销售额"，所以管理团队就拼命地扩大销售额，不管利润、技术、人才等其他的因素。这是不行的，所以复星现在的考核，"利润＋科研投入"是非常重要的一项指标。如果只是利润很高，科研投入下来了，那考核还是不合格。

第二，要注重企业内部的灰度，鼓励内部的竞合。很多企业，尤其是企业大了之后，信息传递一定是失真、不全面的，这就很容易违反商业常识。所以我们鼓励灰度存在，鼓励内部竞合，就是打破信息层层传递、汇报的低效，实现内部信息的透明化和资源利用的最高效。

第三，要经常复盘，尤其要重视对失败案例的复盘。现在复星有 50 多位全球合伙人，大家最主要的工作就是正视我们还没有做好的事情。人性的弱点总是喜欢听好消息，但去看那些血淋淋、失败的东西，才是让我们不断进步的动力。我们要非常清楚地知道哪些地方在流血，逼迫自己知道弱点在哪里。所以复盘非常重要。

还有两个非常好的工作技巧，一个是头脑风暴，另外一个是充分使用更高效的沟通工具。比如钉钉，现在，我一半以上的时间都花在钉钉上，我们有很多钉钉工作群。任何时候、公司的任何人，只要他们觉得讨论的事和我相关、要让我知道，就随时可以把我拉到群里。真的非常高效。

GUO GUANGCHANG

&

FOSUN

INTERNATIONAL

A BUSINESS AND LIFE BIOGRAPHY

TRANSLATED BY DR. ZHU YUAN, XU KUN, ZHAO TIANYU, LIU WENQIAN

CONTENTS

PRELUDE

Guo Guangchang and his Fosun Group are highly regarded by almost everyone in Chinese business circles, as well as many in the global business world. Guo has become an adventurous legend, an enterprising and classic role model, a leading giant, and a guiding star in the business journey.

Guo was born into a poor family in the rural area of Dongyang city, Zhejiang Province. After graduating from Dongyang High School in 1985, he entered the Department of Philosophy at Fudan University. Upon graduation from Fudan in 1989, he remained there to teach thanks to his remarkable academic achievements. In 1992, he collaborated with Liang Xinjun, his Fudan colleague and another Fudan alumnus, and resolutely quit his teaching job. With a loan of ¥38,000, he embarked on a new journey of entrepreneurship and never wavered.

Guo and Liang established Fosun Group, starting with market research and consultation before gradually entering the businesses of real estate, retail, steel and finance, and eventually becoming a large international private enterprise. In 2018, Fosun reached ¥109.4 billion in total revenue with year-on-year growth of 24.4%, and ¥638.88 billion in total assets with year-on-year growth of 20%. In 2018, Guo's personal net worth reached ¥61.7 billion, and Fosun's direct or indirect company holdings amounted to over 1,000.

Many view Guo's life and business experience as amazingly similar to Jack Ma's. Both of them are from Zhejiang Province, except that Guo is from Jinhua and Ma from Hangzhou. They both became outstanding models of Zhejiang entrepreneurs, as well as Chinese entrepreneurs. They both started teaching after their graduation, except Guo both graduated from and taught at Fudan University, while Ma graduated from Hangzhou Teachers College and taught at Hangzhou Electronic Industrial College. They both left their teaching jobs, started their business careers and saw huge success. Guo founded Fosun Group, which is renowned today, while Ma established the now celebrated Alibaba.

Looking at Guo's personal profile, we can see that he made several major decisions at critical moments and turning points in his life.

The first major decision was made when in 1982, after graduation from middle school, Guo resolutely gave up going to a teachers" school and instead turned to the senior high school. This decision became the first turning point in his life. Guo was born into a poor farming family. Like most parents from rural areas, his parents hoped that their son could change his farmer's status as soon as possible through his own effort. Hence, upon his graduation from middle school, his parents urged him to apply for the teachers" school so that he could be a teacher with a secure salary from the state. He conformed to his parents" expectations and gained admittance to the teachers" school with flying colors. However, when he received the admission notice, he felt as if he had received a life sentence. He did not feel that he should just be a village teacher all his life in Dongyang; he felt that he should realize his dream of going to college.

Then he decided to give up the teachers" school and go to the senior high school. He finally finished his three years" senior high school education and successfully entered the Department of Philosophy, Fudan University. Undoubtedly, his university life laid a solid intellectual and ideological foundation for his future success and glory.

The second major decision was made when, influenced by a talk Deng Xiaoping gave on his Southern Tour in 1992, Guo gave up going overseas for further study, resolutely quit his job and ventured into the business sector. After entering Fudan University, moving from Dongyang to Shanghai, Guo discovered a vast world incomparable to his home. During his university days, he spent more time and energy gaining social experiences. Meanwhile, he did two things that surprised his classmates. In the summer of 1987, he went alone by bike on an investigation tour along the canal all the way to Beijing. In the summer of 1988, he organized a bike tour for a group of over ten students along the coast all the way from Shanghai to Hainan. These two events somewhat helped him to understand society and himself, which also led to his employment by the Fudan University Youth League Committee upon graduation. After working at the university, with a youthful heart, he was eager to see a wider world. Thus, he planned to study overseas, for which he actively prepared, passing the Test of English as a Foreign Language (TOEFL) and Graduate Record Examination (GRE), and borrowing money to cover the expense. However, Deng Xiaoping's Southern Tour talk in 1992 changed Guo. He believed that after Deng's talk, Shanghai would surely become a hot destination for investment and entrepreneurship. With huge business potential in one's homeland, why did one have to go abroad? Thus, Guo not only gave up going abroad but also decided to resign from his university post so that he could try business ventures and open up his ideal new world in Shanghai. In exactly the same year, 25-year-old Guo started his business venture in Shanghai and made his first fortune.

The third major decision was made in 1995 when Guo officially changed his company's name from Guangxin to Fosun. By then he had abandoned the family personnel management mode of traditional private enterprises and implemented the modern personnel strategy of recruiting talents, in partnership with his Fudan alumni. In fact, during the early stage of his business venture, Guo had already become fully aware that the core of the competition between enterprises ultimately lay in the competition between talents. He said: "What the young people need most is not individual heroism but collective heroism. In terms of our individual abilities, each of us may only be graded 70 to 80 points, but we must add to and multiply our abilities. In Fosun, our utmost wish is to cultivate groups of young entrepreneurs with common goals and young, vibrant, innovative teams." In the course of introducing and cultivating talents, Guo continued the personnel concept of "attracting talents with promotion, gathering talents with enterprise, cultivating talents with work and testing talents with accomplishment." He insisted on each individual having the spirit of enterprise teamwork and each Fosun staff member taking Fosun as their second home and being a member of a big family. The operation of the company was like a ball game. If any player failed in their role, the game would not be won, so only when each one tried their best could the company develop well.

It took Guo and Fosun only three years to reach more than ¥100 million in assets (in 1995) from their initial ¥38,000 of assets in 1992.

In August 1998, Fosun Pharma (under Fosun Group) was listed on the Shanghai Stock Exchange. It raised funds of ¥350 million, succeeded in connecting the industry with the capital market, and opened up further business expansion through networks of capital.

On 28 November 2001, Fosun Investment, newly established less than a month ago, signed a holding transfer trust agreement with Shanghai Yuyuan Tourist Mart (SYTM). It became the largest shareholder of SYTM. SYTM was one of the earliest A-share listed companies, incorporating national gold and jewellery retail brand ssuch as Laomiao Gold Store and First Asia Jewelry. In 2002, SYTM, then already an enterprise under Fosun Group, reached a net business revenue of ¥500 million,becoming extremely lucrative for Fosun.

In 2003, SYTM, Fosun Investment and two other companies established the joint venture of Tebon Securities, suggesting that Fosun had obtained the controlling interest of Tebon Securities. Afterwards, SYTM and Fosun Industrial Investment once again collaborated and invested in Zhaojin Mining Industry Co.,Ltd., together with Shandong Zhaojin Group. Early in 2006, Zhaojin Mining Industry was listed on the main board of the Hong Kong Stock Exchange. In the same year, the four enterprises of Fosun Group, Nanjing Iron and Steel Group, Fosun Indus trial Investment and Shanghai Guangxin Technology Development Co.,Ltd. established the joint venture of Nanjing Iron and Steel United Co.,Ltd. (NISU). Then NISU acquired Nanjing Iron & Steel Co.,Ltd., the largest steel enterprise in Jiangsu Province, taking 60% of its stock shares and Fosun indirectly almost controlling the shares of Nanjing Iron & Steel Co.,Ltd..

In July 2007, Fosun International was listed on the main board of Hong Kong Stock Exchange with 58% of its shares held by Guo. It had financing of up to HK$12.8 billion and turned out to be the third largest initial public offering (IPO) at the exchange in that year, as well as the sixth largest IPO in the history of the exchange. Soon afterwards, Fosun declared that it would become "the world's first-class investment group." Thus, it started its steady process toward globalization.

In July 2010, Fosun invested €25 million in Club Med, a long-standing French tourist resort business operator, taking up 7.1% of its shares. In March 2015, Fosun offered €958 million and completed the full acquisition of Club Med, holding 98% of its shares. In September 2012, Fosun established the joint venture Pramerica Fosun with Prudential Financial Inc.

In December 2013, Fosun acquired One Chase Manhattan Plaza at the price of US$725 million. This building was one of the two landmarks of the Rockefeller family. The acquisition of the building was aimed at expanding Fosun's business in the world's major financial Centers. In the same month, Fosun, together with the international financial company under the World Bank Group, established the joint venture Peak Reinsurance Company Ltd in Hong Kong.

In January 2014, Fosun offered €1.38 billion for 80% of the stock rights of the Portuguese insurance company Fidelidade, beating a strong rival (Apollo Global Management) at the competitive tender stage. By early 2015, Fosun's holding of Fidelidade's shares had increased to 85%. In the same year, through Fidelidade, Fosun succeeded in acquiring Luz Saúde, the largest private medical group in Portugal.

In June 2014, Fosun acquired 3.9% of the state shares of REN, a Portuguese grid company, at a price of €56.8 million. Then, in August 2014, at a price of US$464 million, Fosun acquired the casualty insurance and property insurance businesses of Ironshore, an American special nature insurance enterprise, amounting to 20% of Ironshore's stock shares. In October 2014, after two consecutively increasing acquisition offers, Fosun finally defeated United Health Group, a global top-500 enterprise, paying €460 million to acquire 96.07% of the stock rights of ESS, a Portuguese medical and health services provider.

In November 2014, Transcendent Resources, a wholly owned subsidiary of Fosun, offered $439 million to acquire 92.6% of the stock shares of the Australian business Roc Oil Co.,Ltd., becoming the largest shareholder of the company.

In July 2015, Fosun declared its acquisition of Meadowbrook, an American labor insurance company. In October 2017, Fosun Pharma offered US$1.91 billion and acquired Gland Pharma, an Indian generic pharmaceutical company. In February 2018, Fosun signed a strategic and cooperative agreement with Arix Bioscience, a British biomedical investment company. In the same month, in Paris, Fosun declared that it had acquired Lanvin, the oldest French fashion brand of haute couture and had become its controlling shareholder while its present shareholders only retained a small number of share rights. Guo Guangchang led Fosun with the core value of "combining Chinese power with global resources," to accelerate the globalization of Fosun and promote integrated and harmonious world economic development. An outstanding entrepreneur with a great enterprise is forever a promising prospect.

CHAPTER

1

BORN POOR BUT AMBITIOUS IN HIS GOALS AND OUTSTANDING IN HIS STUDY

BORN INTO A FARMING FAMILY, HE ASPIRED TO ACHIEVE SUCCESS AT A YOUNG AGE

The town of Hengdian—located in the south-central part of Dongyang city, Zhejiang Province—is a national sustainable development pilot zone, a national film and television industry pilot zone, and a Zhejiang high-tech pilot zone. With a population of less than 90,000, this small town on the south of the Yangtze River has won more than 20 honorary national titles, such as "National Sanitary Town," "National Model Town" and "First Batch of Towns with Chinese Characteristics." In 2010, Hengdian became one of the first batches of small cities to be pilot cities in Zhejiang Province. In May 2018, it was selected as one of the "Top 50 Most Beautiful Towns." In October, Hengdian ranked 29th among the "Top 100 Towns of Overall Strength."

But it was a poverty-stricken place 40 years ago. Surrounding mountains and scarce farmland left the remote town in poverty and lagging behind. The annual per capita income of Hengdian in 1975 was ¥75. A folk song from the local areas goes as follows: "High above are mountains alone, nothing feeds the stomach but porridge, and no girls are to marry Hengdian men." This song was a real reflection of Hengdian at that time.

Today, Hengdian is no longer a stark village. In 2015, the annual per capita income of farmers in Hengdian reached ¥30,020 (US$5,000)—400.26 times higher than that 40 years ago. In other words, a Hengdian farmer's income in 2015 was the same as that of 400 farmers in 1975. Through persistent toil, practical experience and ingenious hard work, these farmers grasped the great chance of reform and opening-up, and achieved a magnificent transformation in Hengdian. In the process of achieving such glorious success, many extraordinary firms and entrepreneurs attracted people's attention. There were companies such as Hengdian Group and entrepreneurs such as Xu Wenrong (chairman of Hengdian Group), Xu Yong'an (president of Hengdian Group Holding Co.,Ltd.) and Xu Yong'an's son. Hengdian Group was a local enterprise in Hengdian. In 2018, under Hengdian Group there were five listed companies, over 200 enterprises focusing on production and service businesses, and more than 50,000 staff members. It became an influential brand in the new era. And out of Hengdian came the outstanding and remarkable entrepreneur Guo Guangchang, the founder and chairman of Fosun Group.

Guo was born into an ordinary rural family in Hengdian, Dongyang, in 1967. In his blood flow the simple but tough, low-profile and pragmatic personality traits of his predecessors. These traits motivated him to leave the countryside to explore his dreams and realize his life's work.

In his childhood, Guo's family was poor. It would be an exaggeration to describe his family as "poor as church mice," but they had nothing spare. However, poverty did not make Guo feel inferior and depressed. In contrast, he became more self-reliant and indomitable. As a child, Guo was very sensible and knew how to solve problems for his parents. He often told his mother, "I am a man now, and I have to be responsible for this family. When there is a problem, I will solve it for you."

Although the family was not affluent, his parents were hard-working and good at housekeeping. Thus, the three children in the family never starved. His father was a stonemason who often followed the collective engineering team in the village to go out to do some construction work, in order to earn some money to support his family. His mother was a vegetable farmer in the production team and planted many kinds of vegetables. When recalling his childhood, Guo remembered clearly: "My mother occasionally went out to borrow food in spring when there was a famine. But she was very capable and planted many sweet potatoes. We could always feed ourselves with those vegetables she planted. Maybe I ate too many sweet potatoes as a kid, as even today I still feel nauseous whenever I smell sweet potatoes." With two older sisters, Guo was the only boy in the family.

Guo's parents knew very well that education could change one's destiny. Even though they were not rich, they tried their best to provide school fees for their children. At that time, as the child of a farmer, there were only a few ways for Guo to rise in life if he wanted to leave the village: to study, to become a soldier or to be a migrant worker. Guo's parents knew their son well, so they put the options in front of Guo and let him make his own choice.

He knew that his parents had good intentions since they gave him the chance to choose. He decided to study without any hesitation. His choice matched the wishes of his parents and two sisters. They expressed joy and said that they would support his decision.

Guo recalled: "At that time, people in Dongyang generally preferred boys to girls. Parents put all their hopes and wishes on their sons. This was indeed a bias against women. Men suffered from the high expectations. In other words, if you were a boy in a family, you didn't need to cook, do the laundry or do any other chores. However, you had to come to the fore because you were a man, and you were responsible for supporting the family in the future."

Because Guo was the youngest child and the only boy, he received special attention from the whole family. Their unanimous wish was that Guo should be able to concentrate on his studies at school without any distractions. At that time, his mother often reminded him: "My boy, you have to win credit for our family. We are poor, but knowledge can change your fate. Only when you advance in society can we finally see the hope of life!"

In fact, Guo did not disappoint his family as his academic performance was always excellent. During his junior high school years, because Guo lived in the countryside and his school was far from his home, he had to live in the school's dormitory. There were both advantages and disadvantages to this. As he didn't have much to do after school, he fell in love with reading. There was a small library in his school, and Guo often obsessively immersed himself in the library for a few hours.

During his first summer vacation of junior high school, Guo wanted to go home to help his parents do some farm work. However, this idea was firmly rejected by his parents and sisters. They only wanted him to wholeheartedly learn from books. They told him: "If you learn more on campus, we'll be much happier. It is no use for you to do farm work." Obviously, he couldn't go against his family's will. With the great support of his family, he vowed in his heart that he would have a successful career when he grew up, in order to better repay his family and his hometown.

One day, Guo happened to find Martin Heidegger's *Being and Time* in the school library, which led him to enter the world of philosophy. As he read more, his insight into philosophy became keener. He was good at thinking and raising corresponding questions. The foundation of his logical thinking was also gradually established, which helped him to surpass other children of the same age. At that time, his teacher always asked him to explain philosophy theories quoted in articles in composition class, which made him very proud. Guo established the ideal of becoming a great philosopher and was determined to do something significant.

BY TURNING TO SENIOR HIGH SCHOOL, HE MADE A DECISION THAT CHANGED HIS LIFE

In the journey of life, we face various choices, and often a decision changes our life. Liu Qing, a well-known Chinese writer, wrote in his long novel *History of Pioneering*: "Although life is long, the critical point lies behind only several vital choices, especially when one is young. No one's life path can be completely straight and without any fork."

In the spring of 1982, Guo, who had graduated from middle school with excellent grades, faced a choice that could change his life: go to the teachers" school or a senior high school.

In 1977, China officially resumed the college entrance examination system, which had been suspended for more than ten years. At that time, after college students graduated, they would be assigned a job. Entering universities became the best way for many young students to change their fate. However, at that time, universities" resources and enrolment quotas were extremely limited. With millions of examinees, the examination was a war in which "hundreds of millions of soldiers wanted to pass a narrow wooden bridge." Because of this fierce competition, rural families were extremely happy if their children could go to college. Setting off firecrackers and having a dinner party were common ways to celebrate.

In 1982, middle school students could apply for teachers" schools, and each of them would be assigned a job after graduation. Guo's family was relatively poor, and his parents hoped that their son could enter a teachers" school and be assigned a job after three years. If he chose to go to high school, he would have to take the college entrance examination after graduation, so the result would be uncertain and there would be no payment in the near future. The family believed that by attending a teachers" school, Guo could obtain the stable and respected job of teaching and would be able to live on his own as early as possible. Students in teachers" schools were exempted from tuition fees and could have some additional subsidies, which directly eased the financial load of families.

Guo acquiesced to the wishes of his parents and decided to go to a teachers" school. He was accepted by a teachers" school after gaining excellent examination grades. After his grades were announced, the whole family was very happy.

However, there was a kind of unspeakable melancholy in Guo's heart when he heard the news. The village men all knew that Guo was a loyal son. He was obedient to his parents and had been grateful to them from an early age. In 1993, when Guo started his business and earned his first million, the first thing he did was to buy a piece of land in his hometown, Hengdian, and build a five-storey building for his parents. As for the choice of the teachers" school, he knew that it was the way to realize his parents" long-standing expectation and that he would quickly obtain a well-paying job for life. So he applied to Jinhua Teachers" School in order to alleviate the poverty of the family.

Being a teacher was a respectable job with a stable income. For many rural children, it was a desirable vocation at the time. But in Guo's view, once he became a teacher, he might have to stay in his hometown for his whole life. In his mind, the images of those great figures described in books emerged from time to time. He tingled with excitement when he thought of them. The deeds of these great people had become the source of his strength. In contrast, he believed that if he were a teacher, he might only educate his students to be a teacher like himself in the future. Teachers and students might say something like this:

"Why do go to school?"

"In order to be a teacher in the future."

"Why do you want to be a teacher in the future?"

"In order to teach students."

"What is the purpose of teaching students?"

"In order to make students become teachers in the future."

With these thoughts in mind, Guo gradually realized that teaching students was not what he wanted to do in his life, and his ambition should not be limited to the local schools. He remembered Lu Xun, a master of modern Chinese literature, who first chose to study medicine and then abandoned medicine to study literature. The Chinese Confucian classics *Book of Rites* and *Great Learning* exhort people: "One should cultivate the moral self, regulate the family, maintain the state rightly and make all peaceful."

Guo knew that there was much knowledge in the world waiting for him to explore. He had a long way to go to cultivate his morality, and there must be a bigger mission waiting for him in the future. He should do more things on a bigger stage to help more people.

After much consideration, Guo made clear his own goals. Although he was grateful to his parents and sisters, for they had supported him and enabled him to focus on his studies, his vision and ambition had far exceeded their initial expectations. At this crucial crossroads in his life, Guo finally made his decision: to give up the teachers" school and go to high school, and then take the college entrance examination.

Feeling that the time was ripe, Guo told his parents and sisters his decision face to face. He wanted to enable them to accept this decision. He said: "I really want to work quickly to support my family. However, if I go to a teachers" school and become a middle school or primary school teacher after graduation, the salary I earn will only slightly improve the living condition of our family and it won't change much." Then, he talked about his ideal of "cultivating the moral self, regulating the family, maintaining the state rightly and making all peaceful." He also cited many examples of great figures who had given up small and immediate profits for long-term benefits in the future. As a result, the more he talked, the more excited he became. Words cascaded in torrents from him.

His parents were in a dilemma. They understood their son, who undoubtedly made them proud. All parents want their children to have a bright future. But, on the other hand, due to their limited perspective, they knew very little about the examples Guo gave or the outside world of which he spoke. The family had been limping along under the pressure of poverty, and they regarded his education in a teachers" school as the best way out.

When Guo revealed all his ideals and aspirations, his family were silent. After a few minutes of stalemate, his mother and two sisters showed their agreement, and then they picked up their farm tools and went to work. Guo's father also stood up, stood behind his son, patted him lightly on the shoulder and then said firmly: "If you decide to take this road, you must finish it. In the future, our family will support you through all difficulties and setbacks." After that, his father also went out to work.

His father's words immediately dispelled Guo's worries. While he appreciated his father's understanding and support, his belief was strengthened. He knew very well that his decision was not only related to his own dream but also to the future wellbeing of the whole family. A real man never went back on his words. He must firmly move toward his goal. A few days later, Guo went to Dongyang High School with a quilt and some rations.

AT THE SENIOR HIGH SCHOOL, A FRAIL-LOOKING STUDENT HAD HIS OWN VIEW

Wang Bo, a famous *littérateur* in the Tang Dynasty, wrote in *A Tribute to King Teng's Tower*: "Poor as one is, he is all the more determined in adversity and by no means gives up his ambition."

When Guo entered Dongyang High School in September 1982, he redoubled his efforts to study in order to fulfil his promise to his family. In his high school years, he followed a routine: morning jogging, morning reading, breakfast, classes, lunch, classes, dinner, evening self-study and sleeping at ten o'clock. He followed this pattern every day.

When he was at the high school, Guo's will-power increased greatly.

From then on, he developed the habit of concentrating on one thing. He believed that the key to success in learning was to illuminate the goal and the purpose of it. Only in this way could students work toward a target in a planned and passionate way with self-motivation.

The determination to work hard not only made Guo's academic performance excellent but also allowed him to read a large number of extracurricular books. His reading habit was formed in middle school, and the library of the high school soon became the ideal place for him to make full use of his spare time. This library had a lot more books than the one in his middle school, and the books were on a wider range of topics. Due to the considerable time he spent reading and the expansion of his vision, he was interested in books on history, literature and biography, in addition to philosophy as always. Through reading, he continuously broadened his horizon and increased his knowledge. The way he looked at a problem was changed, and he established his independent view of the world, life and value. Most of the students around him were not quite sure why they had to study and what they should do in the future, but Guo's goal had become relatively clear.

In the high school, Guo was thin. He was usually gentle and quiet. He had the appearance of a standard frail-looking scholar, but he was quite assertive inside. In class, when there was a discussion session, he would become eloquent, not only logical and careful in language, but also exceptional in thinking, always having different opinions.

He was not afraid of being questioned by his classmates and invited his peers to argue with him. In this way, he could give full play to the knowledge he had accumulated in reading in order to demonstrate his point of view. Although he was young, he was knowledgeable and thoughtful, as seen by others.

At that time, class activities were often held. After the activity was over, the head teacher asked each student to write an essay, such as a summary or a reflection. On one occasion, all the students in the class handed in their essays except Guo. When the teacher called him to the office and asked him for the reason, he replied bluntly: "I don't think it is necessary to write this summary; besides, there is nothing to sum up. Compared with writing empty and meaningless sentences, I'd rather keep silent."

Guo's frank and outspoken words surprised the head teacher. On that very day, the teacher had a long heart-to-heart talk with him. They talked about learning, life, society and many other topics. Guo felt that for the first time in his life he had expressed his thoughts freely. His teacher also found out that this quiet young man had much deeper knowledge and thoughts than his peers, and he was even more incisive regarding some problems than the teacher.

During the conversation, the teacher asked what books Guo usually read. Guo said with some embarrassment that he had recently read several well-known works on philosophy and history. The teacher was very surprised, and he suddenly understood that Guo had always been studying in his spare time. No wonder he had so many sharp points of view and different perspectives.

Finally, the teacher asked Guo what he wanted to do in the future. Without any hesitation, Guo replied that his life's goal was "to cultivate the moral self, regulate the family, maintain the state rightly and make all peaceful." When the teacher heard Guo's goal, he didn't judge it as unrealistic. Instead, this goal made him more confident about his student's future. He encouraged Guo to be dedicated to it and also reminded him not to delay his studies because of reading. The teacher also encouraged him to enter a key university through his own efforts.

AS EXPECTED, HE PASSED THE EXAMINATION AND ENTERED THE DEPARTMENT OF PHILOSOPHY AT FUDAN UNIVERSITY

The high school years are a critical period in which a person learns and grows up. After graduating from middle school, Guo gave up the chance to study in the teachers" school and become a teacher afterwards. He resolutely chose to study in the senior high school, then applied to university and set out for a higher goal. Facts have proven that Guo's choice was certainly wise.

Guo learned a lot in the three years of his high school life. What he learned greatly enriched his mind and made him more confident about achieving his goal in the future. He more clearly defined the standards and principles by which he would conduct himself, deeply learned the truth about life and came to understand how to handle relationships with his classmates. Thus, he became more and more mature in this process. He learned how to solve problems independently and effectively. In his study, he accumulated a set of learning methods and reasonable plans suitable for himself. He could always find happiness in the stressful scholastic life. In terms of mental performance, he could communicate with others properly, treating other people with understanding and tolerance. All these elements promoted his personal qualities of strength, self-confidence and self-esteem, as well as his love for the collective and love for his motherland. He was full of self-confidence and could face failure calmly. During the three years of his high school life, he improved himself all the time. With the progress of his grades, his moral merit and physical fitness also gradually improved.

Three years passed quickly. Guo rushed to the finish line when the college entrance examination finally came, and he had to fill out a form stating his intention to take the exam. He had already made a clear decision to major in philosophy.

Philosophy is regarded as "a subject of useless learning" by some people today. Although philosophy is all-encompassing and exists in all kinds of work, it is debatable whether it should be classified as a major. To this end, some experts even suggest that universities should abolish philosophy as a major and make philosophy a compulsory general course for students. However, in Guo's age, philosophy was the major with the highest number of applicants. At the beginning of the reform and opening-up, the ideological field in China seemed to be in a state of contention. Due to the weak scientific research foundation in colleges and universities, some basic subjects (such as philosophy) were made popular among students and parents.

Later, many people bluntly asked Guo why he chose philosophy. He replied: "Around 1985, the new ideas of the reform and opening-up had affected people in Dongyang, and I began to think as a high school student with childish and enthusiastic characteristics. At that time, most of the articles I read were by Lu Xun, a revolutionary writer in China. Lu Xun said: "It is miserable for the Chinese to have a robust body without a sound mind." I was deeply inspired by his enthusiasm to enlighten the people. I believed that the main target in the early stage of the reform and opening-up was to liberate the thought of people. Therefore, when I filled in the intention form, I made philosophy my first choice."

In fact, the last year of Guo's high school era was indeed a turning point in China's reform and opening-up. In 1984, Deng Xiaoping, chief designer of this policy, made his first Southern Tour and affirmed the policy of establishing a special economic zone in Shenzhen, laying the foundation for China's further progress. That year, Liu Chuanzhi, Wang Shi, Zhang Ruimin and other grassroots entrepreneurs, inspired by the reform and opening-up, started their businesses under this guidance. They were later called the first generation of entrepreneurs or the "84 Group."

Guo had already chosen not only a major but also a university for himself. As a result of his academic performance, he could apply for any national key university in China; however, he chose neither Peking University nor Tsinghua University but Fudan University in Shanghai.

There was no doubt that Fudan University was one of the best universities in China, although it was not located in the capital, Beijing. Guo had been full of yearning for the international metropolis of Shanghai since he was very young, because Shanghai had gathered many accomplished foreigners and was known as the "Paris of the East." It was a city with a relatively developed economy, advanced science and technology, and abundant intellectual resources. When he applied to Fudan University, Guo bound his fate tightly with Shanghai.

Later facts proved that Guo's choice to apply to Fudan University was even wiser than his choice to go to high school instead of a teachers" school. From his point of view, Shanghai was a city with a global gene. Its spirit could be perfectly summarized by the ideas of "embracing diversities, pursuing excellence, staying enlightened and wise, and keeping modest." If his original hometown, Dongyang, endowed Guo with the character of self-improvement and perseverance, then later Shanghai, as his second hometown, gave him a vision of the big picture and insightful strategies. After he entered the city, he grew into a dazzling star in the business circles of China and even the world in less than ten years.

As people expected, in the college entrance examination, Guo ranked first in his class. He successfully entered the Department of Philosophy of Fudan University and brought a satisfactory end to his three years of hard work in high school. Guo still held his great ideal: "to cultivate the moral self, regulate the family, maintain the state rightly and make all peaceful." The four years of study at the university would certainly give his ideal wings to soar.

CHAPTER

AFTER FOUR YEARS AT UNIVERSITY, HE ACHIEVED EXCELLENCE BUT WENT FOR BUSINESS ADVENTURE

FOCUSED ON PHILOSOPHY, HE UNDERSTOOD TAO AND THEN PRACTISED HIS SKILLS

In September 1985, Guo Guangchang took the train to Shanghai with great hope, carrying the luggage his mother had prepared for him. He became a freshman in the Department of Philosophy at Fudan University, and thus started a new chapter in his life journey.

At that time, Shanghai, once the financial center of the Far East and the capital of fashion and culture, was still China's largest economic center and old industrial base. It was also regarded as the world's fourth largest city after New York, London and Paris.

Guo, who had never been to Shanghai before, was soon attracted by the Shanghai-style architecture of combining Chinese and Western features. In the face of numerous buildings, busy streets and endless crowds, Guo was so excited that he found it difficult to calm himself down for several days. He even laughed at himself, behaving as if he had gone abroad. Everything was so fresh.

But, ultimately, Guo was a rational person. He soon put his mind to his studies.

When Guo chose to study philosophy, he decided to learn the truth first and then the associated skills. He believed that compared with other majors, philosophy seemed illusory, but the relevant knowledge existed in all aspects of life. Philosophy could not only enable people to find the essence of things quickly but also broaden their horizons and provide new insights. "Horizons" referred to what could be seen through the eyes, and also referred to human thoughts and knowledge. "Insights" referred to people's cognitive progress. But in terms of practice, this idea was not that easy to enact. In the process of learning the truth, due to not having a clear goal in advance, one's thoughts might stay at the level of abstract cognition, which would lead to empty talk. If so, philosophy might really become a subject of "useless learning."

Guo clearly remembered the scene when he first entered Fudan University. When he enrolled, he was greeted not by a sign saying something like "Welcome Freshmen" but by the slogan "If I Do Not Enter the Inferno, Who Else Will?" Obviously, this was an interpretation of philosophy by the teachers and students in the Department of Philosophy. Although this slogan looked somewhat intimidating, he did not feel particularly surprised. On the contrary, it suddenly dispelled his uneasiness, because he felt that he had found people who shared the same interests as him and who could devote themselves wholeheartedly to the study of philosophy. Since reading his first philosophical book in middle school, he had fallen in love with philosophy and always dreamed of studying it after being admitted to a university. Consequently, he was ready to deal with all kinds of difficulties.

Later, when recalling the scene, Guo said: "At that time, this slogan made me feel more excited than the slogan of "Welcoming Future Political Activists" of the Department of International Politics. Therefore, I also devoted myself fully to the solemn emotion of becoming a "failed hero" and thought about how to accomplish the enlightenment tasks that the May 4th Movement failed to accomplish. Therefore, I was one of those who dressed themselves in old military uniforms and talked in small groups about how to surpass Marx on campus, which was a classic scene in Fudan at that time." Guo even took the slogan as an aphorism to motivate himself, and it gave him a sense of responsibility about learning philosophy well.

Guo believed that compared with most other subjects, philosophy's topics of research were visionary and usually unprecedented. Moreover, no one knew when such questions would be answered, and many of them would remain unsolved despite generations of effort. These problems were just like black holes. You wanted to make a map of it, but you were not sure whether the hole had an exit. But this was exactly what made philosophy fascinating. People continued to uncover mysteries and explore the essence of things step by step through speculation and experiments. Even if one sacrificed oneself in the exploration, one would be trained in the process and become what Guo called a "failed hero."

In fact, the "failed hero," in Guo's words, was not a negative idea at all. He believed that the process of philosophical research was itself a course of growth. It not only broadened people's horizons but also enhanced their insights. The horizon was the width of one's perspective, and insight was the height and depth of it. With width, height and depth, one could see the essence of a problem, more so than others. Especially when facing new problems, one could make accurate decisions quickly.

In the process of studying philosophy, Guo built up his basic thinking and sense of logic. This made him pay more attention to reading and gaining knowledge in various disciplines during his college days. He went to the library of Fudan University almost every day, and his borrowing records could be found in every library section. He did not simply read by following his interests, but summarized many common points in relevant disciplines. Many theories existed in different subjects, but the interpretation methods were the same. Later, Guo concluded that the books he read during his college years foreshadowed the seemingly unrelated fields covered by his industrial empire (worth more than ¥100 billion). No matter how many overlapping products or customers there were in these fields, a considerable degree of convergence could be found in the business logic and operations management.

Four years of philosophy education and companionship with books enabled Guo to read and understand more about society and life. He said: "Some people may say that philosophy is useless. The Department of Philosophy did not teach me any basic skills, but it taught me how to think and learn. What's more, the study of philosophy required plentiful and unbounded reading, which made me see our society and my life more clearly. It was because I was with books that I obtained a rich inner life in my college years. The extensive reading also made me think more about individuals, society and the future of our nation. People often say that college years are a period when one's views toward the world, values and life are established. As a Chinese man growing up in the reform and opening-up, there was still a lot of work for me to do in the future."

RIDING ON A "THOUSAND-*LI*" BICYCLE, HE BECAME ATTACHED TO TSINGTAO BEER

Before going to Fudan University, Guo had never left Dongyang. It was the first time in his life that he had travelled so far. After entering Fudan University, he always dreamed of visiting places other than Shanghai.

During the summer vacation of 1987, in his second year of university, Guo finally had the chance to leave Shanghai. He could go alone to Beijing, the capital of China, to do a survey. In fact, this was an opportunity he created for himself. This survey was special because the transportation he chose was neither a train nor a car, but a bicycle. That was to say, he was determined to ride to Beijing alone.

A bicycle ride from Shanghai to Beijing would still be a big challenge even today, when the road infrastructure has been much improved. At that time, Guo rode his bicycle to Beijing not because he wanted to challenge himself or to exercise. He simply had no money to buy a train ticket. He felt that a train ticket that cost tens of *yuan* was too expensive. Instead of spending money on tickets, he might as well use the money to buy a bicycle and ride it all the way.

In the 1980s, it was a great honor for a Chinese family to own a bicycle. On the campus of a university, everyone would envy a boy who could ride a bicycle with a girl on a tree-lined path. It was also the dream of many college students to have a bicycle of their own, and Guo was no exception. Fortunately, his idea of riding to Beijing to do research was strongly supported by the mother of one of his good friends, who generously lent Guo ¥200. In this way, Guo had his first bicycle. He later recalled: "The moment I bought the bicycle, I was much happier than when I bought a Ferrari later. I proudly declared: 'Once upon a time there was a hero who rode a good horse alone for thousands of *li*, and now there is the bicycle to accompany me for tens of thousands of *li*.'"

After buying the bicycle, Guo meticulously set himself a riding route: the road along the famous Beijing–Hangzhou Grand Canal. The 1,794-kilometer-long artificial canal is the oldest and longest artificial river in the world. It is nine times as long as the Suez Canal and 22 times as long as the Panama Canal. It is ranked as high as the Great Wall among Chinese heritage. As the economic, cultural and political belt of ancient China, the canal runs from Tongzhou in Beijing in the north to Hangzhou in Zhejiang in the south, passing through six provinces. Over the past 2,500 years, it has witnessed the rise and fall of one dynasty after another. As a child, Guo had read about this legendary canal in a book. Since he had an opportunity to go to Beijing, he might as well have a look at this ancient example of historical and cultural heritage.

In this way, Guo embarked on a bicycle journey to the north, more than 1,000 kilometers away. He enjoyed the beautiful scenery along the way while riding. Every time he passed through a city, he would stop to have a look and enthusiastically chat with local people to learn about their living conditions and understand their inner feelings. He also took out his diary and pen from time to time to record the relevant information he had obtained and his thoughts. Seeing the mottled riverbanks and ancient stone bridges in front of him, Guo could always remember the histor-ical pictures he had seen in books, which made him sigh emotionally for the change of the times and the fact that an individual was only a drop in the ocean of history.

After riding for 20 days, he finally arrived at Tongzhou, the end of the Beijing–Hangzhou Grand Canal, with copious notes for his survey. After so many days of travel, he was extremely tired. His skin was tanned, and his legs were aching everywhere. But when he recalled what he had seen, heard and learned along the way, he thought it had really been worth it.

When he regained some of his strength, he rode his bicycle to Badaling, the site of the most visited section of the Great Wall of China, and the excited college student felt a strong emotional connection with the Great Wall. He also experienced its grandeur, feeling the truth of the saying that "he who has never been to the Great Wall is not a true man."

After completing his research mission in Beijing, Guo sold his bicycle before returning to Shanghai. On the way back, he felt that he had enough money to take a detour to Qingdao, from where it was cheaper to go back to Shanghai by boat than by train. After arriving in Qingdao, the first thing he did was to buy a steamer ticket back to Shanghai. After that, the rest of the money was only enough for him to eat a meal. Guo felt that since he had come, he must try the famous Tsingtao Beer. Therefore, Guo went to a canteen at Qingdao Dock to look for the beer.

Tsingtao Beer was invented in 1903 and later became a famous brand in China. In the 1980s, beer supply was limited due to a shortage of grain, and people who had a grain coupon could only buy one bottle. At Fudan University, sharing a bottle of Guangming Beer with his classmates was enough to please Guo. But now he was in Qingdao, the hometown of beer, and the famous Tsingtao Beer was right in front of his eyes. He made up his mind to be extravagant. So he bought a bottle of Tsingtao Beer with the rest of his money and spent the night at the dock. He looked at the bottle with satisfaction and thought to himself that it would be great if he could drink such good beer every day.

This wish was realized a few years later. Moreover, unexpectedly in 2018, Guo's company Fosun acquired 17.99% of Tsingtao Beer (owned by Japan's Asahi Group) and became the second largest shareholder of Tsingtao Beer. In order to commemorate this historic acquisition, Tsingtao Beer specially designed a beer called Lucky Strike, Fosun Forever with red glass bottles. Later, this beer became Fosun's exclusive beer for guests.

Today, Guo is still deeply touched by the experience of that riding journey and having Tsingtao Beer for the first time. He said: "More than 30 years have passed, but every time I go abroad on business, I always find a local Chinese restaurant to treat myself. I'll definitely order Tsingtao Beer, because every Chinese restaurant overseas serves Tsingtao Beer from China. After more than 30 years of ups and downs, many brands that conveyed people's memories disappeared sadly. However, Tsingtao Beer is still full of vitality and it has become a drink that everyone can drink at any time. This was absolutely unthinkable when I rode to Qingdao at the age of 20."

That bottle of Tsingtao Beer formed an indissoluble bond between the 20-year-old Guo and Tsingtao Beer.

BOUND FOR HAINAN, HE LOOKED FOR A PROMISING LAND

In 1988, Guo made the decision to go to Hainan. But let's first look at what he did 30 years later.

On 21 January 2018, Hainan Daily Newspaper Group and Fosun held a signing ceremony in Sanya, announcing the joint launch of

"Hainan and Me—30 Years—30 People" as the major themed event for the 30th anniversary of the establishment of the special economic zone (SEZ) of Hainan Province. Guo Zhimin (Chinese Communist Party secretary and also president and editor-in-chief of *Hainan Daily*), Guo (chairman of Fosun International) and Xu Zhenling (deputy mayor of Sanya) attended the signing ceremony. Hainan Daily Newspaper Group and Fosun co-hosted this event, which aimed to find pioneering figures from all walks of life who had closely connected their fates with that of the SEZ. The event was designed to decode their unique SEZ "genes" and how they used them on their way to success, and also to tap into their "special zone spirit" of joining the reform wave, where they had the courage to think and act, always daring to be the first. The event would contribute to the 30th anniversary of the establishment of the SEZ of Hainan Province and gather strong spiritual strength for Hainan's next 30 years of the reform, opening-up and development. This large-scale event mainly consisted of four parts: "30 People in 30 Years," a series of field interviews with pioneering figures; "The Chinese Dream and Love in Hainan," a large-scale collection of works themed around "Hainan and Me for 30 Years"; "Fosun's Night," the launch ceremony for "30 People in 30 Years"; and a special themed salon for "30 People in 30 Years."

At the signing ceremony for the event, Guo and Weng Chaojian, general manager of Hainan Daily Newspaper Group, hugged each other affectionately, showing that their relationship was unusual. This was indeed the case. More than 30 years ago, they met in the Department of Philosophy at Fudan University and shared the same dormitory. The fact that they were able to get together again on such an occasion made them excited and grateful.

In 1985, both Weng and Guo were admitted to the Department of Philosophy of Fudan University. Weng was from Wenchang City, Hainan Province. After entering Fudan University, his classmates affectionately called him "Jian." During their four years at the university, Guo slept on the upper berth and Weng was right below him. At that time, they often talked about Taoism, Neo-Confucianism and the philosophy of the mind. Their topics ranged from Nietzsche, Kant and Sartre to Marx and Engels, and they also discussed the news that Nie Weiping had crushed his Japanese opponent in a China–Japan Go match, the five consecutive championships won by the Chinese women's volleyball team and Diego Maradona's "hand of God" in the 1986 FIFA World Cup. Obviously, they were close friends who kept no secrets from each other.

In the summer of 1988, Guo made a crazier decision than the one he made the previous summer, to go to Beijing by bicycle. This time, he wanted to go to Hainan by bicycle. That year, Hainan was officially approved by the central government to set up a provincial SEZ. It attracted 100,000 aspiring young people from all over the country with dreams to come to Hainan, hoping to create a new world there.

Hearing the news, Guo was stirred and passionate. As a result, he decided to ride to Hainan. This time, he and 12 other students set forth from Fudan University with ¥3,000 in sponsorship from Shanghai Yongjiu Bicycle Factory and a letter of introduction from the Youth League Committee of Fudan University. Each of them set out from Shanghai on a bicycle and headed south along the southeast coastline. They passed through the four original SEZs—Shenzhen, Zhuhai, Shantou and Xiamen—established in China's reform and opening-up. Their ultimate goal was Hainan SEZ. They travelled more than 3,000 kilometers, riding and researching.

After arriving in Hainan, Guo was amazed at the sights. Although the infrastructure there was still underdeveloped and there was only one traffic light in Haikou, he still used the words "years of burning passion" to describe the attitude of the people he met there. He later recalled: "At that time, every place in Hainan was undergoing a lively start, and more than 100,000 talents went to Hainan. Every day, huge crowds gathered before the "wall of pioneers," many of whom were college students. When they couldn't find jobs, they sold *wonton* (dumplings) in the street and set up stalls under coconut trees. But even when selling coconuts, they showed expectations for the future on their faces, and their youthful faces impressed me deeply."

It should be said that Guo first went to Hainan in 1988 mainly out of curiosity, and it was the exploration of a young man. However, Guo was deeply attracted by the vitality of the reform in Hainan. What he saw and learned in Hainan had a huge impact on him and gave him a new understanding of the SEZ.

Although he didn't stay in Hainan for a long time, it impressed him very much, and he was attached to this land of openness. During the Spring Festival in his fourth year of university, Guo didn't go home and once again went to Hainan to celebrate the festival at his classmate Weng Chaojian's home. That year, for the first time, he ate Wenchang chicken, a specialty food in Hainan. It made Guo appreciate the hospitality and simplicity of Hainan's people, and he became full of affection for this land, undoubtedly falling in love with it. He made a heartfelt oath to himself: "If one day I can do something for Hainan, I will definitely contribute to its development. I believe that one day when the time comes, this hope will definitely come true."

On the eve of his graduation in 1989, Guo affectionately wrote this passage to Weng (Jian) in his graduation album: "Jian, there are not many good memories worth recalling in my life. For me, the enthusiasm of your family, the flavor of Wenchang chicken, and the scenery of Nandao, which consists of white clouds, blue sky and coconut trees, are unforgettable for me forever. When I set foot on my return journey, I thought to myself: 'Someday I will come back to find a piece of land that belongs to me!'" Many might think that Guo wrote this only because of his youthful exuberance. But in fact, he never forgot this promise to Weng. After founding a successful start-up (Fosun), he came to Hainan many times to conduct investigations, and he designed the structure of Fosun's development step by step in Hainan. In 2007, Fosun invested in Hainan Mining and helped it get listed. On 15 August 2007, Fosun established the Fosun Guangcai Education Award Fund in Hainan Province to award local high school students with both excellent academic performance and moral qualities. Over the ten years following the foundation of this award, more than 4,800 Hainan students benefited from it. In 2016, the Sanya Resort of Club Med (invested in by Fosun) was successfully opened. In April 2018, Atlantis Sanya was opened. This was a one-stop tourism, leisure and vacation complex built by Fosun over six years with an investment of over ¥10 billion. It was a benchmark project for tourism in Hainan, with 1,314 guest rooms, Asia's largest aquarium, wonderful water parks and a dolphin bay. At the grand opening ceremony, Guo choked several times during his speech. He deeply felt that the seeds planted 30 years ago had not just taken root but had grown into towering trees. Many people's painstaking efforts and love had been condensed into this project, and Guo had been looking forward to it for a long time.

QUITTING HIS JOB, HE WENT FOR BUSINESS ADVENTURE

In 1989, Guo was given the opportunity to stay at Fudan University and become a teacher in the Youth League Committee by virtue of his outstanding performance. For many new graduates, staying at school to teach was a desirable option. Graduation in this way would not only enable Guo to leave the countryside completely and stay in Shanghai, China's largest city, but also help him to obtain an enviable, stable job. Especially for his family far away in the Dongyang countryside, this result far exceeded their expectations.

Later, while working in the Youth League Committee, Guo met Liang Xinjun, who was two years younger than him and was also a teacher at Fudan. It was this friendship that made Liang one of the co-founders of Fosun Group. Liang's hometown was Taizhou, Zhejiang Province, and he was a straight-A student. In 1987, he was admitted to the Department of Genetic Engineering at Fudan University as the top student in science in the college entrance examination of Taizhou. After entering the university, his academic performance was still excellent and he received the highest scholarship from the university every year.

After Liang chose to work at Fudan University, he and Guo soon became good partners at work and close friends in life. When they were together, their conversations were like diamond cutting diamond but they were also heroes cherishing each other. During that period, they organized students and did a lot of social practice and market research activities in order to broaden their horizons and activate their thinking. Although China's reform and opening-up had only been in progress for a decade, earthshaking changes had taken place in all walks of life. What Guo and Liang saw and heard made them gradually realize that the university was only a place for teaching. If they wanted to build a great business, they must leave this comfort zone and go to the forefront of the reform and opening-up. They felt that as competent people, they didn't have the opportunity to show their talent.

For this reason, Guo once had the idea of pursuing a master's degree in the United States. But what was he going to study in the United States? Should he continue studying philosophy? Or, like other students, should he go abroad with the purpose of finding a job there rather than studying? After making all the preparations to go to the United States, Guo finally calmed down and dismissed the idea.

China's feudal history had lasted for more than 2,000 years, and it was deeply rooted in people's minds that being a public servant was honorable. For this reason, working for the government had become the best choice for intellectuals, while doing business was seen as despicable and a desperate choice. If someone quit their job in the government and was determined to launch a business, few people would understand it.

In the spring of 1992, Deng Xiaoping's speech on his Southern Tour completely changed Guo's life through its message about the vitality of "the great spring of the East." Before 1992, although great achievements had been made in China's reform and opening-up, there was considerable ideological dispute and intense discussion over whether the country was developing in a socialist or capitalist way. It resulted in indecisive reform and limited opening-up. Deng's speech on the Southern Tour completely cast off this ideological shackle. People no longer talked about ideology and accepted the idea that development was the absolute principle.

Deng made it clear in his speech that businesses in the non-public sector were an important part of the socialist market economy. This remark not only defended China's private enterprises but also enabled Guo and Liang Xinjun to make the decision to start up a business. Inspired by Deng's speech, they planned for a short time and then registered and established Shanghai Guangxin Technology Development Co.,Ltd. in Shanghai Administration for Industry and Commerce with registered capital of only ¥38,000. Their main business was market research and consultation.

They gave up their jobs as teachers at Fudan University and started their own business from scratch, which was undoubtedly an act that most people could not understand. For this reason, they hid the decision from their families at first, acting quietly before making their decision public. Liang later recalled: "Although my family understood and supported me, my social status obviously declined. When I met my acquaintances, they always said that I had changed, I had become a businessman, and I was mercenary." Today, China has formed an atmosphere of respecting entrepreneurs and encouraging innovation and entrepreneurship. This is inseparable from the country's economic boom and the improvement of people's living standards brought about by the reform and opening-up.

After choosing to start up a business, Guo landed on the "mundane vast plain" from a "metaphysical castle in the air." When he stayed at university to teach, it seemed that it was not far from his goal of "regulating the family." However, Guo took the initiative to return to the starting point of his ideal ("cultivating the moral self"), and the place of self-cultivation became the vast society. In Guo's eyes, commerce would definitely benefit and transform society, as well as make people's lives better. With such a belief, he changed his original goal of "cultivating the moral self, regulating the family, maintaining the state rightly and making all peaceful" to "cultivating the moral self, regulating the family, maintaining the state rightly and helping the world."

After the birth of Shanghai Guangxin Technology Development Co.,Ltd., Guo said in an open letter that he, Liang Xinjun and several other people had set up a small business called Guangxin. The name was easy to understand. "Guang" stood for Guo Guangchang and "Xin" stood for Liang Xinjun. In 1993, Guo earned his first ¥300,000 by helping Ganso Food with an investigation report. Later, they successively took over projects from companies such as Helios and soon earned ¥1 million.

In 1995, Guo renamed Guangxin as Fosun. With Wang Qunbin and Fan Wei joining the company, the emerging industries of real estate and biomedicine had become new options for Guo to advance the development of Fosun.

As a representative of the "92 Clique" (a group of entrepreneurs who started their businesses after Deng Xiaoping's Southern Tour), Guo had been working tirelessly with the mentality of "treading as if on thin ice, acting with extreme caution, and working conscientiously." But Guo did not walk alone on the road to wealth. In the early days of Fosun's establishment, Guo and his four cofounders (Liang Xinjun, Wang Qunbin, Fan Wei and Tan Jian) were called the "Fosun Five" and even the "Fudan Five Tigers" because all five of them were Fudan alumni. To this end, Liang Xinjun said: "The five of us are like five fingers of one hand, and everyone is indispensable. When the five fingers clench together, there is a fist. Moreover, apart from our friendship, which was established at school, the spirit of Zhejiang businessmen also influenced several of us, and the corporate culture formed according to this common cultural background was the biggest foundation for us to work together."

3

CHAPTER

SETTING SAIL, FOSUN INITIATED A NEW AGE OF BUSINESS INNOVATION

SUCCESSFUL AT THE OUTSET, HE WON HIS FIRST BID

We all have countless firsts in our lives, and here is the story of Guo Guangchang's first bid. Although Guo is a very rich person, he has always been a modest and prudent businessman with Confucian manners. On many occasions, he has modestly said: "Fosun is still a small company." His modesty came from the legendary performance of Guangxin Technology Development Co.,Ltd., which was registered with only ¥38,000 and exchanged small amounts of funds for large assets over and over again.

When Guangxin was founded, it was pioneering. During his years working at Fudan University, Guo had often taken students on trips to do surveys during the holidays. The professional social statistical methods and practical experience they had accumulated laid the foundation for the birth of Guangxin. When it was founded, there were no more than ten such consulting companies nationwide, and four in Shanghai. As a leader in the industry, Guangxin quickly occupied the consulting market in Shanghai with keen insight. As more and more enterprises entered Shanghai, the growing demand for market surveys in Shanghai undoubtedly provided opportunities for Guangxin to develop.

However, the process of starting a business was very tough. Guo rode a bicycle to work to run the business. This iconic style was later talked about by many business allies in loving detail. At that time, Guangxin was indeed as small a company as it could be. In a bungalow of less than 15 square meters, there was a 586-chip computer, the company's most valuable asset. The "company car" was the old bicycle that Guo often rode.

In the face of tough business conditions, Guo did not flinch. In fact, when he left Fudan University, he had already made up his mind: "Once I choose a career, I cannot retreat. Retreating is what cowards usually do. I, Guo, am an indomitable man. I will use my wisdom to create a bright future." With this belief, he rode that bicycle every day, continually passing through the streets and alleys of Shanghai. Sweat flowed down his forehead and into his eyes, even blurred his vision, but in his heart, he was always hopeful.

To put it bluntly, in ancient times, the market research and consultation industry played the role of military advisers when armies were marching and fighting. In China in the early 1990s, there were not many people working in this industry; therefore, Guo chose to start his business in this field. He said: "If one wants to start a business, one needs to choose a new industry. The old ones do not need start-ups but innovation. However, a brand new one is not a good idea either. Once you are a half step ahead of others, you are a pioneer, but if you are one step ahead of others, you may become a martyr."

In 1993, Taiwan Ganso Food Company, which had just entered the Shanghai market, was seeking further diversified development and urgently needed a specialized consulting company for advice. To this end, Ganso had issued a tender notice seeking consultation and aimed to find a consulting company that could satisfy its needs.

After seeing the tender notice from Ganso, Guo was very excited. In his heart, he had always been looking for such an opportunity. He rode his bicycle back to Guangxin immediately and told several colleagues the news of the tender notice. All of them were delighted after hearing it.

They took action straight away to prepare the company's qualification materials for the qualification process. Soon, Guo brought the materials to Ganso to be registered for bidding.

In the bidding office of Ganso, three consulting companies had passed the qualification examination before Guangxin. In this situation, as the legal representative of Guangxin, Guo was anxious. He forced himself to calm down and handed over the documents to the staff responsible for the examination. He had been very careful, because this opportunity was very important for him and the Guangxin team. The Ganso staff took the documents, briefly glanced at them and put them aside. Compared with the documents submitted by the other three companies, what Guo had submitted was very brief, which suggested no advantage at all. Therefore, Guo comforted himself over and over again: "Don't be too nervous, and don't take it too seriously."

Although Guo comforted himself, he could not hide his desire to be successful. He even tripped over the doorsill when he walked out of the office. He stumbled and almost fell, but his partner Liang Xinjun seized his hand behind him and supported him.

Fortunately, two days later, Ganso called Guo and informed him that Guangxin had passed the qualification examination and could prepare the corresponding documents to participate in the bidding. After Guo answered the phone call, both Guo and Liang were excited. Guo soon had a premonition that this opportunity must belong to Guangxin. At this thought, his heart beat violently.

On the day of the public bidding, the weather was very hot. Guo and Liang came to the meeting room of Ganso with two other staff members. The head of the marketing department of Ganso gave them some information, such as the background and development plan of Ganso, and then briefly explained the purpose of the tender. Guangxin was required to explain its understanding of Ganso's project and the method of investigation within 20 minutes.

Before Guangxin's bid, two consulting firms had already been eliminated. After the head of the marketing department of Ganso stated the requirements, Guo and Liang conferred quietly for a while and then took a pile of papers out of their bag. These papers were the market investigation strategies formulated by Guangxin, including sampling, investigation methods, investigation cycle and so on, all of which were explained in detail. Guo immediately submitted the working plan to Ganso, and then gave a brief introduction and explanation.

Guo introduced himself and Liang, as well as the story behind Guangxin. They had given up the job of university teaching, which was stable and decent, and started their own business. The people of Ganso were impressed. In particular, the investigation strategy Guo and Liang presented was insightful. During the conversation, the market leader of Ganso found that these two young people not only had broad knowledge and logical thinking, but also quite profound opinions on the current development situation in China. Finally, they believed that it was worth giving these two aspiring youths a chance. Twenty minutes later, it was announced on the spot that Ganso would cooperate with Guangxin.

After winning the bid, Guo immediately calmed down. He realized that winning the bid was only a starting point, and the next step must be carrying out the work in a down-to-earth manner to ensure the satisfaction of the other party.

FOR GUANGXIN'S CONSULTATION, HE GAINED REVENUE OVER ¥1 MILLION

After Guangxin signed a cooperation agreement with Ganso, Guo led the company's employees to immediately begin intense work. He took the lead and did everything by himself, from designing the questionnaire to sending the copies out, conducting onsite interviews and collecting the questionnaires. He performed his duty in every detail. In the process of designing the questionnaire, Guo and Liang worked out the survey questions in person, and other relevant personnel were responsible for classifying and analyzing Ganso's previous operation mode and sales performance. In Guo's view, the questions in the questionnaire should be limited in number;

otherwise, the respondents would not have the patience to answer them all. The purpose of this market research for Ganso was to gain as comprehensive an understanding of Shanghai's food and beverage market as possible. How to understand the market as a whole without making respondents impatient was a real problem to Guo.

Winning the bid to conduct a market survey for Ganso made Guo understand what it meant to flexibly use what he had learned. The excellent learning and comprehension ability he acquired during his education, especially in his university years, enabled him to quickly understand and master knowledge in a new domain and combine it closely with his own work. This kind of ability, possessed by Guo, should be one of the major characteristics of emerging talents. In his view, without a strong learning ability, one could never keep up with the fast changing pace of the times.

At the end of the sixth working day after signing the contract, the questionnaire was completed ahead of schedule. The questionnaire as a whole and each question it contained were skilfully related to the key points that people paid attention to when purchasing food. The demand ratio (which Ganso cared about) and salient factors for respondents were all combined perfectly into it. Although the content was comprehensive and rich, only ten questions were included. In this way, when the questionnaire was distributed, people could fill it out on the spot. As such, Guangxin could quickly master the first-hand investigation data and ensure comprehensive and accurate analysis of the results.

At 7 am on the first day when the questionnaire was handed out, when people were just getting up to eat breakfast, Guo was already standing at the gate of Lu Xun Park in Shanghai to conduct written and oral surveys of passers-by. He patiently and politely asked everyone who passed by on his side of the road to do the survey and gave them relevant explanations. The smile on Guo's face made everyone who was surveyed feel very relaxed. Some people even asked Guo questions. It was in these conversations that Guo obtained a lot of inspiration and new ideas.

Guo was busy from 7 am until dark. At noon he only ate a piece of bread and drank a bottle of water. His selfless working spirit also deeply affected other employees of the company. According to the statistics collected in the evening, Guo alone issued 10,000 copies of the questionnaire on that day, which meant he handed out 700 to 800 copies per hour.

After the work was over, Guo forgot to eat and began to excitedly read the returned questionnaires. He could not hide his joy and his heart was filled with gratitude. Looking through the neatly filled questionnaires one after another, Guo had a new idea.

The next day, he went into the street early according to his plan. He bought a lot of small gifts in advance and placed a prepared table at a street junction instead of the gate of Lu Xun Park. There was a small sign on the table reading: "Fill in the questionnaire and get a gift." This move attracted more curious passers-by to stop and participate in this activity, and their enthusiasm was immediately aroused. In just half a day, all the gifts Guo had prepared were handed out, and almost 10,000 questionnaires were completed.

Just as Guo was immersed in the joy of victory, three security patrol officers came over to him. Without much ado, they loaded everything that belonged to him into their patrol car. Guo was worried, because the table did not matter, but the questionnaires that had already been filled out were priceless. He immediately went forward to communicate with the security patrol officers. They saw him wearing glasses and looking like an intellectual, so they asked him to go with them to be interrogated. They said that then they would return the questionnaires.

After arriving at the street security management office, they told Guo that the market economy system was established and various economic models were on the rise. As long as people did not violate the laws and regulations, they were all encouraged to go about their business according to the principles of China's reform. However, such activities as issuing questionnaires should be approved by the street management office. Otherwise, if a large number of people crowded in downtown areas, it would be neither easy to manage nor safe.

Guo repeatedly apologized to them and promised to go through the application and approval procedures before conducting such an investigation again. His attitude won the sympathy and understanding of the patrol officers and the two bags of questionnaires were soon returned to him.

When Guo left, a security patrol officer said to him with great concern, "I think you are a scholar. Why don't you stay in the office rather than do such work on the street?" In the view of the security patrol officer, intellectuals should stay in their offices and live a safe life, and should not go outside to suffer. This was a question that Guo has remembered vividly ever since.

In the evening, Guo threw himself into the intensive reading of the questionnaires. The returned questionnaires and the information obtained through interviews fully reflected a trend of market development in China at that time. Specifically, products with local characteristics would be greatly welcomed once they had been properly processed. Moreover, if foods from all over the country were refined in plants, they would also be more welcome.

A month later, Guo and his team drew up a detailed and comprehensive investigation report for Ganso. The report drew inferences and put forward three suggestions. First, the traditional moon cakes were too big for people to eat, so they should be smaller. Second, Ganso should develop new tastes in addition to traditional ones such as "bean paste" and "five kernels." Third, moon cakes were gradually being bought more as gifts than as groceries. The packaging of moon cakes should be designed more luxuriously to make them more attractive. In short, with the improvement of people's living standards in the new era, moon cakes should be both delicious and elegant.

Surprisingly, Ganso greatly appreciated the investigation methods and professional terminology adopted in this report. When the detailed and logical report was sent to Ganso's leadership, the boss spoke highly of it and immediately decided to add an investigation fee of ¥20,000 to the original contract amount. This could be regarded as a kind of recognition for Guangxin.

In Guo's mind, the ¥20,000 voluntarily added by the boss was worth more than the ¥280,000 agreed in the contract. In his view, the ¥20,000 was a recognition of Guangxin that showed trust.

It was because of the honesty and high-quality services provided by Guo and his colleagues that Guangxin began to flourish. Many famous domestic brands, including Helios, Le Kai Film and Angel Ice King, came to them and asked to cooperate. By the end of 1993, the business income of Guangxin exceeded ¥1 million. There were many stories behind that ¥1 million.

FOR REAL ESTATE SALES, HE EARNED ¥10 MILLION

At the end of 1993, when Guangxin's annual business income exceeded ¥1 million for the first time, both Guo and Guangxin were making a real impression on people. At that time, ¥1 million was a lot of money—incomparable to the current ¥1 million.

However, just when Guangxin was doing well, Guo suddenly announced that it was quitting the market research and consulting industry. He said: "When there is a large crowd, it is almost time for the crowd to disperse."

This was indeed the case. After more than two years of boom in this industry, more and more peer companies had joined in, and there were less and less profits. Later, professionals spoke highly of how far-sighted Guo was when he chose to quit the consulting industry.

In the beginning, when he chose to start a business, he made a pledge: "Only cowards retreat. I will never do that." Since then, Guo, a man who did not look very strong, had always played a pioneering role in the business world. From the birth of the market research and consulting industry, Guo undoubtedly took roads that no one else had ever taken.

As Guangxin grew bigger and bigger, the three other people mentioned in the previous chapter—Wang Qunbin, Fan Wei and Tan Jian—joined Guo and Liang Xinjun to form the group later called the "Fosun Five." Wang, Fan and Liang had been classmates, graduating from the Department of Genetic Engineering at Fudan University. Tan was the only woman among the Fosun Five and had graduated from the Department of Computer Science at Fudan University in 1993. Since all five of them had been graduates of Fudan University, Guangxin was officially renamed as "Fosun," which means "Fudan's Stars" in Chinese.

After more people joined the company and the name was changed, its overall strength was improved, and it began to focus on medicine and set foot in real estate. Before long, Guo became one of the first real estate developers in Shanghai.

At first, Fosun's main focus was the real estate industry. At that time, China's real estate industry was not yet market oriented, and it could not be compared with the booming real estate market that came later. The housing systems in the country could be roughly divided into three types. The first was welfare housing distribution. Houses built by institutions would be allocated to their employees for free or in the form of welfare. The second was commercial housing for domestic sale, which was built by the municipal construction companies affiliated with the government. The land was free of charge and the housing was available to local enterprises and residents. Its selling price was relatively low. The third was commercial housing developed and built by real estate companies at home and abroad. The land was obtained by lease. It was available to overseas Chinese, foreigners, and Chinese from Hong Kong, Macao and Taiwan. The price was relatively high, but it was of a good quality.

The first building Fosun took over was one that previously could not be sold at all. At that time, people's average salary was relatively low, and everyone expected to buy a house from the welfare housing distribution or to purchase low-priced domestic houses. Therefore, there was a long-term shortage in the welfare housing distribution and domestic housing supply system. However, the commercial houses were not only expensive but also only available to limited buyers, and in some cases they were unsellable. The first project that Guo took over was the exportation of commercial buildings. Since the sale of real estate did not require capital in advance and the commission was relatively high, it would be a typical case of gaining profit for very little risk. Guo was able to sell the property.

After this project, Guo formulated an advertising plan aimed at highlighting the advantages of the buildings, reformulating the sales methods and then developing the market. This advertising effort had remarkable results and the unsellable buildings were soon sold out. The sale of unsellable buildings had given Guo a new understanding of policies and markets.

The key link in real estate sales was to find customers. Guo believed that customers who could buy apartments should fit two criteria: first, a high income; second, a strong demand for housing. But where could they find such customers? An advertisement in a newspaper led to higher advertising costs and it was not effective enough to attract the target customers.

Liang Xinjun gave Guo a suggestion. He said: "Let's track these people down by following clues. Everyone who studied abroad is on file and we should be able to find out who they are." Only Guo understood the meaning of this suggestion. Previously, when he'd had the idea of studying abroad, he'd had to wait in line for a visa, and no one could skip this step. What Liang meant was that all the immigration records were held in a central office. If they could go there to check, they could easily find their customers.

The next day, Guo and Liang ran to the immigration department together. After they stated their purpose, the man in charge told them that personal information about overseas students couldn't be obtained without a referral. However, they didn't have one with them. But, as the saying goes, some people are naturally auspicious. Guo was embarrassed, but suddenly one of his former college classmates came out of an inner room and Guo recognized him at a glance. When they had been at Fudan University, they had attended a poetry recital together.

Guo immediately stepped forward and tapped his old classmate on the shoulder. But this man was surprised and didn't initially recognize Guo. After thinking for a while, he finally recognized Guo and the two talked enthusiastically. It turned out that this classmate had been assigned to the immigration control center after graduation, and there had been no contact between the two men since then. After listening to Guo's story, the classmate immediately spoke to the staff responsible for managing the files, and Guo obtained the corresponding information successfully.

After returning to the office, Guo summarized the information about the buildings that were for sale, their sup-porting facilities and the aftersales services, and wrote it all up into a concise brochure. Then he put his employees into five groups to distribute the brochures to the regis-tered addresses he had obtained of families with overseas students. Each group was responsible for one district.

This method received immediate results. The buildings that had been unsellable began to be sold. Because of the sale of these buildings, Fosun's operating income exceeded ¥10 million for the first time at the end of 1994, marking a new start for the development of the company. Guo and his colleagues had almost started from scratch, but they had grown the company's annual income from ¥1 million to ¥10 million in less than three years. In this way, Guo quickly emerged into the business circle despite people's doubts.

FROM BIOPHARMACY, HIS DREAM OF ¥100 MILLION CAME TRUE

It should be said that from the moment Guo decided to start a business, he never doubted his ability to gain wealth. His diligent pursuit of anything he tried would always make his income exceed what might be expected.

Guo had an extraordinary ability to predict the market and had always adhered to the principle of "walking into the market and learning about what it demands." People who were familiar with him all knew that his method for operating in a market, when summed up, was to make full use of ready-made resources. For example, he would choose to rent instead of purchasing and building. Following this rule, Guo led his colleagues in Fosun to achieve exponential growth of the company's income over the next ten years.

In 1993, Guo seized the opportunity to earn his first "bucket of gold" from Ganso through market research and consultation, and accumulated ¥10 million in the real estate agency business. However, Guo was not satisfied with this. He invested almost all of the company's assets in the research and development of genetic engineering testing products. At that time, the national economy was in a period of recovery, and all walks of life were booming. However, everyone knew that everything was difficult before it was done, and no one was sure which project to choose or which one had a bright prospect.

But in Guo's mind, the type of project that would be beneficial was already clear. He believed that modern medicine must be a competitive sector in the market, and one of the main directions of modern high technology was bioengineering. After the company earned ¥10 million, Guo resolutely decided to take genetic engineering as the main focus of the company's future. He finally determined upon modern biological medicine, a high-tech and risky industry, as its main business segment.

As mentioned, Liang Xinjun, Fan Wei and Wang Qunbin had all graduated from the Department of Genetic Engineering at Fudan University. After joining Fosun, Fan and Wang provided technical support for Guo's strategic transformation. Fan was a typical scholar who focused on the research of biological products. When he was studying at Fudan University, he had often immersed himself in the laboratory.

At the warm invitation of Guo, Fan brought his latest research and development technology on biomedicine to Fosun. He brought Fosun not only technology but also a large number of corresponding resources. If technical difficulties were encountered in an experiment, they could be solved through the academic network established by Fan, thus creating intangible value for Fosun.

Guo attached great importance to the help brought to the company by Fan. In the process of marketing, he always modestly said that he was "useless and engaged in the exploitation of others," to express his sincere respect for Fan and other experts. In fact, marketing was no easier than the research and development of products. To some extent, the grasp of the market really determined the direction of the research.

Industry insiders knew that Guo's accurate grasp of the market came from his hands-on, pragmatic spirit. To "walk into the market and learn about its demands" is the cornerstone of Guo's unique vision. Lu

Xun, one of the greatest writers of modern China, said: "Even a genius's first cry, when he is born, will still be an ordinary cry and never a good poem." However, in Guo's mind, no matter how superb the vision was, it could not be developed in a single day. What it needed was a long-term process of understanding the market.

Guo's mastery of market research came from his practice and grew from his experience. He pursued the development of new genetically engineered medicine for complicated diseases related to Chinese people. With high entry points and a need for significant investment, he regarded this industry as the new prospect for his company.

In addition to Fan Wei and Wang Qunbin's excellent research and development capabilities in biopharmaceuticals, Liang Xinjun was also a genuine expert. As cofounders of Fosun, Liang and Guo knew well that market development was an important foundation of the company's future. Therefore, Liang had been assisting Guo in understanding the market and his own professional knowledge had not been put to good use.

When Guo decided to pivot Fosun into bioengineering, he and Liang had been contesting with the market for many years. Obviously, it would never be wise to abandon the market and simply conduct experiments. What's more, Guo's grasp of the market at this time was inseparable from that of Liang, his right-hand man.

In 1995, under the leadership of Fan and Wang, Fosun developed a key product after six months of day-and-night effort. This product was a polymerase chain reaction (PCR) hepatitis B diagnostic reagent, which is well known in Fosun's history.

People in the industry knew that hepatitis B was highly infectious and difficult to cure. The traditional detection method was not only complicated in its procedure but also not effective enough in leading to a cure. The lack of effective treatment left patients in misery and presented doctors with a great challenge. If there was a convenient medical kit that could quickly and accurately detect hepatitis B, it would certainly represent great progress in applied medicine.

The research topic of Fan and Wang was this hepatitis B test kit. When they had been studying at Fudan University, they had studied hard and repeatedly conducted experiments on this topic. They had already obtained a degree of experimental success. However, due to the shortage of funds at that time, there was no further financial support for them. It was because of the invitation to join Fosun which was given at a party held by Liang Xinjun that they regained the chance to do the necessary research, leading to this achievement. Following that gathering, Guo decided to make biopharmaceuticals Fosun's main focus after careful consideration.

Subsequently, Guo and Fan held a deep talk and eventually reached a consensus on cooperation. Fan and Wang invested with their technology, while Guo invested all the funds accumulated previously by Guangxin into the research and development of the hepatitis B reagent.

This was undoubtedly an enormous gamble. If the experiment was successful, the return would be huge. If it failed, all the investment would be wasted and the consequences would be ruinous. However, Guo was very calm. In his view, young people could afford to lose anything, and it was no big deal if he became poor again.

Guo had paid close attention to the development of PCR reagents and the construction of the sales network. He promoted both aspects at the same time. Without any hesitation, Fosun invested heavily in setting up a sales company, thus ensuring that the PCR hepatitis B diagnostic reagent developed by Fosun soon had a nationwide sales network with overwhelming advantages. By the end of 1995, Fosun had achieved the goal of ¥100 million in the sale of PCR reagents, thus becoming the leader in the biomedical industry in China and constructing a valuable national sales network.

Later, there was a lot of speculation about Fosun's "myth of wealth accumulation," to which Guo responded:

"Fosun's first ¥1 million was brought about by consultation. The first ¥10 million was made through real estate marketing. The first ¥100 million was earned through biopharmaceuticals, and the first ¥1 billion was achieved through the combination of capital and industry. Fosun's development trajectory is actually very clear. How can it be a myth? Opportunity means making a decision with determination at the right time and in the right situation."

CHAPTER

4

LAYING THE FOUNDATION, HE SEIZED THE OPPORTUNITY

TAKING THE ADVANTAGE, HE OCCUPIED THE LEADING ROLE WITH HIS SUCCESSFUL BRAND

In 1992, 25-year-old Guo Guangchang not only gave up the opportunity to go abroad but also resigned from Fudan University. With ¥38,000 borrowed from relatives and friends, he started his own business. Of course, his effort paid off. At the end of 1995, Fosun, founded by Guo, had earned more than ¥100 million.

Since then, the development of Guo and Fosun has never stopped. In addition to further progress in the biopharmaceutical industry, his business has gradually expanded further into real estate, steel, insurance and other fields, and these businesses have also made Guo great profit. Thus, he has been called the "Chinese Warren Buffett" by foreign media.

In the eyes of many people in the mid-1990s, Guo had keen eyes like an eagle, the fighting spirit of a tiger and a decisive executing style like a cheetah. As the blockbuster of Guo and Fosun, Fosun Pharma showed the extraordinary entrepreneurial spirit possessed by Guo.

From its establishment in 1994, Fosun Pharma focused on modern biopharmaceutical health products, seizing the chance offered by the rapid growth of the Chinese pharmaceutical market and the huge opportunities for Chinese enterprises to enter the world's mainstream pharmaceutical market. It strategically covered many important links in the pharmaceutical health industry chain, such as research and development, manufacturing and distribution, with medicine research and development as the core. At the same time, it held a leading market position in the fields of medical services, medical diagnosis and medical devices, and formed a large-scale professional medical industry group with competitive advantages in research and development innovation, marketing, mergers and acquisitions, integration, and talent recruiting.

In August 1998, Fosun Pharma made its first leap: it was listed on the Shanghai Stock Exchange. Since then, it has become a leading pharmaceutical company and a star in the Ashare market with its rapid development and excellent financial performance. It was also one of the first companies to be listed in the CSI 300 Index. In 2017, Fosun Pharma's total market value soared from ¥55.1 billion at the beginning of the year to ¥106.6 billion on 20 December, and it joined the ¥100 billion club in the pharmaceutical industry. In 2018, its revenue was ¥24.9 billion, up by 34.45% year on year. One of its sources of income, the business of drug manufacturing and research, made ¥18.7 billion, up by 41.57%. Medical services earned ¥2.6 billion, up by 22.72%, and medical devices and medical diagnosis reached ¥3.6 billion, up by 13.22% year on year.

Fosun Pharma followed the strategic deployment of "innovation, internationalization, integration and intelligence" and adhered to the development model of "endogenous growth, expansion and integrated development." Focusing on unmet medical needs, it continuously improved the quality of its products and the popularity of its brand. It was committed to the improvement of its capabilities in terms of innovation, service, integration and internationalization in order to achieve long-term, fast and effective development.

Fosun Pharma took innovation, research and development as the core factor driving its development. It focused on investing in the research of superior products with specific curative effects in line with the development direction of modern medicine, and insisted on improving its full-chain research and industrial development capabilities. In 2018, it invested ¥2.5 billion in research (up by 63.92% year on year), formed an internationalized research and development structure, and built strong research and development capabilities. It had established interactive and integrated research systems in China, the United States, India, and other countries and regions, and it also introduced innovative technologies from around the world into its company through diversified cooperation methods to promote the global development and transformation of cutting-edge products. The company continued to increase research investment, including in monoclonal antibody bio-innovative drugs, biosimilar drugs and small molecule innovative drugs, and actively promoted the consistency of evaluation standards for generic drugs. In 2018, Fosun Pharma's research and development investment in the pharmaceutical business reached ¥2.3 billion, up by 76.49%. The company was working on 215 projects, including new drugs, generic drugs, biosimilar drugs and generic drugs consistent evaluation. The company had also introduced many cutting-edge products and technologies at home and abroad through product cooperation and permissions relating to market rights and interests. Together with Kite Pharma, the world's leading research and manufacturing enterprise for T-cell immunotherapy products, it jointly built the first product, FKC876, of Fosun Kite, an immunotherapy platform. This product had obtained the approval of the National Medical Products Administration for clinical research and trials. At the same time, Fosun Pharma, as the company's incubation platform for scientific and technological innovation, had taken the lead strategically in a number of promising areas, including research and development of innovative drugs, mobile portable medical imaging devices and gene therapy.

In 2018, Fosun Pharma earned ¥19.0 billion in China, up 25.22% year on year. Its operating income overseas reached ¥5.9 billion, up by 76.26%, with this accounting for 23.70% of its total income, up by 5.62%. Gland Pharma, which was acquired by Fosun Pharma in 2017, performed well, benefiting from the growth of its core products, such as vancomycin, enoxaparin injections and caspofungin. Its operating income increased by 26.62% and its net profit increased by 39.92% compared with the previous year.

As Fosun Pharma had established an efficient international research and development team, it ensured that the company's main products occupied a leading position in their respective market segments. In the domestic market, it gained competitive advantages in products relating to liver diseases, diabetes, tuberculosis and clinical diagnosis in various segments of the market. Fosun Pharma also became a leader in antimalarial drugs in the global market.

PARTICIPATING IN THE MIXING SYSTEM REFORM, HE VITALIZED A STATE-OWNED ENTERPRISE

On 1 December 2017, when attending the Yabuli China Entrepreneurs Forum, Tianjin Summit, Guo said that Fosun had participated in 35 mixing system reform projects of stateowned enterprises in the past 20 years and was very optimistic about the importance of such projects in economic development. He also hoped to seize the opportunity of the era and actively participate in the reforms. He said: "We feel confident that through this flexible mechanism, we can deeply empower and create value for enterprises."

Guo believed that the reform and opening-up of the joint-stock system had allowed private enterprises like Fosun to spring up at a fascinating pace. Similarly, he believed that the subsequent rise of China's capital market and mixed ownership had given Fosun the opportunity to participate fully in the reform process and become part of China's rapid growth.

Guo said: "In 1986, Deng Xiaoping, chief designer of the reform and opening-up, gave a stock certificate to John Van Erlin, Chairman of New York Stock Exchange in the United States, who was visiting China, to express his determination to build Shanghai into an international financial center. At that time, I never expected that in 12 years, Fosun would become the first private enterprise listed in Shanghai. At that time, IPOs were subject to approval. After hearing Fosun's report, the leaders of the Shanghai municipal government and the planning committee spoke highly of our company, which was founded by college graduates and was designed to develop medicine independently. In order to support the development of local science and technology of private enterprises in Shanghai and also to support college graduates to start their own businesses, the Shanghai municipal government gave Fosun the right to launch an IPO. In this way, Fosun was officially listed on the Shanghai Stock Exchange in August 1998. Here, I would like to thank the municipal government once again for offering such a good opportunity of development to young college graduates who had run their business for only a few years. We also want to thank the city of Shanghai for its tolerance, with which we built our career here."

Fosun's successful listing had provided the company with capital with which it could promote the rapid development of the industry. At that time, against a background of large-scale losses, debt restructuring and overcapacity removal of state-owned enterprises, Fosun's listed capital enabled the company to participate in the historic process of state-owned enterprise restructuring, thus rejuvenating those companies. In 2003, Fosun and China National Pharmaceutical Group Corporation (CNPGC) jointly funded the Sinopharm Group Co.,Ltd., to which Fosun contributed ¥500 million, accounting for 49%, while CNPGC contributed 51% with the stock assets of its pharmaceutical circulation business. This was the first mixed ownership enterprise jointly established by a state company and a private enterprise in the Chinese pharmaceutical industry.

At that time, the pharmaceutical circulation business of CNPGC was facing operational difficulties. Fosun expected that CNPGC's nationwide interprovincial sales network could work well with the pharmaceutical business of Fosun.

Together with the investment, Fosun's market-oriented management concepts were introduced into Sinopharm with remarkable results. These concepts included decision making mechanisms, market awareness, management methods and incentive mechanisms. Over the following years, Sinopharm's sales surged almost every year. As a non-controlling shareholder, Fosun defined itself as a responsible long-term strategic shareholder, which, in Guo's words, should neither exceed its duties nor engage in negative actions.

In 2009, Fosun helped Sinopharm to be successfully listed in Hong Kong, in the largest IPO in the global pharmaceutical industry since 2000. In 2018, Sinopharm's sales revenue reached ¥344.5 billion, up by 11.73% year on year. This figure represented a 43-fold increase over the sales revenue of only ¥8 billion in the first year of Sinopharm. Sinopharm had thus become the largest pharmaceutical distribution and supply chain service provider in China and it was also among the world's top three such companies.

Fosun's participation in the mixing system reform of state-owned enterprises established many successful companies in the pharmaceutical industry, including medical companies such as Yao Pharma (in Chongqing), Wanbang Pharma (in Jiangsu) and Guilin Pharma. These all became important, innovative, leading enterprises in the pharmaceutical industry. Artesunate injections, developed and produced by Guilin Pharma were, at the time, the only drug for severe malaria certified by the World Health Organization. Over the ten years from 2007, artesunate injections saved more than 20 million lives in Africa.

In addition to medicine, Fosun has gradually entered other industries through similar means, such as Nanjing Iron & Steel Co.,Ltd. and Shanghai Yuyuan Tourist Mart. In 2016, a private consortium led by Fosun Group signed an agreement with the Zhejiang Provincial People's Government to jointly build the Hangzhou–Shaoxing–Taizhou Intercity Railway with a total investment of ¥46.2 billion through purchasing power parity. This was China's first intercity railway controlled by private capital, allowing the resources and advantages of the government, state-owned enterprises and private enterprises to complement each other. This project started at the end of 2017, and its total construction period was forecast to last for four years. This transportation infrastructure project was intended to greatly improve the urban function and transportation efficiency of the covered areas.

Guo said that by keeping a finger on the pulse of the country's industrial development and understanding how people's demands were increasing, Fosun had participated in more than 30 mixing system reform projects of state-owned enterprises since it was listed. Fosun had injected vitality into state-owned enterprises and central enterprises in various ways, such as corporate governance, strategic management, connecting sources of capital and operations management to achieve win-win results. Through the system of mixed ownership, Fosun had also benefited from China's growth momentum and achieved rapid expansion of its own industry. From medicine and real estate to steel, retail, insurance and many other industries, it had become a group with diversified industries. Through improving the operation of mixed ownership enterprises, Fosun's industrial foundation had been gradually consolidated and its strategic vision had been incrementally upgraded, laying the foundation for Fosun's globalization strategy.

By the beginning of 2019, Shanghai Fosun High Technology (Group) Co.,Ltd., led by Guo, controlled more than 100 companies directly and indirectly. Its investment scope covered industries relating to information, real estate, biopharmaceuticals, commercial and trade circulation, finance, steel, securities, banking, automobiles and other fields. Most of Fosun's rapidly expanding wealth came from the enterprises it had acquired. Guo defined Fosun as the integrator of resources in different industries. He said: "First, China's current economic development has made integration a necessity. Second, competition barriers are decreasing and Chinese society is moving toward industrialization, urbanization and privatization. This process makes integration possible."

AFTER D'LONG'S CRASH, HE WAS WARNED TO AVOID THE SAME FATE

In 2004, the collapse of Xinjiang's D'Long Industrial Company taught Fosun an extremely profound lesson in investment and management. Fosun was warned, and it also learned from the tragedy. Guo conducted a comprehensive examination of the enterprise in a timely manner, thus ensuring the healthy development of Fosun.

In 1992, Tang Wanxin registered and established Xinjiang D'Long Industrial Company in Xinjiang. Later, he issued ¥500 million of new shares on the Shenzhen Stock Exchange through subscription lottery forms. However, he hired thousands of people to queue up in Shenzhen to get the forms. Three days later, the forms became cash in Tang's pocket.

In 1994, D'Long developed agriculture and animal husbandry in Xinjiang. Since then, investment in agriculture had become a long-term and stable source of funds for D'Long.

A year later, Tang controlled the listed companies by buying corporate shares. He made profits by investing in his own stocks in the secondary market. At the same time, he tried to achieve a transition in industrial devel-opment. In October 1996, D'Long made its debut in the capital market and accepted parts of the corporate shares of Xinjiang Tunhe. In 1997, it became the largest share-holder of Tunhe Group.

Suddenly, D'Long was the most powerful player in the stock market, which was experiencing a peak. Tang had been seeking industrial integration with ketchup processing as its core, and had achieved significant results in fields such as cement, auto parts and electronic tools.

However, the ketchup industry had not become D'Long's main business.

As a result, the folk rumor that D'Long was a "banker" had become increasingly influential. Among both ordinary investors and the media, D'Long was regarded as a scourge, and people were angry with the company. However, during this period, Tang chose to remain silent. The mystery this generated had a further negative impact on the situation, and it eventually became the trigger of the D'Long crisis.

Since July 2003, China's securities market had frequent-ly seen big news: "Hops," "Southern Securities," "Qinghai Trust" and a series of other crisis events had erupted one after another. D'Long's financial enterprises had almost no income, and the company faced a perfect storm of prob-lems. In August 2003, more than a dozen banks across the country suddenly announced that they would not give D'Long any loans.

At the beginning of 2004, D'Long's executives made the decision to sell the outstanding shares held by the enterprise in order to ease the current cash flow shortage. Since D'Long had the majority of the shares, the selling behav-iour immediately led to a continuous fall in the stock price in the secondary market, thus causing greater doubts and more denunciations from investors and the media.

In mid-April 2004, D'Long's stock fell into a decline, and adverse conditions (such as illegal guarantees of listed companies) were exposed. A great problem was also fully revealed in how D'Long had been entrusted with the financial management of financial institutions. As a result, the crash crisis quickly destroyed D'Long.

Four months later, the State Council of China issued relevant documents to the central bank, formally approving an overall market-oriented solution to the D'Long crisis: D'Long would be entrusted to

Huarong Asset Management for overall custody. Immediately, D'Long International, Xinjiang Tunhe Group and Huarong signed the asset custody agreement, by which D'Long and Xinjiang Tunhe Group irrevocably and fully entrusted all their assets to Huarong. Huarong could fully exercise management and disposal rights over all their assets. As a result, Tang Wanxin completely lost control of D'Long.

Tang regarded finance as a platform on which to play the game. With his extraordinary courage and boldness, he had quickly accumulated a lot of wealth. However, in terms of practical operation, he was often obsessed with means and forgot the purpose to be achieved, which frequently caused him financial dilemmas, meaning that he had to obtain the financial resources he needed indirectly.

Industry analysts pointed out that D'Long was a "real" family business. Everything in the company relied on Tang Wanxin's decisions, so D'Long's decision-making was obviously fairly personal. However, the shortage of profes-sional talent required to enter the industry ultimately led to a lack of control over the acquired enterprises and the inability to carry out operations management within the target enterprises. D'Long originally relied on the stock market to accumulate capital, but this method later became impossible due to a broken capital chain. This was a tragedy with a strong color of fatalism.

The collapse of D'Long was greatly intensified by the media's wanton spread of the reputation of D'Long as a "banker." Like D'Long, Fosun had a diversified industrial structure, and it also carried out mergers aggressively. For these reasons, Fosun was drawn into this crisis. What's more, Fosun was regarded as "the second D'Long" by some people. Rumours about tensions in Fosun's capital chain began to spread across society.

At the critical moment, Guo made a decision: he asked Ernst & Young Global to carry out a financial analysis report of the company and make the report public. This decision was undoubtedly wise. At that time, explanations without evidence would have been considered camouflage by the outside world, which would only have aggravated the suspicion and made the situation worse.

This active examination let Fosun out of the crisis. Since then, Fosun has paid more attention to its debt ratio and stable operation. Compliance thresholds and strict discipline became the most important aspects of Fosun's corporate culture.

Due to Fosun's timely transformation, Guo gained a chance to be famous nationwide: he was elected CCTV China Central Television (CCTV) China Economic Person of the Year in 2004. At the award speech, CCTV described him as follows: "He is rational and innovative with the spirit of seeking the truth. He leads the enterprise to operate in the sunshine. He seeks gold in the era of the knowledge-driven economy, and is a creator of capital investment. His story tells us that wealth gained in the sunshine is healthier."

At the award ceremony, Guo had humorous and far-reaching conversations with a number of experts. Cao Yuanzheng, chief economist of Bank of China International, asked: "It is said that you hired auditors to do audits for the non-listed parts of Fosun. And you even submitted the audit results to the banks. Ordinary enterprises are afraid of auditing, and even more afraid of handing the audit results to banks, their rivals. Why did you do that?" Guo said: "After a person catches a cold, the last thing he wants is to be suspected of SARS [severe acute respiratory syndrome]. If he is sure that it is just a cold, a physical examination is the best proof. Similarly, if the small problems encountered by enterprises cause certain illusions to the public, the best solution is to make an audit report. It is impossible for a person to have no shortcomings. We can better find out where our shortcomings are and then make up for them. In addition, this approach can gain the trust of others, which is very valuable."

An economist asked: "As a successful person, you have done a lot of public welfare undertakings. Why have you done so?" Guo replied: "I think it is related to the plan of my life. Before I was 20, I mainly devoted myself to studying. After I turned 25, I concentrated on creating wealth. After the age of 50, I'm going to return most of my wealth to society, so I set up various funds, and do all kinds of valuable things. Now I only pay some of my attention to charity, because I am still creating wealth. You can see that after I am 50 years old, I will definitely fulfil my promise and return my wealth to society. I hope to contribute to society until I am 70 years old."

An expert asked: "What are the vital factors in the development of enterprises?" Guo said: "The market. I think if the market is right, it doesn't matter if there is a little mistake in any other aspect. But if the market is not suitable for the products and the whole direction is wrong, you will be abandoned by others, so I will always pay attention to the market."

The host asked: "Today we should not only focus on the market but also on wealth. You mentioned wealth many times today. I know (your) father is a stonemason, and your family was not very rich. Can you tell us what is the greatest wealth your father left you today?" Guo said: "Characteristics of being hard-working and kind-hearted. Apart from my father, I want to talk about my mother. She is very kind-hearted. She sold vegetables to support me in finishing my college education, but she never used toxic pesticides. She was very opposed to farmers using pesticides that should not be used when planting vegetables. My gratitude (goes out) to her, and the kindness I inherited from my mother became the unique feature of Fosun, and she is also the most important motivation for me to achieve what I have today. So, I should say thank you to her."

Guo's answer aroused a burst of warm applause.

BOLD AND RESOLUTE, HE EXCELLED IN THE STEEL INDUSTRY

Fosun set foot in the steel industry at the end of its process of industrial integration, but Guo obtained the relevant knowledge at an early age. When he was a junior in the Department of Philosophy at Fudan University, he began to dabble in knowledge around iron and steel metallurgy, and he read some professional works. But at that time, he never expected that he would invest in the steel industry a few years later.

In 2003, Fosun bought and reorganized Nanjing Iron & Steel Group at a price of ¥1.7 billion. This acquisition was the first stock market tender offer in Chinese history. Before that, there was no private enterprise in charge of the transformation of a giant state-owned iron and steel enterprise.

It was 9 April 2003 when the first tender offer was announced in the Shanghai and Shenzhen stock markets. Nanjing Iron & Steel Group, Fosun, Fosun Industrial Investment and Shanghai Guangxi Fechaology announced the joint establishment of United Nanjing Iron & Steel Co.,Ltd.. Fosun invested ¥300 million in the company as the initial capital injection, accounting for 30% of the entity's equity, while the state-owned enterprise Nanjing Iron & Steel Group held 40% of the equity. After the news spread, the stock market almost exploded and the "tender offer" was widely discussed.

Guo's investment philosophy is that if there is an industry that Fosun needs to set foot in, there are two ways to achieve this goal. First, it is to train its own management team, which integrates the resources in the industry. Second, it is to invest the industry with the best performers and then use Fosun's industrial resources to help it strive for a bright future.

For the investment in the steel industry, Guo chose the second option. He invested in the steel industry because he met a group of top talents in this industry, and he had always been optimistic about it.

In March 2004, Jianlong Steel Group, Fosun Industrial Investment and Jilin Jianlong Steel respectively transferred 5%, 20% and 10% of the shares of Ningbo Jianlong Steel to United Nanjing Iron & Steel Group at a total price of ¥463 million. As a result, the shares held by Jianlong Steel Group and United Nanjing Iron & Steel Group each amounted to 35% and they became the major shareholders, while Fosun Industrial Investment and Jilin Jianlong Steel were no longer shareholders of Ningbo Jianlong Steel.

In January 2005, Nanjing Iron & Steel Group raised ¥786 million through the issuance of 120 million A-shares.

The sale resulted in the reduction of the united company's shareholding from 71% to 60.6%. From May to July 2006, the united company purchased 40.64 million Ashares at a total cost of ¥153 million, increasing its stake to 64.9%. In October 2006, Nanjing Iron & Steel Group completed its sharetrading reform plan, and all non-tradable shares held by the united company were converted into tradable shares. From October to December 2006, the united company purchased 64.03 million of it's A-shares at a total cost of ¥1.3 billion, increasing its stake to 71.8%.

In the summer of 2007, Fosun International (a subsidiary of Fosun) and Hainan Steel Group decided to establish a joint venture company called United Hainan Steel Co.,Ltd. to engage in the mining and processing of iron ore, including ferrous metals, nonferrous metals and non-metals. The total investment of the joint venture company was ¥1.6 billion. Of this figure, two subsidiaries of Fosun International [Shanghai Fosun High Technology (Group) Co.,Ltd. and Shanghai Fosun Industrial Investment Co.,Ltd.] jointly invested ¥900 million, holding 20% and 40% respectively, while Hainan Steel Group held 40% of the equity with ¥600 million.

On the next day, when Fosun took over Hainan Steel Group and

Jiangsu Steel Group, which was run by Shen Wenrong, the "King of Private Steel in China," successfully bought an Australian iron ore company. As the head of China's largest private steel producer, Shen had long taken notice of Guo. Guo, who was 20 years younger than Shen, took only seven years to reach second place in China's private steel industry. This speed greatly surprised Shen.

For Guo, entering Hainan Steel Group was undoubtedly very cost-effective. Hainan Steel Group hoped to complete its shareholding system reform through this cooperation. At the same time, Guo also hoped to take this opportunity to increase investment in Hainan to expand the development space of Fosun.

At that time, "scarcity" was a key word in the steel industry. In East Asia, Europe and the United States, there had been a simple quantitative change in the steel industry. At the same time, in China, a revolutionary change was quietly taking place.

When the company Baosteel relocated to Zhanjiang, Wuhan Steel moved to Fangcheng Port and Shougang moved to Caofeidian, a number of steel projects with annual outputs of over 10 million tonnes had surfaced. As a result, some people predicted that the shortage of steel in China would turn into a huge surplus in a few years. However, in the short term, such a surplus had not occurred. Under the leadership of industry integrators such as Guo, the Chinese steel industry was moving toward the international market, and this triggered a reshuffle in the global steel industry.

From Guo's point of view, there would always be emerging enterprises as well as outdated ones. No industry could have bright prospects forever. When integration in the steel industry was actively promoted in China, authoritative figures in the world's iron and steel industry predicted that by the end of the first decade of the 21st century, European and American iron and steel enterprises would all withdraw from the historical stage, leaving Japan with little profit.

In China, half of the enterprises would disappear and the rest would become international giants. However, the cost of this was extremely high, and tens of billions of dull assets would be abandoned for a dying sunset industry.

Facing these predictions from world authorities, a group of large iron and steel enterprises, represented by Jiangsu Steel Group, explained (and took practical actions to demonstrate) that as long as there were enough raw materials, China's iron and steel enterprises would not decline. In fact, Chinese steel giants had completed or were completing capital acquisitions of raw material suppliers. Many Chinese steel companies signed huge contracts with BHP Billiton, acquiring nearly half of the shares in an Australian mine subleased by that company. As a result, 12 million tonnes of iron ore could be purchased there every year for the next 20 years. Moreover, Baosteel already owned half of a new mine of Rio Tinto Zinc Corporation Ltd.

As is widely known, Fosun's steel business relied on the speed of it mergers and acquisitions. The company's sweeping mergers and acquisitions accelerated the improvement of the industrial chain. Fosun, while contributing to the main sectors of its businesses, had made the industrial "machines" run more quickly and stably through mergers and acquisitions of the "parts." When many state-owned enterprises were trying to form complementary industries through cooperation, Fosun's steel business had been playing the role of a big buyer in the mergers and acquisitions market.

CHAPTER

5

DEVELOPING MULTIPLE INDUSTRIES, HE ACHIEVED BUSINESS LEGEND THROUGH WISDOM

WITH FORTE GROUP DEVELOPING, HE EXPANDED THE NEW WORLD OF REAL ESTATE BUSINESS

In 1994, when Shanghai's real estate industry was gradually warming up, Guo Guangchang led Fosun to seize the opportunity to enter the real estate industry. Initially engaging in real estate sales, the company soon earned its first ¥10 million. Since then, along the Huangpu River, Guo and his people have created a new world of real estate industry.

As a Chinese real estate dealer who began selling real estate property early in his career, Guo has undoubtedly been a witness to the development of the Chinese real estate industry over the past decades. His company Forte has become a real estate empire based on the famous development called Fosun Garden.

Forte's initial development of Fosun Garden was accidental. At that time, the Shanghai real estate market showed an ascending trend, but it had not yet built any scale, and many real estate companies lacked direction. Guo and his Fosun start-up team had gained insight into the broad prospects of the real estate market while building the pharmaceutical business, but they were not sure how to sell houses to customers. At this time, the emergence of a group known as "Petty" and the rise of the internet gave Guo and his team great inspiration and opportunity.

"Petty" was a popular term in the mainland of China in the 1990s. Its original meaning was a short form of "petty bourgeoisie," referring especially to those young people who yearned for a Western lifestyle and focused on inner experience, materiality and spiritual enjoyment. Members of the Petty group were generally white-collar workers in the city and had a certain status and wealth in society, but there was an economic gap between them and the middle class.

In 1995, China's internet developed rapidly and a large number of internet users emerged, opening a convenient door for luxury consumption. When the internet expanded into mainstream use, the Petty, with their special identity, had more opportunities to obtain access to the internet than others.

The formation and growth of the Petty group reflected the initial maturity of the middle class. The Petty group not only had the ability to purchase but also pursued special tastes. In choosing food, clothing, housing and transportation, especially housing, they had extraordinarily personalized needs.

In order to understand demand in the real estate market, Guo decided to conduct a real estate market survey of the Petty group through the internet. Guo led Forte's people to interview potential customers through the internet using four different methods. After two months of intensive work, the results of the investigation were collected. The survey results showed that the respondents had a strong interest in apartments that reflected their unique tastes, but not in luxury villas.

Obviously, what the Petty valued was personal taste, not high-grade luxury. According to them, as long as a residence (even if it was an apartment rather than a house) was of good quality and the decoration and design of the room highlighted the resident's attitude toward life, they would be greatly satisfied. This result deviated from Guo's original idea of building villas, but it reduced the difficulty as well as the cost of the development. What Forte needed to do was focus on the details of house construction and the Petty group's pursuit of taste.

The result of this survey was that Forte began to develop houses in restored areas. They immediately began to carry out real estate development planning, with the goal that half a year later all necessary real estate would be in place.

Next, to attract customers and expand the popularity of Forte, the most important thing was to give a name to the real estate it was developing that would attract customers and expand the company's popularity. Some people suggested calling the building "White-Collar Apartment," which was concise and straight to the point. Some people suggested that it should be called "Beauty's Home," a warm and profound name. Others suggested that it should simply be called "Fu Yu" (whose pronunciation sounds like "Rich Apartments" in Chinese), a pun that would not only represent the identity of the residents but also reveal the nature of the property.

Guo had his own ideas. He believed that "White-Collar Apartment" was relevant to the theme but not poetic enough. Although "Beauty's Home" was warm, it couldn't reflect the high quality of the building. While "Fu Yu" had deep meaning, it was not straightforward enough. In particular, these names did not contain any mention of the developer. At that time, Forte was just a newly registered company, and its publicity could not be compared with that of Fosun, which was already a celebrity. Guo felt that if the enterprise's characteristics were to be shown, the first half of the new project's name should be the word "Fosun" and the second half should be a word that positioned the quality of the housing.

One day, while walking in a garden, Guo had an idea and the word "garden" immediately appeared in his mind. He made a prompt decision and named the development project "Fosun Garden."

Six months later, the name showed great vitality. It took less than two months for the real estate to be sold out. This development for the Petty group in Shanghai enabled Guo and Forte to rise rapidly in the real estate arena in Shanghai.

Forte was officially launched in August 1998 in the form of Shanghai Forte Real Estate Development Co.,Ltd.. In September 2001, Forte was transformed into a joint-stock limited company and its name was changed from Shanghai Forte to Shanghai Forte Land Co.,Ltd.. Following the development and construction of Fosun Garden, Forte invested in 11 more real estate projects.

On 6 February 2004, Forte was listed on the Hong Kong Stock Exchange's H-share main board, selling a total of 600 million shares, of which 90% were international placements and 10% were public placements. This raised a total of HK$1.7 billion. After ten years of development, Guo had multiplied his wealth. It had increased 10,000-fold and won him the title of "Bill Gates of Shanghai" from the media. After ten years of hard work and accumulation, Forte had gradually formed its unique core source of competitiveness in China's real estate industry with accurate product positioning, mature multi-project management capability, quick turnover of capital operations, and a perfect sales and service system.

As mentioned, in December 2004, Guo was elected CCTV China Economic Person of the Year of the China Central Teleuision. After ten years of hard work in the real estate industry, the formerly scholarly young man had become calm and profound. As Guo appreciated the view of the Huangpu River from the window of his office, Forte was gradually growing into one of the best real estate companies in China.

In 2004, thanks to the joint efforts of Guo and several senior partners, Forte's stocks were all rising. There was no doubt that this year was not only "the year of Forte" but also "the year of Guo." It was this year that Guo and Fosun's co-founders—Liang Xinjun, Wang Qunbin, Tan Jian and Fan Wei—were ranked on *Forbes*" China Rich List. Guo himself won 14th place on the list.

ACQUIRING SYTM, HE MARCHED INTO THE RETAIL SECTOR

In the beginning, Guo established Guangxin Technology Development Co.,Ltd. with registered capital of ¥38,000. Its main business was market research and consultation. Later, the company's strategy became more inclusive, extending to real estate, biopharmaceuticals, steel and other industries, and then entering the retail sector on a large scale.

Fosun's aggressive entry into the retail sector began with the acquisition of Shanghai Yu*yuan* Tourist Mart (SYTM). SYTM was an A-share listed company located in Yu*yuan* Commercial Tourist Zone, a famous tourist area in Shanghai. SYTM's business mainly included the retail of precious jewellery, catering and commercial property rental. SYTM owned time-honored gold jewellery shops such as Liaomiao Gold and First Asia Jewelry, as well as more than 400 shops and over 500 retail outlets.

SYTM was a subsidiary of the State-Owned Assets Supervision and Administration Commission of Shanghai, and it was also a rare listed company with relatively dispersed shares. At that time, the shares held by the largest shareholder accounted for only 13%, and the shares held by the two largest shareholders added up to only 25%. The basic conditions of SYTM, such as stable cash flow, abundant land assets and dispersed shares, made the enterprise a very good choice for acquisition.

SYTM was a large-scale commercial retail enterprise that had obvious location advantages and a brand with 700 years of cultural inheritance. Its daily average customer flow volume was more than 100,000 people and the annual average customer flow volume was more than 45 million. SYTM had a net operating cash flow of several hundred million *yuan* every year, while the cash expenditure invested in its main business was only ¥20–30 million. At the same time, the enterprise also had a large number of undeveloped commercial land rights and interests. These land resources had an unlimited cash flow value.

Realizing the impact of foreign retail enterprises on the domestic retail industry, Guo was anxious. Therefore, he had the idea of becoming a rejuvenator of China's traditional retail industry in the new era. He reasoned that Fosun had started its business in Shanghai, which was one of the most economically developed cities in China. If it could integrate a number of old and famous retail enterprises in Shanghai with modern management, it would surely achieve fruitful results in competing with foreign retail giants.

After several setbacks, Fosun finally bought a 14% stake of Yu*yuan* Tourist Service Company in 2001 and 7% of SYTM in 2002 at the price of ¥4 per share. In this way, Fosun became the largest shareholder of SYTM with a 21% stake, and Guo also joined the board of directors of SYTM.

In 2002, SYTM achieved a net operating income of ¥500 million, while its investment cash expenditure was less than ¥70 million. The huge profit margin and large amount of operating cash laid a very solid foundation for Fosun to make a multi-channel strategic investment in SYTM.

Just as Fosun was preparing to make more aggressive moves in relation to SYTM, an accident quietly occurred.

In 2003, during the SARS outbreak, the operation of SYTM was greatly affected. However, it still saw some achievements under Guo's leadership. SYTM invested ¥300 million in Tebon Securities and acquired 30% of the shares, while Fosun's subsidiary company invested ¥200 million and acquired 20% of the shares. In the same year, SYTM cooperated with Fosun's financial strategy and invested another ¥23 million to buy shares in the Bank of Shanghai.

After SARS, the cash flow of SYTM jumped to ¥200 million. In 2004, SYTM and Fosun jointly took a stake in Zhaojin Mining Industry Co.,Ltd., investing ¥168.7 million and acquiring 21% of the shares. Meanwhile, another investment company owned by Fosun invested ¥160.7 million and acquired 20% of the shares.

SYTM had gradually changed its role while consolidating its position in retail since Fosun became its largest shareholder. Through controlling SYTM, it was also more convenient for Guo to carry out industrial mergers and acquisitions in the retail industry.

In addition to entering the retail industry, SYTM extended its reach to financial investment and the real estate industry (as outlined above). One of the projects was its joint acquisition of Shanghai Old City God Temple Square with Fosun Commercial Company and *Yuyuan* Real Estate Development Company.

Fosun's acquisition of SYTM would not easily stop once it had taken off. In 2005, SYTM's cash flow reached ¥340 million. That year, SYTM invested another ¥30 million to buy shares in Tebon Securities and some land, resulting in a net cash investment of ¥60 million. These investments paid off in 2006, with SYTM's annual net income reaching ¥95 million. It sold the previously acquired Shanghai Old City God Temple Square, obtaining a cash return of ¥600 million at one stroke.

In purchasing SYTM, Guo also made and completed the acquisition of Friendship. First, Guo and Friendship's major shareholder, Friendship Group, jointly invested ¥400 million to form Shanghai Friendship Fosun (Holding) Co.,Ltd., of which Friendship Group accounted for 52% of the shares and Fosun accounted for 48%. Subsequently, Friendship Fosun and Friendship Group jointly signed an equity transfer agreement, transferring some shares of Friendship Group, thus making Friendship Fosun a major shareholder in Friendship.

In Guo's view, sometimes acquisitions are more feasible than defeating rivals. For example, as a time-honored retail enterprise, SYTM still had strong vitality and a huge profit margin, and its relatively dispersed equity made acquisition the easier option. In addition, compared with the world retail giants, China's retail enterprises had not yet gained a large scale. Only through integration could Chinese retailers counter the huge impact of retail giants on the world stage.

Guo believes that with the fierce competition in the retail industry, an enterprise cannot simply rely on opening new stores, as this will make it hard to keep pace with its development. Expanding market share through mergers and acquisitions will be the only way for an enterprise to participate in competition and cooperation in the business world. Guo has said: "The essence of business is economy of scale. Without scale, there would be no competitiveness. Only when there is scale can domestic enterprises establish advantages of goods supply and channels and form strong competitiveness. Compared with the scale of advantages of foreign funded enterprises, the only method for domestic enterprises is to choose the chain operation mode, to expand rapidly and to improve their ability to resist market risks."

OPERATING MULTIPLE BUSINESSES, HE STRENGTHENED HIS COMPREHENSIVE POWER

In 1993, just over a year after Fosun's predecessor, Guangxin, was founded, the company successively entered the real estate industry, the biopharmaceutical industry and the retail industry under the leadership of Guo. In this way, the company vigorously promoted multiple business strategies and continuously strengthened its comprehensiveness.

It has been proved that Fosun's multiple business strategy is successful, and the business indicators for diversified businesses are healthy. Even so, Guo always warns himself that this current success does not mean that diversified operation is the only strategy for an enterprise. As a mature enterprise, Fosun should work hard to develop its core industries to cultivate core competitiveness. Specialized management is a solid strategy, whereas diversified management is more like a sweet trap.

Because of his awareness of this defect, Guo can always walk cautiously around the trap in the process of implementing diversified business strategies.

From Guo's point of view, the acceleration of urbanization and industrialization will certainly provide corresponding opportunities for the growth of comprehensive companies. Fosun's diversified management efforts will also redefine the image and core of diversified enterprises and gain respect from society.

Guo never deliberately evaded external doubts about Fosun's diversified business strategies. Such doubts became strongest in 2004. At that time, Xinjiang's D'Long Group, famous for its diversified operations and founded in the same year as Fosun, suddenly collapsed (see Chapter 4). President Tang Wanxin was arrested by the police on suspicion of illegally absorbing public deposits and manipulating stock trading prices to make profits. As a result, many rapidly expanding diversified enterprises in China faced the heavy pressure of control by the state, while such enterprises as Home Inns Group and Baidu, which specialized in one field, were rapidly rising.

As for diversified management, Guo had his own interpretation: "Diversification does not oppose specialization, but unification. Specialization does not mean doing one thing; you can also do one thing in an amateur way. A company can be involved in many fields at the same time, and it can also be very professional in every field."

Fosun's diversified operation had unique characteristics. What it pursued was diversification in investment and specialization in operation. For Fosun, diversified operations clearly reflected industry choices. The fields that the company had entered and invested in for a long time were all based on China's huge market demand, with comparative advantages and great potential.

In terms of the choice of direction to take within industries, Guo led Fosun to get ahead of others and rarely made big mistakes. In 1994, Fosun entered the real estate and biopharmaceutical industries. In 2002, it went into the commercial retail industry. In 2003, it marched into the steel and securities industries. In 2004, it invested in the gold industry and in 2007 the mining industry. Later, as these industries showed upward trends, Fosun gained great returns.

If we say that Fosun's early success in diversified operations was somewhat accidental, then what happened after 2004 effectively proved its comprehensive strength. At that time, Fosun went through two crises related to external questioning and control by the state, and then it gained recognition by the capital market on the Hong Kong Stock Exchange in virtue of Forte. This happened only through the growth of the company's comprehensive strength.

In 2007, Fosun formally adopted the development strategy of building a "professional diversified industrial group."

Then, at Fosun's 2008 annual conference, Guo creatively proposed Fosun's "three value chains" for the first time. These were continuous financing, continuous discovery of investment opportunities and continuous optimization of management. He also summarized the Fosun model for enacting the three value chains. This model was a positivecycle operation model formed by entrepreneurs and teams who identified with Fosun's culture as the core and the three values as the operation methods.

There is no doubt that it is the positive cycle of the three value chains that has made Fosun a successful enterprise. Guo said when laying out Fosun's future development that Fosun's people would certainly follow this model. He said that Fosun's development strategy for the future was aimed at becoming a world-class comprehensive company with Chinese characteristics and Fosun's character.

Guo believed that to maintain the three value chains of continuous financing, continuous discovery of investment opportunities and continuous optimization of management, it was essential to have three teams: a professional financing team, a professional investment team, and a professional team for continuous management and operation. He said that a talent gap had emerged in Fosun, and Fosun's first task was to spend more time introducing and training talents. In Guo's mind, when a company owns capital and has a framework and a strategy, the most important thing is human resources.

As an outstanding businessman, Guo always says modestly that his business intelligence is not excellent. However, when he invested in Tebon Securities and entered the financial field, people were convinced by his extraordinary business intelligence.

Tebon Securities Co.,Ltd. was established in May 2003. It was a national comprehensive securities company with a standardized operation and was also the private securities company with the largest net capital in China. Investing in Tebon Securities was Fosun's touchstone for entering the financial field. Guo's aim in entering the financial field was to cooperate with the best securities companies in the world, thus reducing the business risks of enterprises and increasing the economic benefits.

At first, Fosun injected ¥501 million and held 20% of Tebon Securities. In April 2010, Fosun's Xingye Investment bought a 32.73% stake in Tebon Securities for ¥550.61 million. The goal of Guo's investment in Tebon Securities was to accelerate its capital increase and listing process, thus promoting the rapid development of the securities business.

From Guo's investment behaviour, it can be seen that Fosun chose to enter the real estate industry and the steel industry when the industry was in a trough, and he did the same when entering the securities industry. Guo's choice to enter an industry when it was at a low point was based on the long-term strategic consideration of enterprise development. Guo believed that the domestic securities industry was still in its infancy and that its potential far exceeded that of other forms of financial investment, such as commercial banks.

After investing in Tebon Securities, Guo actively contacted the top ten securities companies in the world to seek cooperation and better promote the securities business.

In Guo's view, Fosun's development strategy of "diversified industrial groups" needed to be supported by the financial industry, and Tebon Securities could accumulate a large amount of financial resources for the whole of Fosun. When Fosun starts a new undertaking in the securities industry, it always emphasizes professional operation and market segmentation, thus forming core competitive advantages. After investing in a securities company, Fosun can participate in fund issuance and make joint ventures with investment banks.

Due to the solid promotion of diversified business strategies, Fosun realized its dream of becoming a powerful empire that was worth trillions—the "Fosun Empire." By the end of 2017, Fosun owned 142 subsidiaries, including six listed companies: SYTM, Fosun Pharma, Nanjing Steel Stock, Zhaojin Mining Industry, Mysteel Group and Hainan Mining.

ESTABLISHING ZHAOJIN MINING INDUSTRY, HE WAS QUICK AND RESOLUTE

There are many good businesspeople, but outstanding ones are rare. Guo is an outstanding businessman. There are three extraordinary things about Guo: extraordinary courage, extraordinary wisdom and extraordinary intuition. As an outstanding businessman, Guo has a keen business sense and responds quickly. That is why his Fosun team can always achieve brilliant results and surprise everyone.

Since Guo has always followed a diversified enterprise development strategy, when an industry shows signs of warming up gradually, Fosun's team will appear on the stage.

In 2004, when the price of gold showed a rising trend after the gold industry had lingered in a trough for a long time, Fosun took decisive action again. In April of that year, Fosun's SYTM and Fosun Industrial Investment jointly invested ¥400 million to launch Zhaojin Mining Industry Co.,Ltd. in cooperation with Shandong Zhaojin Group. In the newly formed Zhaojin Mining Industry, Shandong Zhaojin Group held 55% of the shares and Fosun held 45%. The new company was mainly engaged in gold mining.

Guo was sure that Fosun's SYTM, which had the largest gold and jewellery retail industry in the country, could further strengthen the gold industry and improve the gold jewellery marketing industry chain after taking a stake in Zhaojin Mining Industry.

According to SYTM's 2005 annual operating results, it had a net profit of ¥100 million; in 2006, the net profit exceeded ¥150 million, showing an increase of more than 50%. Fosun's investment in Zhaojin Mining Industry yielded relatively rich returns.

In addition to investing in Zhaojin Mining Industry, Guo held cooperation talks with precious metal merchants of other countries, including large gold-processing enterprises in South America and South Africa. Guo aimed to enter the primary processing of gold, an important node in the gold industry chain, and then form an effective gold industry chain covering the upper, middle and lower reaches.

Under the leadership of Guo, SYTM invested in Zhaojin Mining Industry while expanding into other industries. SYTM Real Estate Development Co.,Ltd., a subsidiary of SYTM, invested ¥3.6 billion and obtained the right to use 800 *mu* of land of Wuhan Heavy Duty Machine Tool Group (WHDMT) through bidding. Promoting real estate with gold was another brilliant move by Guo.

Guo chose SYTM to engage in bidding instead of Forte because he anticipated that SYTM would completely redefine the gold market once it held shares in Zhaojin Mining Industry. The land of WHDMT was located between East Lake and Shahu Lake in Wuchang, in the city of Wuhan, close to the administrative center of Hubei Province.

It was hard to find another piece of land like this in the prosperous center of Wuhan. After Fosun acquired SYTM, the projects of the shops Liaomiao Gold and First Asia Jewelry, and the combination of a large number of shops and real estate projects in Yu*yuan* Old Street, became parts of a chain strategy through which Fosun would upgrade its gold brand value. It is not difficult to see that SYTM bid for the land of WHDMT to better follow the development path of promoting real estate with the gold industry, giving each complementary advantages.

In December 2006, Zhaojin Mining Industry was successfully listed on the Hong Kong Stock Exchange at an opening price of HK$13, driving up the price of SYTM. After deducting the investment cost in Zhaojin Mining Industry, SYTM earned more than ¥2 billion.

After its listing, Zhaojin Mining Industry vigorously implemented acquisition, merger and expansion strategies to continuously increase its reserves of gold resources. In 2007, Zhaojin Mining Industry purchased 16 projects outside Zhao*yuan*, Shandong Province, expanding its business to 12 major gold-producing provinces and cities in the country. By the end of 2008, Zhaojin Mining Industry had 58 exploration rights and 21 mining rights across the country, with a total gold resource of 253.06 tonnes and mineable gold reserves of 165.29 tonnes.

Fosun's bid for the land of WHDMT would surely become the main profit growth point of SYTM and would also bring new financing channels, laying a solid foundation for the sustainable development of SYTM.

The idea of "seeing the strong when weak and seeing the prosperous when declining" is a value to which Guo and Fosun's people have always adhered. Guo believes that a fast-growing emerging economy will surely support several diversified industrial investment enterprises. Therefore, he has always stressed the need to build a multi-industry holding company. In the face of all kinds of ridicule from all sides, Guo has always firmly believed that the world is not in the hands of those who ridicule, but in the hands of those who can stand the ridicule and keep moving forward.

Industry insiders know that managing a diversified industrial company is a major undertaking. Faced with this difficult challenge, Guo has shown extraordinary courage, leading Fosun's people to conquer the challenge with extraordinary business wisdom. Guo has a belief in his heart: those who try to do something but fail are much better than those who do nothing but succeed.

The courage to go against the trend and a keen business vision have helped Guo to build up a huge "Fosun enterprise kingdom" and gradually create a diversified holding group with ¥100 billion annual sales revenue.

In June 2007, during Fosun International's IPO road-show, some overseas investment banks raised doubts about the bid price (which was in the range of HK$6.48 to HK$8.68). For a diversified comprehensive enterprise, the bid price was somewhat high. Faced with this challenge, Guo made no concession and delivered an impassioned speech at the roadshow: "Look at China with your own eyes, and you will not question Fosun's pricing. After 30 years of rapid development in China's productive forces, I believe there will be more vigorous momentum. If you don't believe me, it's no use talking to you. Please believe in Fosun's team, the company that has created the myth of private enterprises in the mainland of China, and the team's judgement and decision-making ability on investment and its capability of enterprise management. If you don't believe it, don't invest, but if you do, there is no reason to care about a 5% increase in price. The value of an enterprise is not determined by this small 5%." As a result, Fosun International's offering was more than 100 times oversubscribed internationally, and its public offering in Hong Kong was oversubscribed by a large number of retail investors. On 16 July 2007, Fosun International was successfully listed on the Hong Kong Stock Exchange amid this frenzy. The amount of financing reached HK$13.2 billion, with new shares accounting for 22% of Fosun In-ternational's expanded total share capital.

The listing of Fosun International undoubtedly brought people a new image of Fosun: a multi-industry enterprise empire with great development prospects.

CHAPTER

6

BY INNOVATING TECHNOLOGICALLY, HE WON SUCCESS WITH LONG-TERM INVESTMENT

WITH PRECISE TIMING, iFLYTEK DISPLAYED ITS PROWESS

At Fosun, almost everyone knows that Guo Guangchang is a man who will firmly grasp an opportunity once it comes, and he will not easily let it go.

On 30 November 2000, just as the global internet business bubble burst, under the leadership of Guo, Fosun's subsidiary Shanghai Fosun High Technology injected one-time capital of ¥16.77 million into iFLYTEK, acquiring a 21.5% stake and becoming its largest shareholder. This investment marked Fosun's formal entry into artificial intelligence (AI) technology, more specifically, speech technology in AI.

The name Liu Qingfeng is widely associated with iFLYTEK. In 1999, Liu Qingfeng, a PhD student at the University of Science and Technology of China (USTC), led 18 students to set up iFLYTEK, and enthusiastically joined the entrepreneurial milieu of the time.

Not long after its establishment, iFLYTEK experienced the upsurge and bursting of the global internet bubble, and the company soon fell into the dilemma of a shortage of funds. Just when Liu felt cornered, the company was lucky to receive investment from Shanghai Fosun High Technology.

There is an interesting story to tell about Guo's investment in iFLYTEK. At that time, Liu Qingfeng and his colleague Jiang Tao went to Guo with a heavy Toshiba laptop to demonstrate how to use their newly developed voice-tech-based software, Chang Yan 2000, through which users could listen to music, surf the internet and open a browser by speaking. However, before their presentation started, the laptop suddenly began to talk incessantly, which made both sides feel very embarrassed. Jiang later recalled: "At that time, we didn't know how to explain it to Guo and had to leave despondently."

This failed presentation made Guo almost give up investing in iFLYTEK. However, Guo still believed in its development prospects and ultimately invested without hesitation, becoming its largest shareholder.

Later, iFLYTEK was lucky to receive another $3 million in investment by Lenovo. Having received these two injections of funds, seeking listing became one of iFLYTEK's goals. In order to be listed as soon as possible, iFLYTEK adjusted its development strategy after careful analysis and research. The company decided not to develop new products by itself but to provide Lenovo, Huawei, ZTE and other clients with core voice technology modules and apply its technology to PCs, call Centers, intelligent networks and other fields. In this way, in 2002 and 2003, iFLYTEK successively introduced a series of solutions for telecom, desktop and embedded chips, thus finding a suitable development model and achieving initial success. In 2004 iFLYTEK turned losses into profits at one stroke, and in 2005 it entered a period of rapid improvement in performance. Therefore, listing was put on the company's agenda.

When iFLYTEK was busy planning its listing, Fosun implemented a share transfer of iFLYTEK. On 10 June 2005, Shanghai Fosun High Technology signed an equity transfer contract with Fosun. Shanghai Fosun High Technology transferred its ¥12.9 million equity in iFLYTEK to Fosun at the price of ¥20.7 million.

At the beginning of the planning phase for the listing, iFLYTEK preferred to list on the Nasdaq. However, considering the Nasdaq's pursuit of high risk and high growth, it was not suitable for iFLYTEK. The company finally chose to be A-share listed and landed on the small and medium-sized board on 12 May 2008. On the day of the listing, iFLYTEK opened at ¥28.21 per share, up by 122.83% from the issue price, and finally closed at ¥30.31 per share. By choosing to be A-share listed, iFLYTEK not only enabled Fosun and Lenovo to obtain rich returns on their investments but also made great progress in terms of the company's performance and market value.

In August 2010, when Guo recalled investing in iFLYTEK, he said with great pride: "Innovation and entrepreneurship are the basic components of entrepreneurship. We invested in iFLYTEK, a company born out of the national speech laboratory of USTC. A group of young doctors left the campus with their achievements. With the support of major shareholders (Fosun and Lenovo), it took only ¥60 million and six years to achieve the world's leading position in Chinese speech technology and regain 80% of the market share of the Chinese voice industry from foreign companies. They also applied a market mechanism to effectively integrate a number of national phonetic re-search institutions, such as USTC, the Chinese Academy of Sciences and Tsinghua University, to gather national speech technology research resources. At the same time, iFLYTEK led the setting of standards of speech technology on behalf of the country. For a long time, the research and development team members received only a small salary, but they devoted themselves to the continuous promotion and application of intelligent speech technology. After six years of entrepreneurship, they finally grew into the world's leader in Chinese voice synthesis with an annual profit of ¥30 million and an annual growth of more than 60%, enabling the Chinese people to attain achievements and monopolize the Chinese voice industry. In Blizzard Challenge, a global English speech synthesis competition, iFLYTEK won first place, which indicated that China's multilingual intelligent speech technology research had reached the world's leading level." Guo also said: "Although Fosun's investment in iFLYTEK is not the highest, the output and benefits of iFLYTEK are the highest because it is a private enterprise with a good mechanism and a great team. In this team, there is always the spirit of entrepreneurship and the pursuit of maximum output for every input."

Under the leadership of Guo, Fosun pays attention to long-term investment, accurately judges general trends and keeps a very good overall rhythm. From 24 June 2011 to 17 May 2012, Fosun sold about 12.9 million shares of iFLYTEK through the Shenzhen Stock Exchange, accounting for 4.79% of the total share capital. From 1 June 2012 to 4 June 2012, about 745,200 shares (accounting for 0.2% of the total share capital) were sold through the bidding trading system. In this way, during the two periods of concentration, Fosun's accumulated reduction accounted for 4.99% of the total shares of iFLYTEK and the accumulated recovered capital was about ¥474 million, which represented huge investment returns.

In a series of reductions to its holding shares after July 2012, Fosun's early investment of ¥16.77 million totalled about ¥1.7 billion by the end of 2013, with a return of more than 100-fold. Fosun was able to obtain such a high return due to two factors: first, because Fosun invested a lot of their funds, and second, because Fosun valued long-term investment. On 23 April 2013, China Mobile, the world's largest mobile telecommunications company, announced that it was investing almost ¥1.4 billion in iFLYTEK and acquired 15% of the shares, becoming the single largest shareholder. In the future, the two companies would cooperate in areas such as intelligent voice portals, intelligent voice technologies and related products. Previously, Fosun had only invested ¥16.77 million to acquire 21.5% of the iFLYTEK shares. This shows that Guo has deep insight.

As a leader in intelligent speech technology in China, iFLYTEK has been making great efforts in the field of AI. By contrast, Baidu and Sogou, which have a significant influence on AI technology, are latecomers. According to Guo, it is difficult for AI businesses to become established. New AI technologies have not yet generated huge profits, and the realization of innovative projects is progressing slowly; all of these problems need to be solved urgently. However, Guo believes that AI is bound to change all industries, and the competition in these industries is becoming more and more fierce.

The speech technology introduced by iFLYTEK has achieved human–computer voice interaction, making communication between people and machines as simple as that between people. Speech technology mainly includes two key technologies: speech synthesis and speech recognition. Speech synthesis technology involves making machines speak, while speech recognition technology is about making machines understand people. In addition, speech technology includes speech coding, timbre conversion, spoken language evaluation, speech denoising and enhancement technologies, which have broad applications.

In June 2017, in the "50 Smartest Companies in 2017," published by *MIT Technology Review*, iFLYTEK surpassed Baidu, Alibaba and Tencent (commonly known as "BAT") to become the smartest enterprise in China.

On 10 August 2017, the iFLYTEK investor forum was held in Hefei, Anhui Province. The meeting attracted more than 300 investors and over 200 institutional investors. Liu Qingfeng, chairman of iFLYTEK, said at the forum that the development of iFLYTEK and AI should be viewed in the light of future dreams, and greater dreams and space lie ahead.

During the forum, Liu proudly claimed that iFLYTEK was unique in two aspects. First, it had been listed for nine years and the chairman of the board had never sold any shares. Second, since its listing in 2008, none of the company's 30 core members had left the company.

At the forum, Liu mentioned more than once that the global AI industry was facing an unprecedented window of opportunity. He said that iFLYTEK had potential in education, medical treatment, customer service and transportation systems. The challenge was how to grasp the opportunity. He said: "We don't just want to be China's BAT. In the next three to five years, the pattern of AI will be fixed. In five to ten years, a lot of work now will be replaced by AI, and HKUST (The Hong Kong University of Science and Technology) will continue to make breakthroughs."

When it was first listed in 2008, iFLYTEK had a market value of only ¥3.2 billion. By late August 2017, the market value had reached ¥88.6 billion, an increase of over 27 times.

On 9 November 2017, iFLYTEK held its annual conference in Beijing. From education to medical care, from customer service to the smart home, and from mobile phones to car-mounted systems, iFLYTEK released more than ten AI products in many fields at one breath, making the industry sit up and take notice.

On 15 March 2018, as the only representative of the AI field among Chinese enterprises, the iFLYTEK Open Platform (owned by iFLYTEK) appeared on the Nasdaq Advertising Screen in the famous landmark of Times Square in New York. Once again, iFLYTEK showed itself to be the leader of the industry.

WITH STOCK PRICES SOARING, MYSTEEL GROUP WORKED MIRACLES

Guo's investment decisions always give people a decisive and wise impression, catching the attention of the investment business field over and over again. The investment in iFLYTEK was large, and so was the investment in Mysteel Group.

In January 2007, Fosun's Xingye Investment invested ¥36.9 million to gain a 60% stake in the steel e-commerce company Mysteel Group. The full name of Mysteel Group is Shanghai Ganglian E-Commerce Holdings Co.,Ltd. and it was established on 30 April 2000. Mysteel Group is a national large-scale comprehensive information technology industry service enterprise integrating steel information, e-commerce and network technology services. It is an interactive platform that mainly provides professional steel information and one-stop steel e-commerce services. Mysteel Group has established Mysteel.com, which has five major information sections: steel, furnace burden, special steel, nonferrous metals and international channels. The site provides comprehensive information, industry and economy news, statistical data, steel mill information, downstream news, and other informative content. With the help of its English website, the company cooperates with world-renowned steel mills and dealers. The company has its own research center, which publishes a series of research publications, such as *Steel Market Dynamics and Analysis, Mysteel.com Research Report, Mysteel Weekly, Mysteel Daily* and *Mysteel Monthly*— that act as reference points for enterprises and governments when they are making decisions.

In 2005, Mysteel Group won the title of Shanghai Famous Brand and passed the ISO 9000 management system certification. In 2005, 2006, 2007 and 2008, Mysteel Group was placed in the Top 100 E-Commerce Companies in China list.

In August 2008, the revenue of Mysteel.com (under Mysteel Group) surpassed the China Chemical Industry Network, ranking first among the vertical business to business (B2B) websites in China's steel industry. At the same time, the main indicators (website page views, website users, website visit time, website traffic, etc.) ranked first in the domestic ranking list of the same industry for three consecutive months.

In 2010, Mysteel.com's income reached a record high of ¥122.8 million. The increase in revenue of the website directly boosted Mysteel Group's operating income to ¥160.7 million, with net profit after deducting nonrecurring gains and losses reaching ¥23.7 million.

On 8 June 2011, Mysteel Group was listed on Shenzhen Growth Enterprise Market. That year, the company achieved a record operating income of ¥350 million, and the net profit after deducting nonrecurring gains and losses was ¥32.4 million.

After Mysteel Group went public, Xingye Investment's shareholding in Mysteel Group fell to 39.69%. At that time, Guo's goal was to turn Mysteel Group into China's most internationally influential market information provider and e-commerce service provider for commodity production, trading and demand data. However, to Guo's disappointment, Mysteel Group's net profit began to show signs of a rapid decline in 2012, when it was striving to seize market share, despite the fact that its revenue was soaring. While the revenue surged by 172.66% to ¥954 million, the net profit after deducting nonrecurring gains and losses fell by 14.36% to ¥27.7 million.

In July 2013, Mysteel Group's first half financial report showed that the company's operating conditions had not improved at that time, and its net profit after deducting nonrecurring gains and losses was ¥10.7 million, down by 38.76% year on year. But at the same time, the company had built up the concepts of "internet" and "e-commerce," and its stock price soared. On 1 July 2007, Mysteel Group had closed at ¥8.59. After a two-day trading limit on 2 July and 9 July, the price increased to the limit on 11 July and stayed there for four consecutive days. On 24 July, Mysteel Group rose as high as ¥21.25, becoming the most dazzling star stock at that time. In September 2013, the share price of Mysteel Group exceeded ¥30. On 30 January 2014, the company's stock price reached ¥55.83. A month later, on 24 February, the stock price hit a new high of ¥60.94.

Under the leadership of Guo, Mysteel Group called 2014 a key year for the company to develop commodity e-commerce. Based on its continuous exploration and achievements in steel e-commerce, the company proposed to build an integrated e-commerce ecosystem online and offline and was committed to creating a closed trading loop. In addition to continuing to vigorously develop the steel and iron online trading platform Banksteel, it began to build a service system that integrated payment and settlement, warehousing, logistics, data and financial services. It was committed to promoting seamless docking and accommodating the development of various platforms to form a complete e-commerce ecosystem.

The Banksteel platform played an important role in boosting the stock price of Mysteel Group. This platform, which integrated many popular concepts such as e-commerce, the internet and finance, gave the capital market unlimited scope for the imagination. In July 2014, Mysteel Group even began to proclaim the slogan that they would "build Mysteel Group into the Alibaba of the commodity trading market," once again inspiring the capital market.

On the one hand, the stock price was rising; on the other hand, performance was declining. Mysteel Group's 2013 financial report showed that the company's revenue reached ¥1.6 billion, up by 62.73% year on year, but its net profit after deducting nonrecurring gains and losses was ¥13.9 million, decreasing by 49.72% year on year. In 2014, the company's net profit after deducting nonrecurring gains and losses was ¥10.7 million, down by another 23.44%. In 2015, the company's net profit after deducting nonrecurring gains and losses was negative, with a loss of ¥255 million.

In response to the continuous decline in performance, Mysteel Group cooperated with HC International Inc, a Hong Kong listed company. The two sides said that they would continue to seek breakthroughs in B2B in order to achieve an improvement in the company's performance as soon as possible.

Around this time, Mysteel Group was famous for operating Mysteel. com and had become the largest e-commerce operator providing information services about steel and related industries in China. At that time, Mysteel Group was the only absolute holding company of Guo that invested in the technology, media and communications industries. For this reason, looking to the company's future development, Guo positioned Mysteel Group as the most internationally influential market information provider and e-commerce service provider of commodity production, trading and demand data. The company would build three platforms, namely a commodity information platform, a commodity trading platform and a commodity research platform.

To Guo's great distress, Mysteel Group's stock price had been rising continuously while its performance had been declining over the past few years, taking the company further and further away from the ambitious goals he had designed for it at the beginning of his investment. The poor performance made the small and medium shareholders of Mysteel Group feel disappointed.

HAVING PREPARED FOR DECADES, HENLIUS FULFILLED ITS DREAM OF TECHNOLOGICAL INNOVATION

On 25 September 2019, Henlius, a subsidiary of Fosun Pharma, went public on the Hong Kong Stock Exchange. Henlius issued a total of around 64.7 million shares at a price of HK$49.6 per share, raising about HK$3.2 billion (about ¥2.9 billion). On that day, Henlius opened at HK$47.45 per share and closed at HK$49.45 per share, with a market value of HK$26.7 billion.

Henlius is known as the "unicorn of Chinese biomedicine." Its successful listing in Hong Kong was an important milestone in Fosun's deep cultivation of scientific and technological innovation in medicine over the past decade. After more than ten years of unrelenting investment, Guo was self-mocking about Fosun's failure to acquire Henlius, saying that Fosun had tried again and again after being defeated. However, it was this "stubborn" insistence that enabled Henlius to break the monopoly of the influence of foreign research in medicine in China, thus greatly reducing drug prices and enabling more patients to use more reasonably priced anti-cancer drugs.

As the creator of HLX01 (a kind of rituximab injection), the first biosimilar drug approved to enter the market in China, Henlius was the industry leader in research, development and commercialization of biosimilar drugs, innovative drugs and combination therapies. Therefore, its listing was expected by the industry and the capital market.

Henlius had gone through a full ten years of hard work and development from its inception to its eventual listing. At the start of the 21st century, Chinese local pharmaceutical enterprises had had to fight to the death on price and hurt each other because of the serious homogenization of their products. Fosun, one of whose first businesses was a generic drug company, decided to settle down and focus on research and development in order to avoid this competition around homogenization among domestic pharmaceutical companies while looking for opportunities overseas. At one time, Fosun tried to acquire innovative research and development technologies through overseas mergers and acquisitions, but it ultimately failed. This strengthened Fosun's determination to choose the innovative road of independent research and development.

Henlius was born in 2009 through cooperation between Liu Shigao and Jiang Weidong. Liu Shigao, whose family's origin is Xuzhou, Jiangsu Province, was born in Taiwan. He was the top student in the Department of Microbiology at Soochow University in Taiwan and received a PhD from Purdue University in the United States. Later, he engaged in research, development and management in the field of biomedicine, accumulated rich industry experience and became a senior expert in biomedicine.

Jiang Weidong graduated from the Department of Biology at Hangzhou University and was admitted to the Institute of Cell Biology of the Chinese Academy of Sciences after graduation. Subsequently, he won second place in the academy's selection of state-financed students to study abroad and chose to go to Germany to study for a PhD. After obtaining a doctorate in microbiology and molecular biology from the University of Giessen in Germany, he went to California as a postdoctoral fellow and then chose to enter a pharmaceutical company in Boston.

Liu Shigao's father and Jiang Weidong's sister had both died of cancer, which had caused each man a great spiritual trauma. In October 2008, Liu and Jiang met at the California Bay Area Alumni Association of Zhejiang University. They had a congenial conversation and became friends. Soon, they reached a consensus on starting a business and recognized each other as partners. From then on, they fought together in the business world, sharing both prosperity and adversity.

In February 2009, Liu and Jiang officially registered and established Henlius. But at that time, they faced a once-in-a-century financial crisis, the US economy was in recession, and Henlius was soon in trouble.

It was at this juncture that Fosun Pharma appeared. Fosun Pharma and Henlius showed a high degree of consistency in their concepts, values and goals. Therefore, in December 2009, Fosun Pharma signed a cooperation agreement with Henlius, represented by Liu and Jiang. In February 2010, Fosun Pharma invested $25 million to jointly form Shanghai Henlius Biotech Inc.

Henlius was determined to be the world's best pharmaceutical enterprise and sell its products around the world from the very beginning of its establishment. Since then, in addition to continuous capital investment, Fosun has invested a large amount of human, material and financial support in enterprise management, research and development strategy, market access, commercialization and other aspects in Henlius, making every effort to build a world-leading biopharmaceutical enterprise.

In terms of strategy, Henlius established the market position of "innovation affordable to patients" and had various advantages at home and abroad. It developed high-quality and reasonably priced biological drugs to serve ever more patients. The company conducted a study of the number and proportion of patients using biological drugs in China each year and found that the needs of a large number of patients were not met. This was commonly due to exorbitant costs.

For this reason, Henlius adopted various approaches such as independent tests, widespread research and development, and a series of technological innovations (including one-off production systems) to significantly reduce its research, development and production costs.

On 25 February 2019, Henlius's biosimilar drug HLX01 was approved by the State Drug Administration for registration for marketing. As mentioned, HLX01 was the first biosimilar drug approved in China, and it was mainly used for the treatment of non-Hodgkin lymphoma. So-called biosimilar drugs are therapeutic biological products that are similar to approved and registered reference drugs in terms of quality, safety and effectiveness. The approval of the marketing of HLX01 achieved a breakthrough for domestic biosimilar medicines, bringing a price cut of 40% for domestic patients. This was good news for the many patients who could not be treated due to price issues and it also saved considerable funds in national health insurance, which could be used to support other medicines.

Since its establishment, Henlius has gradually established an efficient and integrated global research and development platform, distributed across Shanghai, Taipei and California. Henlius has actively implemented a global structure; signed commercial cooperation agreements with Accord, Cipla, Biosidus and Jacobson; and granted authorization to 82 countries and regions in the world. By the end of March 2019, the company had built a research and development team of 239 senior employees. The global research and development platform, with its strong independent R&D capability and full-process development capability, enabled Henlius to fully control the whole process of a drug, from discovery, development and production to clinical research after the product goes on the market. At the same time, Henlius conducted 11 clinical trials on eight kinds of candidate products in multiple clinical trial stages, plus two tumour immunotherapies, in six jurisdictions: the mainland of China, Taiwan, the Philippines, Ukraine, Poland and Australia.

Henlius always puts quality first in terms of product standards. The company always adheres to high international standards regarding product and production quality.

Another core product of Henlius, trastuzumab HLX02, became the first locally developed and produced biosimilar drug in China on 24 June 2019, after completing phase three clinical trials in international Centers across locations such as the mainland of China, Ukraine, Poland and the Philippines. The company has established a version of the total quality management system that fully conforms to the quality standards of the United States, the European Union and China, laying the foundation for the commercialization of the company's products in many jurisdictions and regions. The company's Shanghai Xuhui production base passed a Qualified Person inspection by the European Union, showing its production capacity relating to the Good Manufacturing Practices certification. Henlius has also actively participated in the establishment of China's biosimilar drug regulatory system with an international standard quality system, helping domestic regulatory agencies to establish a biopharmaceutical regulatory system in line with international standards.

Henlius's scientific team includes a large number of returnees, most of whom have worked in internationally renowned pharmaceutical factories. Of the 80 medical experts, 60% have overseas working experience. On the one hand, these talents can bring in the most advanced technologies from leading enterprises. On the other hand, they can bring in the business philosophy and management experience of those enterprises, thus accelerating the healthy development of local enterprises.

Behind the research and development of HLX01 is a series of numbers: more than 10,000 monitoring tasks, which took more than 600,000 hours, produced about 20 batches, and took ten years. HLX01 is only a microcosm of Henlius's deep scientific and technological innovation.

Henlius's success is due to its successful global operations in many dimensions, such as talent, research and development, and marketing. Biomedicine is a relatively new technology, and the leading technologies are mainly overseas. In Guo's view, if Chinese companies do not recruit talents from all over the world, set up research and development institutions globally, and become immersed in the most advanced technologies, they will not be able to catch up and attain the leading international level. In terms of independent incubation and research and development, Henlius focuses on macromolecular biological drugs and maintains innovation of small molecular chemical drugs, for which purpose it established Fochon Pharmaceuticals Corporation together with overseas scientists. This initiative developed the new anti-tumour drug FCN-437, approved by the Food and Drug Administration via clinical trials in the United States.

Competition between enterprises in the future will be about competition for technological innovation and globalization. How many fruits like Henlius will be born from Fosun's global technological innovation platform in the future? There is much to be excited about.

VERTICALLY INTEGRATING, HE BUILT A GIGANTIC PLATFORM OF ¥1 TRILLION

While Mysteel Group's stock price kept rising, its performance was continuously declining. This was moving the company further and further away from the ambitious goals Guo had designed for it at the beginning of his investment.

Facing this abnormal situation of a rising stock price and declining performance, Guo began to implement a new round of the integration of Mysteel Group. Mysteel Group acquired ZOL from HC International Inc through a combination of issuing shares and paying cash. The aim was to create a bright future where the company could adopt the principles of B2B 2.0.

Mysteel Group is the largest information and e-commerce platform in China's steel industry, while ZOL is the largest information and e-commerce platform in China's IT industry. Guo believed that when the endogenous growth of Mysteel Group began to lack a foundation, extensions, mergers and acquisitions became the inevitable choice.

In December 2014, the share price of Mysteel Group rose again, reaching a peak of ¥85.46. In May 2015, amid a growth enterprise bull market and the "Internet+" craze, Mysteel Group's share price reached ¥157.95, once again becoming a superstar stock.

On 15 May 2017, when giving lectures to students at the former Hupan University (established by Jack Ma), Guo mentioned two companies, one being China National Medicines Corporation Ltd and the other being Mysteel Group. Guo said: "I am very optimistic about the prospects of these two enterprises: their annual sales revenue could ex-ceed ¥1 trillion within three to five years."

Guo believes that a good enterprise must be focused on accumulation and have industrial depth and excellent product strength. He said: "China National Medicines and Mysteel Group are good companies that meet these conditions." In the lecture, Guo gave a detailed explanation of Mysteel Group's business model and strategic evolution, as well as its successes and future strategic direction.

Guo pointed out in his lecture: "Many people always like the enterprises in the limelight. I prefer enterprises that are not in the limelight and do not look very trendy. As a matter of fact, a lot of money has been made in the steel industry in the past. Everyone can live without e-commerce, but none can live without steel. Is there any product that can be produced without steel? No! Manufacturing is the core and foundation. Originally, we thought that we might give up the steel industry, but in fact, there are a lot of opportunities for the steel industry in virtue of IT. I said these are based on one purpose: we should pay more attention to traditional industries, those industries that are not properly valued, and we should focus more on the depth of these industries, and do not always go with the tide."

Guo said: "The model I least like is the one that everyone can understand and everyone is rushing to. The model I like is the one that needs accumulation and is not understood by ordinary people. It is very interesting to observe Mysteel Group's development step by step. The development of Mysteel Group is almost the road taken by Taobao and Alibaba. What is it doing recently? Data consulting, including collecting data at the steel mill and selling it to customers. Then its research and consultation are like Ali's Yellow Pages at that time. A few years ago, it began to do electronic transactions, including launching spot trading platforms. How will it proceed now? Mysteel Group will become a trading platform for commodities. Currently, e-commerce is B2C e-commerce. The volume of commodities trading is very large, but there is a lack of a closed-loop enterprise for commodity trading services." Guo continued: "Mysteel Group will achieve about ¥100 billion this year. We hope to build an efficient ecosystem of commodities and become a trillion-dollar industrial platform if it keeps developing. What everyone dislikes in the steel trade is loan fraud. Why is there loan fraud? Because the transaction process is not a closed loop, storage is provided by a third party and the third party is not honest, so it is easy for loan fraud to arise. What shall we do next? We will enter the supply chain of financial services and provide financial services in a trillion-dollar commodities platform, which is equivalent to a current service of Alipay, Ant Financial. Fosun attaches great importance to commodities and industrial depth. C2M [customer to manufacturer] is very important in industrial depth, and supply chain transformation is an important point in C2M. Of all the supply chain transformations, the most important one is the transformation of the commodity supply chain. There is huge potential here."

The industry knows that Mysteel Group acquired ZOL mainly to open up the upstream and downstream parts of the industrial chain, while ZOL and its marketplace belong to the downstream users of steel. Mysteel Group and ZOL are both focused on information and transactions and will extend from transactions to warehousing, logistics and financial services. Media information is a means of attracting attention, transaction information is the core and financial services are profits. The cooperation of Mysteel Group, HC International and ZOL is conducive to the mutual benefit of the three parties. For Mysteel Group, this cooperation could lead to the extension of its internet business, thus avoiding it needing to rely on the commodities business long term and improving the company's ability to withstand risk. HC International would gradually change from a media company to a trading company, relying on the strong trading volume of Mysteel Group to help build a "trading closed loop". ZOL's popularity in the e-commerce industry was not high, and there was an urgent need to expand its business sector and seek greater development.

Investment in Mysteel Group was only the beginning, and opening up the whole commodity industry chain to realize C2M was Guo's ultimate goal.

CHAPTER

7

EXPANDING OVERSEAS, FOSUN DEEPENED THE GLOBAL STRATEGY

CHINESE POWER COMBINED WITH GLOBAL RESOURCES

On 14 November 2014, Fosun announced that its wholly owned subsidiary Transcendent Resources had offered A$439 million to acquire a 92.6% stake in Roc Oil Company Limited, Australia's leading upstream oil and gas company, becoming the largest shareholder of the company.

Guo Guangchang's decision to buy Roc Oil was based on Fosun's strong industrial operation experience in mining and energy. By bringing Roc Oil within its remit, Fosun would make full use of its expertise in industrial operations and fully integrate upstream oil production resources into the overall energy industry chain, helping Roc Oil to maximize its synergy along the entire value chain. Alan Linn, CEO of Roc Oil Company, said: "It is exciting to be part of Fosun's strategic entry into the oil and gas industry. With the support from Fosun and Roc's industry expertise, we look forward to building a leading oil and gas business platform."

After the acquisition, Fosun fully retained Roc Oil's existing management team and continued to operate under Roc Oil's brand name, based on the results of a strategic assessment of Roc Oil's operating conditions.

The acquisition of Roc Oil is only a microcosm of Fosun's global structure. The core of Fosun's global structure is "Chinese power combined with global resources."

On 25 and 26 April 2015, the Duke International Finance Forum was held at Duke University's campus in Kunshan. The theme of the forum was "Cross-Border Mergers and Acquisitions." Business leaders and well-known scholars from all over the world gathered at the forum to discuss topics such as how to successfully make strategic investments in China, how to help Chinese enterprises successfully carry out overseas mergers and acquisitions, and what new success factors would be needed.

During the forum, Guo said in his keynote speech: "In the past, when we saw large global funds investing in Chinese enterprises, the most common thing they said was that they didn't come here to make money; they came here to take us to the world and give us international ex-perience. How can Chinese investors compete with them? Therefore, one of the key problems Fosun encounters when making investments is that we don't have a global capability but must face global competition, which will make us vulnerable. What should we do? *The Art of War* says that we should attack the rival's shortcoming with our strength. Therefore, in 2007 we considered what our advantages and disadvantages were compared to those of the multinational investment enterprises. In short, our advantage is that we know China, we plough deep into China, and we have a deep industrial foundation in China. Thus, at that time, we put forward a slogan: 'Chinese power combined with global resources.'"

He continued: "What is Chinese power? You should know that half of the global gross domestic product (GDP) growth now comes from China. Although China's GDP is still the second largest in the world, half of the growth in the global economy comes from China. Growth is the driving force, the power, and the rest is the stock. So-called power means growth. You are rooted in China, and that is the advantage. It can be said that the initial power and engine of global growth is the land where everyone is located. So, let's think, how can we combine this power with good resources around the world? Fosun's best path is to develop globalization. Who are you looking for? Our idea is to find those enterprises that want to develop in China. Fosun can offer help. However, at first many people did not believe this. Therefore, in the first three years, we only invested in one project, Club Med in France. At that time, it was really difficult for us to make these investments."

Guo pointed out: "There is a good chance now. We have the goal of achieving an international cross-border merger every month or two. What is the reason? Why did everyone approve of us? In my opinion, the main reason is that our proposal of "Chinese power combined with global resources" has touched people's hearts. For example, Club Med, after our investment, accelerated the development of enterprises in China, as well as the global development of enterprises. Therefore, many enterprises now say they want to develop in China and hope to find an enterprise that can help them in China. They think such an enterprise could be Fosun. As a result, we have now solved at least one key problem—that is, turning our previous position of searching for others into others searching for us—and others believe our story. A slogan can't solve a problem. I feel what is more important is that you should get things done. In this way, the subsequent investment speed will be greatly accelerated."

He continued: "We want to be a value creator in the industry. Therefore, Fosun is very clear that we hope to be able to stand on the land of China in the industrial sector and be an industrial integrator on the global scale. In this industry integration, we want to do three things most: the first one is the health industry. At present, we are deeply involved in two of the top five listed companies in China's pharmaceutical industry, Fosun Pharma and China National Medicines. Therefore, we will increase investment in pension, hospital and health insurance. The second and third are the entertainment and fashion industries. We have invested in Club Med and Atlantis, and recently Cirque du Soleil, Studio 8, Bona and others. I think that we will gradually build this industry up ... I feel that all traditional industries should be combined with the internet and gradually transformed. Therefore, we must be the integrators of these industries."

Guo's speech on this topic mainly concerned how to combine Chinese power with the world's resources and how to graft the world's resources onto Chinese power. Combining Chinese power with global resources was Fosun's best way to develop globalization. Guo also shared his experience of how to build a global investment group and proposed that enterprise development should adhere to the principle of "standing on the floor of value and dancing in circles." He said that capital should honestly serve industry, a topic that attracted extensive attention during the forum.

GOING OVERSEAS MEANT RETURNING HOME WITH BETTER BUSINESS

On 11 September 2016, Guo, together with Xiang Wenbo, president of SANY Heavy Industry Co.,Ltd., and Liu Yonghao, chairman of New Hope Group, shared their thoughts behind their respective enterprises" international investment in the 2016 International Investment Forum Special Program on CCTV's financial channel. They explained in depth the opportunities and challenges faced by Chinese enterprises in the process of globalization.

In the programme, Guo mainly answered questions from the host.

The host asked: "How do you view the change from "made in China" to "owned by China"?" Guo replied: "China's so-called globalization in the past was passive. In most situations, people came to integrate us. What we are observing now is reverse globalization. Our enterprises have the strength to gain access to global resources and make use of them. This stage has just begun."

"Fosun announced four acquisitions in July. Is this crazy shopping?" Guo replied: "In fact, each of Fosun's acquisitions had been in progress for a year or two, so this was a completely deliberate result. It seems that they all took place in July, but this was purely a coincidence. The total of these four acquisitions was below US$2 billion, which is not much compared with our previous purchase bills."

"Will the lack of "foreign relatives" hinder the development of enterprises" overseas investment?" Guo replied: "The relatives you mentioned are external consulting agencies, investment banks and lawyers. This is very important. Of course, these services are also very expensive, so it is important to know how to save money on "foreign relatives." At the same time, we must make our judgement and never follow their words blindly. As for Fosun, we feel that we are now in a stage of deep globalization, so we cannot rely solely on these institutions but must rely more on local teams, such as in Japan, Brazil and India. We have all found local teams, and these have been in operation for 10 or 20 years and have helped us to achieve control. These local teams have very strong experience, which means no longer just relying on others but deep localization. Only when you have your team can you take root."

"Fosun has many investment fields. What is the logic of Fosun's investment?" Guo answered: "Fosun's investment logic is very clear and has two main lines. The first is that, from a global perspective, Fosun insists on "insurance + investment." We need to build an investment group with comprehensive financial capability and industrial depth around the world with insurance as the core, with special emphasis on coordination between the two. One reason is to obtain better long-term funds, while the other is to obtain long-term returns. As for the second line, it is also very simple. It is to build a solution that can meet the needs of families around the world for "abundance, health and happiness" using the core idea of "Chinese power combined with global resources." Therefore, Fosun's investment is scattered in form but not in spirit. Fosun cannot be understood as a kind of superficial martial art. Fosun is practising Tai chi magic kung fu."

"Some people say Fosun invests to make money. What do you think?" Guo replied: "I have always believed that Fosun is a very passionate and humanistic enterprise. Investment is a way for us to run our business. Our goal is not to invest in one thing or another. Our goal is to provide a closed-loop solution for the "abundance, health and happiness" of family life through these investments. We are providing an all-round guarantee of the healthy and happy life of all people. How humanistic is this!"

"What do you think of Wang Jianlin's idea of "catching the white wolf using your bare hands [getting something for nothing]"?" Guo replied: "I don't believe it is possible to get a free lunch in the world. Behind the so-called bare hands, there must be invisible hands you can't see. Let's take Disney as an example. Don't think that having money or buildings is to "own something." These are actually the second most important things. The most important thing is Disney's intellectual property. For pharmaceutical enterprises, factory buildings and capital are secondary; in first place are drug R&D capability and patent certification. These are invisible, but they are the most valuable things. I think another important thing is persistence, effort and patience. You have created something that others do not have. You can leverage other people's money and other people's assets. If this is done in such a way as to catch the white wolf with bare hands, I will admire it."

"Now that more and more investments are being made in the United States, what do you think should be paid most attention?" Guo replied: "The most important thing is to choose the right partner. The overall rules of the United States are still relatively transparent, but the problem is that if your partner is not good, they will use these rules to hinder you, which is the worst possible outcome. Therefore, I think choosing the right partner is as important as a girl finding a good husband, especially in the United States."

"What do you think of "bottom fishing" (i.e. looking for low-cost stocks)?" Guo replied: "In investment, everyone says you should do the opposite. Buffett's most well-known saying is: "When others are greedy, you have to be afraid; when others are afraid, you have to be greedy." Isn't this bottom fishing? It is normal for an investor to want to buy stocks at a relatively low price. We aim to invest our money, so we will think carefully about how to use every penny and try not to make stupid decisions. We want to be prudent and long-term investors. We also care about how to manage and create value for each enterprise after investment. We also want each enterprise to be responsible for its employees and the local community. I believe that the greater the enterprise is, the greater the responsibility will be."

"Have you ever failed to buy an enterprise that you wanted?" Guo said: "We have had several such cases. We wanted Prada, for example, when we started to do the fashion industry. And there is also a brand called Moncler, which we like very much. An insurance company we talked about for a long time is AIA, a very good insurance company, but at that time we did not buy it in the end for various reasons. The main reasons for not buying AIA were as follows. First, Fosun's capital structure was not sufficient at that time. Second, Fosun was not ready for internationalization in such a big acquisition. Third, the timing was not necessarily good. Finally, they chose to go public directly. I think it is very normal to succeed or fail in investing in an enterprise."

"What is the idea behind Chinese enterprises going overseas and then returning?" Guo answered: "I think the basic logic of Fosun's globalization is "Chinese power combined with global resources." Therefore, the purpose of our going overseas is to come back better. For example, we have invested in Club Med, Cirque du Soleil and the Indian company Gland Pharma. At the same time, Fosun has invested in three R&D Centers in Silicon Valley in the United States. We have also invested in Fidelidade (a Portuguese insurance company) and also an excellent hospital. One of the most important factors in our investment is that we can bring these technologies and brands back to China, which can enrich family life in China. This is our basic investment logic. Therefore, China is our starting point and our ending point."

"What are Fosun's overseas investment tips?" Guo said: "I think "wholeheartedness" is essential. Whether in a global context or when doing domestic business, you must listen and learn wholeheartedly. Listen to the voices of your clients, your partners and all other sources. I think it is very difficult to obtain everything easily, but once you put your heart into it, you will find that it is not as difficult as you think."

THE PHILOSOPHY OF INVESTMENT WAS TO DEEPEN GLOBALIZATION

From 8 to 11 September 2016, Guo attended the opening ceremony of the 19th China International Fair for Investment and Trade in Xiamen, Fujian Province, as a guest. In his keynote speech, "Fosun's Investment Philosophy," he said that Fosun's next stage of development should seek win-win globalization and deep globalization. Guo's speech was full of passion, rationality and conciseness:

Today, I want to share with you my thoughts on globalization. China is a beneficiary of globalization and now faces many challenges. Moreover, there is a wave of antiglobalization today that is also very strong. What should we do? What can we do?

In the process of globalization, China has had many advantages over the past 30 years of rapid development, such as cost advantages and strong government ability to attract investment overseas. Now, I realize these two advantages are facing great challenges. Compared with India, China's current labour cost is not low. India's labor cost may be only one third or one quarter of China's. Similarly, the United States has more ability to attract foreign investment than China. For example, one of our brother enterprises goes to the United States to do projects. The state government provides free land, well-laid water and electricity networks, supporting railway facilities and favorable tax. In the face of this situation, how Chinese enterprises can continue to maintain competitiveness in the process of globalization is a problem we have to face.

Fosun has invested in Canada's "national treasure" Cirque du Soleil. When the Canadian prime minister came to Fosun to discuss the issue of globalization together, we reached a consensus on globalization: that it is beneficial to the global economy. However, this benefit does not reach everyone. Can we make more examples to convince everyone? How to make globalization benefit more people, not just those who benefit from a job transfer or a pollution transfer, is the focus of Fosun's thinking and efforts. In the process of globalization, Fosun has implemented the development model of "Chinese power combined with global resources." China's momentum is still strong. Professor Lin Yifu, the vice-chairman of ACFIC (All-China Federation of Industry and Commerce), has just mentioned many figures in China showing that we still have huge potential. We can find our comparative competitive advantage through innovation, investment in science and technology, etc.

I don't think we can rest on past achievements on the road of globalization. In fact, we have just started. Although China now invests overseas directly more than US$100 billion a year, the total stock is less than US$1 trillion. Therefore, for many enterprises, the process of globalization has just begun and has not entered the stage of deep globalization. In the past, we were globalized more passively. Now, more of our enterprises are actively and positively globalized under the leadership and guidance of the government. This deep and active path of globalization has only just begun.

We are not aiming at investing overseas. We aim to integrate the different potentials and resources of various countries around the world through global investment and a global structure, and use them to enhance the creativity and competitiveness of enterprises. Gland Pharma, a pharmaceutical company recently invested in by Fosun in India, started to set up a pharmaceutical research and development in-novation base in the United States seven years ago. A large number of innovative R&D achievements will come out in the next few years. Gland Pharma's innovative investment in China and Israel has also been very large in recent years, basically forming a 24-hour medical research and development system. Fosun, through its investment in Gland Pharma, has linked together India's low-cost and high-quality pharmaceutical manufacturing, the world's two largest consumer markets (the United States and China), and the strongest R&D Centers, Israel and the United States, thus forming the most powerful win-win complex in the pharmaceutical industry.

For example, Cirque du Soleil did not reduce its Canadian artistic elements because of Fosun's investment. All the clothes are handmade by Canadian craftsmen. But our investment is helping it speed up its development in China and share the growth of the Chinese market. At the same time, Cirque du Soleil has cooperated with Club Med, a French global vacation brand invested in by Fosun, combining unique cultural and artistic elements with French vacation services. I also believe that, as Wang Jianlin said, China's Cirque du Soleil will bring more overseas tourists to China.

Fosun will pay more attention to investment in developing countries. My own experience is that we used to invest more in developed countries. What does it mean to invest in developed countries? It means we already know where we are going in the future. Now, we invest more in developing countries, which means you can only have expectations about where they are going. Chinese enterprises have advantages in investing in developing countries, because we have faced and dealt with the same problems as a relatively backward country will face when it is beginning to develop. It is worthwhile for developing countries to learn the practices of both enterprises and the government.

Developing countries will face many problems, as do emerging markets. However, China has faced many development problems, such as high inflation, and it is not that terrible. Therefore, we see the investment opportunities in Brazil, India, Russia and Southeast Asia and believe this is a good time.

Guo's speech is not only a feast of wisdom in the field of international investment but also a comprehensive outlook on the current global investment trend and an interpretation of Fosun's participation in deep globalization.

THE ULTIMATE GOAL WAS TO OWN BOTH CHINESE POWER AND GLOBAL POWER

In Guo's heart, he had a very deep understanding of why Fosun wanted globalization. In June 2018, on the eve of commemorating the 40th anniversary of China's reform and opening-up, Guo gave a speech:

If you want to develop in the world, you must understand China, because China is already the world's second largest economy. If you want to develop in China, you must understand the world, because China is now very international. This is my most basic view of the future of business. Equipped with Chinese and global power, we will have the strongest competitiveness in the future.

2007 was the first year of Fosun's globalization and was also approaching the 30th anniversary of the reform and opening-up. With the successful listing in Hong Kong, we entered an international capital market for the first time, adopted international standard financial and accounting systems, accepted the tests of global investors, and looked at the world from our perspective. At that time, I felt that China's economy had reached a stage when the best enterprises in the world came to China. If Chinese enterprises could not "go out" and had no ability to integrate global resources, they would not be able to compete with others. So Fosun put forward the globalization strategy at that time, and we believe globalization is the inevitable choice for China's economy and enterprises when they have developed to a certain stage.

In 2008, the US sub-prime mortgage crisis broke out and the global economy fell into recession over the next few years. At that time, the pace of globalization in China was still relatively cautious, and there were not many enterprises that really "went out," so the impact was relatively limited. On the contrary, a large number of overseas assets experi-enced a deep correction in valuation, thus creating a large number of investment opportunities with mismatched values. However, even though there were many opportunities, overseas investment was still fraught with risks, especially when Fosun was still a "newcomer" in the field of overseas investment. It was not only difficult to find the target but also more difficult to evaluate the value of the target. Therefore, in the beginning, we only tested some excellent Chinese enterprises with seriously underestimated value in overseas secondary markets, because at least when evaluating Chinese enterprises, we knew something about them. At this time, Fosun was in urgent need of a guide to "introduce" and help to "determine" as much as possible overseas. At the same time, at the strategic level, our "going out" was not intended to buy low and sell high, but to use the rise of China's consumer market to "bring back" quality overseas brands and products. At that time, I felt that the 30 years of reform and opening-up had enabled the Chinese government to accumulate rich experience in the operation and management of the market economy. China's continuous industrialization and urbanization process over the years, as well as the huge consumption and investment demand gradually released in China, would provide strong and lasting momentum for Fosun's future development. As "China experts," we should make good use of "Chinese power combined with global resources."

At the beginning of 2010, former US Treasury Secretary John Snow first joined Fosun as a consultant to the board of directors to share his experience in senior administrative work in Fortune Global 500 enterprises and government departments. Then, Fosun and Carlyle Group, the world's largest private equity fund, announced a strategic cooperation around the world to focus on the opportunities brought about by China's rapid economic growth, and then established China's first partnership fund with foreign investment. Through such cooperation with leading international individuals and teams, Fosun began to learn from world-class enterprises in global investment, financing, operations management and human resources, gradually turning into a global enterprise. Soon, we also welcomed Fosun's first major overseas investment in its history—the French tourism and holiday chain group Club Med. Before this, Fosun had never formally set foot in tourism. In order to make this investment, we had done a lot of research and found that the global tourism industry was very large, especially leisure vacation. But this largest part of the tourism industry was almost nonexistent in China. Therefore, we decided to introduce foreign brands and experience to help China do something on the tourism supply side.

Club Med at that time had been losing money for five consecutive years. The troubled board of directors agreed to let us take a small percentage of shares, but we had to help them enter the Chinese market. In terms of the tourism industry, we were not as professional as they were at that time, but in terms of the Chinese market, the knowledge and resources accumulated by our industrial operations over the years were simply priceless to them. In 2010, just six months after we became a shareholder, we successfully helped Club Med open its first resort in Yabuli, Heilongjiang Province. This efficient cooperation impressed French people, and trust has been established between us since that time. After that, we continued our efforts to help them expand in China. The number of Chinese tourists increased rapidly and soon China became the world's second largest market after France. At the same time, after gaining a fairly deep understanding of the tourism industry, we proposed to privatize Club Med in 2013 and completed the privatization in 2015.

Through our management output and resource empowerment, Club Med successfully turned losses into profits after privatization and achieved a compound annual growth rate of 26% in the operating profits of its resorts in the past three years.

Throughout the Club Med project, we were understanding and studying, exploring the path and methods of globalization, accumulating talents, and gradually forming the rudiments of Fosun's going out mode through cooperation with the world's best investment institutions and individuals. This project is a process in which our model has been verified and matured. Subsequently, our globalization strategy has been fully implemented by continuously replicating this model. Today, we have conducted in-depth business in 17 countries and the industry is becoming more and more extensive. We already have dozens of international brands in many fields, such as medical treatment, tourism, fashion and insurance. Fosun has transformed itself into a global enabling platform, creating value through the coordinated integration of its enterprises with its accumulated industrial operation capabilities over the years.

Looking back over the past ten years or so, Fosun's globalization might not have been the fastest, but it has always been very stable. Its success is based on our accurate judgement of China's future economic development trends and also on our industrial development concept of step-by-step operation and steady progress. Besides, with the continuous progress and upgrading of China's industry today, we have been able to export products, technologies and models to the world in many fields, especially to emerging markets such as Africa and India.

Therefore, our globalization strategy today is no longer just Chinese power combined with global resources, but a China–global two-way drive.

CHAPTER

8

WITH FOOTBALL AS THE STARTING POINT, FOSUN'S STRATEGY WAS STEADY AND SURE IN THE EUROPEAN MARKETS

VENTURING INTO THE SPORTS INDUSTRY, FOSUN INTEGRATED MARKETS WITH RESOURCES

On 18 January 2016, Foyo Culture & Entertainment Co.,Ltd., controlled by Guo Guangchang, announced that the company had agreed a strategic cooperation with a well-known European sports brokerage company, Gestifute, to enter the football industry together.

Regarding the cooperation between Foyo and Gestifute, Guo said that the first goal was to make full use of Gestifute's top stars and coaching resources to represent the Chinese business and to host various business and publicbenefit activities, such as meetings of key individuals. The second was to introduce excellent foreign players into the Chinese market. The third was to assist excellent Chinese players in transferring to European clubs. The fourth was to set up youth football training institutions to train potential players to study abroad. The fifth was to carry out derivative business operations around star player intellectual property (IP), such as IP authorization for online games and exclusive brand sales.

Following Fosun's large-scale international expansion into the tourism, health and fashion industries, this time Guo's business empire had entered the sports industry, specifically the football industry, through strategic cooperation with Gestifute. With this move, Guo once again linked Fosun with Portuguese markets and resources.

Gestifute is one of the most famous sports agencies in Europe, with top coaches and stars such as José Mourinho, Ronaldo, James Rodríguez, David de Gea and Diego Costa. The founder of the company is Jorge Mendes, who is recognized as a person who can influence the entire European transfer market.

As an influential financial investment company in the global capital market, Fosun's interest has never been limited to one field. Guo has said that Fosun would not miss any possible investment opportunities.

From the beginning of 2014, Fosun's investment direction gradually shifted to overseas markets. It especially made big investments in Portugal, making Fosun the most active Chinese company in that country. Guo believes that Portugal is an attractive and important market that fully conforms to Fosun's globalization strategy and layout. Portugal is one of the most suitable countries for investment in Europe. Fosun pays close attention to investment opportunities in Portugal in various fields, including real estate, tourism and brand products. Once an investment opportunity arises, Guo and Fosun act decisively.

In January 2014, Fosun beat its powerful rival Apollo Global Management, an American investment fund, to acquire a controlling stake in the Portuguese insurance company Caixa Seguradora for €1 billion. In June 2014, Fosun bought 3.9% of the state-owned shares of the Portuguese power grid company REN for €56.8 million. In October 2014, after raising the bid price twice in a row, Fosun finally defeated United Health Group, one of the top 500 global companies, and bought 96.07% of ESS, a Portuguese healthcare service provider, at a price of €5.01 per share and a total of €460 million. Fosun received strong support from the country in the process of acquiring these Portuguese enterprises.

In a series of large moves in Portugal, Guo followed the strategic thinking of Warren Buffett in his investment model for Berkshire Hathaway and also paid attention to the needs of Chinese consumers. He has been considered one of the outstanding figures in Portuguese politics and business, and appeared on the "Portugal Top Influencers 2015" list, ranking 30th.

When Guo made his high-profile announcement that Fosun had chosen to cooperate with Gestifute, he made no secret of Fosun's ambition to enter the sports industry. He said: "We are facing a sports market with great development potential, passion and creativity. Working with a world-class master like Mendes, with his abundant resources and influence in the world sports arena, we will bring more positive changes to the development of China's sports industry, especially the football industry."

History shows that from entering industries including insurance, power grids, medical treatment and now football, Guo has not missed any worthy investment opportunity in Portugal. He has been paying close attention to all investment possibilities and has invested intensively.

Guo has said that Fosun will expand into various kinds of performance, movies and other fields in the future.

With good news frequently coming from Portugal's good economy and the willingness of Li Ka-shing, Wang Jianlin and other tycoons to put their money into Portugal, the confidence of Chinese domestic investors in investing in Portugal has also been greatly enhanced. Portugal's introduction policy for investment is very favorable. As long as €500,000 is invested in Portuguese real estate, it takes only three months for an immigrant family of three generations to begin enjoying Portuguese welfare, thus realizing a win-win situation of "investment + immigration." With a large number of Chinese investors investing in Portugal, Guo has further strengthened Fosun's "Portuguese Strategy."

BY ACQUIRING WOLVES, FOSUN EXPANDED ITS BUSINESS CHAINS

In January 2016, after Fosun agreed a strategic cooperation with the Portuguese company Gestifute, Guo planned to acquire top European teams. After much negotiation, Fosun bought 100% of Wolverhampton Wanderers FC (Wolves), an English Championship team, from Steve Morgan in July 2016 at a cost of £45 million, marking a substantial step into the football industry.

In December 2015, six months prior, the British media had reported that Ding Lei, chairman of the board of directors and CEO of the Chinese company NetEase, was interested in acquiring Wolves, claiming that the relevant acquisition negotiations had been going on for several months. Morgan, the owner of Wolves, who was eager to sell the team, was positive and intended to facilitate the transfer of shares in the club as soon as possible.

Ding Lei held nearly 45% of NetEase's shares. At that time, NetEase's market value was US$23.7 billion; thus, Ding's market value should have been US$10.7 billion, equivalent to ¥69 billion.

Wolves is a professional football team in England. It was established in 1877 and was a founding member of the English Football League. In the 2009–2010 season, Wolves played in the Premier League, but in May 2012 it was relegated to the Championship (the second tier) due to its poor record.

In the end, Ding was unable to complete the acquisition of Wolves for some reason. This result left an opportunity for Guo.

After Fosun acquired a 100% stake in Wolves, Morgan said in a farewell letter to Wolves" fans, employees and the media: "It is the right time to be handing the baton on to someone else to take Wolves forward, and to that end I am delighted to have completed the transfer of the ownership to Fosun International Group. Leaving the right legacy is hugely important to me and I am delighted that as part of my deal with Fosun they have made a commitment to invest between £20–£30m over the next two years into the club. They have also agreed to maintain our local charitable work by continuing to financially support Wolves Aid for at least one year. I am confident that with Fosun, the club is in very good hands. I wish them well, as I do everyone connected with Wolves both now and for the future."[1]

As Morgan stated, Fosun promised to invest £20 to £30 million into Wolves over two years, which was 2.5 to 3.75 times more than Morgan's investment of less than £4 million a year, so it represented a doubling or even quadrupling. This was enough to make Wolves" fans optimistic.

Although this figure was not as high as that of the top Premier League clubs, it was still the highest in the Championship.

During Fosun's acquisition of Wolves, Jorge Mendes, the boss of the Portuguese company Gestifute, undoubtedly acted as a middleman.

Regarding Fosun's purchase of Wolves at a price of £45 million, the *Financial Times* said: "But a secondtier Midlands club that has not won a trophy in 36 years represents something of a departure for Fosun, which boasts a number of glamorous brands such as Club Med and Cirque du Soleil."[2]

As time went on, Wolves, under Fosun's ownership, were featured in Britain's *The Guardian*, *The Times* and *The Independent*, which stated that Mendes had intervened in the management of Wolves and caused dissatisfaction among the Championship teams.

The speculation in the media and the dissatisfaction of the league mainly came from two factors. First, Wolves had signed players affiliated with Mendes's Gestifute over the past four transfer windows: in August 2016, Ivan Cavaleiro for £7 million; in January 2017, Hélder Costa for £13 million; in June 2017, Miranda for £2.7 million; in July 2017, Rúben Neves for £15.8 million; also Diogo Jota, who joined on loan; and in January 2018, Thomas Raymond, who joined the team for no fee. As a result, Wolves" first team had seven Portuguese players, accounting for almost one third of the squad. Second, Nuno Espírito Santo (known as Nuno), who became Wolves" coach in May 2017, is Portuguese and an old acquaintance of Mendes. Mendes, who was a nightclub owner in 1997, entered professional football by being employed by Nuno. For more than ten years, Mendes, who was trying to repay Nuno's kindness, had been working as the latter's voluntary agent. The two have an extraordinary friendship.

According to the British media, Mendes had replaced Fosun as the actual controller of Wolves, overseeing everything from players and coaches to the transfer market.

In response, Wolves said in an official statement: "It is a matter of public record that Fosun have a percent-age stake in the Gestifute company headed up by Jorge Mendes. Jorge is available as an adviser to the owners, in the same way as many other agents and influential figures within football are."[3] Wolves did not respond to questions about economic affairs and agency fees in the statement.

Despite the fact that Wolves were featured by many me-dia outlets, Guo never stopped cooperating with Mendes. Guo believed that Mendes was the agent of top stars such as Ronaldo and had high-level contacts in football, which was exactly what Fosun valued. Fosun's alliance with Gestifute was an important step in Guo's Portuguese Strategy. As early as June 2015, Guo declared Portugal to be "one of the most suitable countries in Europe for investment." Fosun also focused its European investment on Portugal first.

Before and after the acquisition of Wolves, Fosun had been steadily promoting the group's investment in Portugal, winning a controlling stake in the Portuguese insurance company Caixa Seguradora, acquiring the hospital business of the troubled Espírito Santo Group, and acquiring nearly 17% of Millennium Bank.

Regarding Fosun's aforementioned major acquisition, *Portuguese Trade Weekly* pointed out that in 2015, Guo did his best to expand Fosun's industrial chain in Portugal, especially in the fashion and media industries. Fosun's goal was very clear: to graft Chinese power onto global resources.

In Guo's view, Fosun had no reason to give up this resource because Mendes had extremely high-level connections in Portugal. Fosun needed to make full use of Mendes's resources to enact its Portuguese Strategy.

Over time, Guo and Mendes gradually prepared for Wolves to enter the world's foremost stage. In the Championship League in 2017–2018, Wolves won the competition three rounds in advance, thus enabling them to return to the Premier League after six years.

Within two seasons, Wolves" Portuguese coach, Nuno, turned them into a team with Latin style. Neves, Jota, Cavaleiro and other players from Portugal all performed well in the league and became the team's greatest heroes, helping Wolves back to the Premier League. In the 2018—2019 season, Wolves won the chance to take part in the UEFA Cup, having ranked seventh in the Premier League with 57 points, creating history for the team. In September 2018, Nuno was elected Premier League manager of the month. Not only that, the team proclaimed that they would win the Premier League within seven years.

CONFIDENT IN ITSELF, FOSUN SAW THE PROMISING PROSPECT IN PORTUGAL'S ECONOMY

In 2017, the April issue of the Portuguese magazine *Exame* used ten pages for a special report on the investment and development of Guo and Fosun in Portugal. It was the first time that a mainstream financial magazine in Portugal had featured Chinese entrepreneurs and enterprises so prominently.

The report pointed out that Fosun had already achieved remarkable fame in Portugal. In the past three years, Fosun had become a shareholder in leading enterprises in banking, insurance and medical services, including as a major shareholder in Fidelidade, Luz Saúde and the bank BCP. Fosun was also involved in real estate and energy and would enter the tourism market next.

The magazine reported that when Fosun had just bought Fidelidade in 2014, people might not have expected Fosun to become one of the foreign companies that would invest the most in Portugal. Today, Fosun's investment in Portugal has exceeded €2.3 billion and it is still looking for suitable targets. For Fosun, Portugal is a gate way to the European market and helps the company to strengthen its presence in Portuguese speaking countries such as Brazil, Angola and Mozambique. Guo said in the interview that he was full of confidence in Portugal's economic situation and full of praise for the Portuguese people, calling it a diligent nation.

Exame even positioned Guo as the "best spokesperson" for Chinese private capital in Portugal. In an interview with *Exame*, Guo said that health, happiness and abundance would be Fosun's investment priorities, including in the sports and entertainment businesses. In recent years, both football and tourism have attracted the attention of many Chinese investors.

When talking about Fosun's investment in Portugal, Guo said: "At the beginning of the investment, we were very cautious, because at that time Europe had just experienced the economic crisis and Portugal was also in an economic downturn. With deepening understanding of the Portuguese people and economy, our confidence became more and more strong. Portuguese society is very stable and also very friendly to foreign investment. It is a very hard-working nation. Therefore, I am very optimistic about Portugal's economic prospects."

The facts have proved that Fosun's investment in Portugal achieved very satisfactory results. In 2016, Fidelidade and Luz Saúde made a total net profit of €229 million, of which €211 million came from Fidelidade. Luz Saúde's annual report showed that Angola's healthcare institutions had been approved and would be put into practice, with a planned opening in 2018. Jorge Correia, CEO of Fidelidade, said that Fidelidade's development strategy was "overseas expansion" with the goal of "digitalizing the company and establishing a leading position in the insurance field."

In Guo's view, Fosun's globalization strategy continues to advance steadily, and Portugal is the key to opening up the markets of Portuguese speaking countries. He has said: "We have investments in Brazil, such as Rio Bravo. We hope that Luz Saúde and Fidelidade can also promote their development in the Brazilian market in the future. In addition, we are seeking more opportunities in Africa. Fosun Pharma is the largest supplier of malaria treatment drugs in Africa. At the same time, we also have many innovative businesses in the field of general health."

Fosun has operating assets in many fields, such as finance. Fosun holds a 23.9% stake of BCP and 5.3% of REN. Guo has said: "Portugal is our gateway to investing in Europe. At the same time, it is also our gateway to investing in other Portuguese speaking countries. Apart from Portugal, we have made investments in other European countries including Germany, Britain and France." He also said: "Fosun is very willing to help BCP enter Macao and the mainland of China."

As early as 2013, Fosun came to Lisbon, Portugal. At that time, Portugal was facing a severe shortage of funds and the unemployment rate had reached a record high of 17%. It was during this year that Guo, who closely followed overseas investment opportunities, found suitable opportunities in the Portuguese privatization reform and launched many projects. By the summer of 2015, Fosun had become the largest Chinese private enterprise to invest in Portugal and one of China's most outstanding investment groups in Portugal, thus dominating the pack.

On 21 November 2016, Fosun acquired 16.7% of BCP at a cost of €174.6 million through a capital increase and became a major shareholder. The bank, founded by Jorge Jardim Gonçalves, has since become a member of Fosun's businesses.

Before that, as mentioned, Fosun had acquired Fidelidade with an 80% stake in 2014. Guo did not choose investment projects at will. He was looking for high-quality enterprises with strong brands and growth potential.

Another example was the acquisition of One Chase Manhattan Plaza in New York, built by David Rockefeller. This Wall Street building was previously the headquarters of JP-Morgan Chase.

By 2015, Fosun had invested in 12 overseas projects.

According to Fosun's financial report for the first half of 2016, its total assets exceeded US$59 billion and it had achieved an annual growth rate of 7.4%. During this period, the company's revenue reached US$4.3 billion, increasing 9.3% year on year. Profits reached €590 million, increasing by 21.4%. The company's financial report showed that Fosun's asset–liability ratio improved and its debt structure was further optimized. In an interview with *Expresso*, Guo said: "Our debt remains at an appropriate level, but we also think we should further reduce the level of debt and reduce costs."

COMPLIMENTED BY THE FRENCH PRESIDENT, FOSUN BECAME THE MODEL OF CHINA–FRANCE BUSINESS COOPERATION

On 9 January 2018, French President Emmanuel Macron held a special forum for Chinese entrepreneurs in Beijing during his visit to China. Guo was invited to attend the forum. During the discussion, Macron called the Club Med investment by Fosun a "textbook" success story in Chinese and French cooperation.

France's Club Med, established in 1950, founded the concept of a one-stop tourist resort. It was listed in Paris in 1966. It is the world's largest tourist resort chain. The group has a total of more than 80 resorts, covering more than 30 countries and regions on five continents and providing high-quality one-stop vacation services to more than 1.2 million people worldwide every year. It generates annual revenue of more than €1.3 billion. Club Med's striking trident logo has covered almost all of the most beautiful corners of the world.

Fosun first bought shares in Club Med in 2010. On 13 June 2010, Club Med and Fosun jointly announced that Fosun, China's largest comprehensive private enterprise, had acquired a 7.1% stake in Club

Med at ¥210 million, thus becoming one of the largest strategic investors in the enterprise.

Subsequently, the two sides signed a memorandum of cooperation on the establishment of a strategic partnership and decided to cooperate in depth on the construction and operation of high-end resorts in China and to collaborate in the global business world.

Guo said: "The cooperation with Club Med will not only bring higherquality tourism and holiday experiences to Chinese consumers but will also provide opportunities for stakeholders to share China's growth. Data shows that China's tourism industry is experiencing rapid growth and has brought huge business opportunities. As the global economy enters an adjustment period, the transformation of China's economic growth pattern has caught the attention of the world. Economic growth driven by the upgrading of China's domestic consumption will bring a new round of business opportunities to the world."

In March 2015, Fosun completed its acquisition of Club Med with an offer of €24.6 per share and a total acquisition amount of more than €900 million. It took nearly five years from the first acquisition in June 2010 to the acquisition of the whole company.

Just one day before President Macron visited China in January 2018, Fosun was awarded the honor of "Best Investment Management Company in Asia" by the British magazine *Global Banking & Finance Review*. This award undoubtedly shows Fosun International's value in providing high-quality products and services, focusing on post-investment management, adding value, improving industrial operation capabilities and fostering continuous innovation, thus bringing benefits to Fosun-invested member enterprises.

Guo knew in his heart that opening up Chinese and even Asian markets to Club Med would be Fosun's most important strategy since it had started its globalization journey in 2007. Behind it was the rapid development of China's economy and China's rapid integration into the world. With the help of the strong momentum of China's rapid development, Fosun hoped to seize the opportunity to gather high-quality resources around the world and use them to serve the growing consumption needs and higher demands of Chinese people. Guo always has very clear goals in implementing Fosun's globalization strategy: first, to become a shareholder; second, to help enterprises expand in the Chinese market; and third, to explore the world market together with those enterprises. Fosun's investment in Club Med achieved all three objectives.

Fosun's implementation of its internationalization strategy has a strong industrial and capital foundation. By the beginning of 2018, Fosun's total assets exceeded ¥500 billion and it was a huge ecosystem. Fosun's abundant resources were fully connected with the enterprises it had invested in, and its huge user database would open up all its industrial sectors in the "C2M" strategy (see Chapter 6).

In the process of managing Club Med after the investment, Fosun pushed its group resources to interface with Club Med both at home and abroad. For example, Cirque du Soleil in Montreal, Canada, cooperated deeply with Club Med, and some of its projects quickly landed in Club Med resorts in France, Dominica and other countries. These Cirque du Soleil-themed events allowed tourists to experience the feeling of hanging from ropes and rings under the guidance of the Club Med staff. This immersive experience has undoubtedly enriched Club Med's activities and connected the two major intellectual properties.

Since taking a stake in Club Med in June 2010, Fosun has successively invested in the women's clothing brand IRO SAS, the asset management platform PERAF, the margarine producer St Hubert and the pharmaceutical distribution company Tridem Pharma, with a total investment of €2.5 billion. The chosen fields embody the pursuit of health, abundance and happiness. Fosun has become one of the most influential Chinese private enterprises to invest in France and the European Union. In France alone, Fosun's assets under management are nearly €10 billion, accounting for a quarter of Fosun's overseas assets of this kind.

Speaking at the forum where he referred to Fosun's investment as a textbook example of Chinese and French cooperation, Macron said that Fosun's acquisition of Club Med had once caused concern in France. However, after repeated accommodations, French anxieties had gradually been calmed and the two sides had even expanded their cooperation to achieve mutual benefits and a win-win situation. This investment case showed that the solution to the trade imbalance between China and France was not to "block" but to "drain". Only by further expanding trade and exchange and by enhancing communication and understanding differences could unexpected fruits be achieved. Finally, Macron called Fosun an example of a Chinese enterprise that had "gone out" from China.

In the face of Macron's positive evaluation, Guo said that by the end of 2017, hopefully there would be six Club Med resorts in China, and by 2020 the number of resorts would be more than 20. He forecast that the number of customers would increase more than ten-fold, from 20,000 to 250,000 per year.

There is no doubt that Fosun has become the core driving force of Club Med's global business recovery. It has also become a key means for Club Med to strive to become world number one in the leisure and vacation field.

President Macron has always been an active advocate of globalization. He says that when it comes to Chinese—French cooperation, either a wall or a windmill can be built. Walls are built to keep out the wind, but windmills can make use of the wind and create more value. Macron actively encourages Chinese enterprises to join hands with French businesses to strengthen cooperation in artificial intelligence, big data exchange and energy transformation.

At the end of the forum, Macron took the initiative to walk beside Guo and shook hands with him.

1. Steve Morgan, "Open Letter from Steve Morgan" (Wolves.co.uk), last modified 21 July 2016, https://www.wolves.co.uk/news/ club/20160721-open-letter-from-steve-morgan.
2. Tom Mitchell, "China's Fosun to Pay £45m for Wolverhampton Wanderers" (FT), 21 July 2016, https://www.ft.com/content/7a7f3d4a-4fc9-11e6-8172-e39ecd3b86fc.
3. Nathan Salt, "Premier League Target 'Urgent Talks' with Wolves Over Relationship with Agent Jorge Mendes as Concerns Grow" (Daily Mail), 13 April 2018, https://www.dailymail.co.uk/sport/ football/article-5612249/Premier-League-target-urgent-talks-Wolves-relationship-agent-Jorge-Mendes.html.

CHAPTER

9

MAKING GOOD PRODUCTS IS THE SOUL OF ENTERPRISE DEVELOPMENT

TO INVEST IN INDUSTRIES IS TO INSIST ON FOUR MATTERS

Every Monday, Fosun's employees attend a regular morning meeting to learn about the latest investment hot spots and go through trading investment cases shared by the investment teams.

On 15 August 2016, Guo, who had just returned to Shanghai after spending over a month travelling across the United States, Russia, Brazil and Europe, brought Fosun employees the latest insights into the company's investments: that is, Fosun should stick to four principles:

First, it must be emphasized that one needs to be present to discover value. In the past two months, I have visited the United States three times, Brazil one time, India one time, Russia one time, Britain one time and Portugal one time. This does not include domestic business trips. Why do I want to talk about this? Because I know that we can easily get the latest information on the internet now, but the best information comes from face-to-face communication. Therefore, I would like to remind all Fosun colleagues that you must not just sit in the office and only analyse the information given to you by others. You need to find it out by yourself and talk with others face to face. In Fosun's investment philosophy, we always stress deep understanding of the industry and the capability of in-depth localization. Therefore, Fosun's colleagues must go to the local area, go deep into the market, find suitable candidates, and listen, see and communicate by themselves when doing projects. Moreover, this is not only a requirement for the investment teams but also for our middle management and backoffice personnel, such as HR. Most of the time, you will receive more useful information by having a cup of coffee with someone else than by merely relying on public information or just making a phone call. Being present is very important. And from my own feeling, what I saw in Russia and Brazil is different from the information I got from the news. This is normal. If we get the same information as other investors, make the same judgement and invest in the same way, then how is Fosun different from others? Therefore, we must go deep into the front line, seeing and listening, communicating and discovering the value. This is a basic requirement for all Fosun colleagues: be present and discover values that others do not see.

Second, stick to doing the right things, the important things and the difficult things. Enterprise development is like sailing against the current; when insisting on doing the right things, important things and difficult things, we often feel bad. However, if you feel that everything is going well, you may get worse every day. I think Fosun now is sailing against the current. There are indeed many things that need to be broken through. This is because we are choosing to do the right things, the important things and the difficult things, which are different from others. Take our investment in the football industry as an example. I think we are just trying a different approach and of course it will be more difficult. What we have to do is buy a promising team at a relatively low price. Then we should make full use of our advantages to improve the team. This is not an easy thing, but it is valuable. Therefore, Fosun's path is to do things that others don't do. If we all do the same thing, what is our value?

Third, breakthroughs should be made in important areas. This year, Fosun has made two breakthroughs in its core strategy. First is Fosun's big health strategy. We bought India's Gland Pharma with a large sum of money and increased Fosun's investment in India. Most of Gland Pharma's products are sold to the United States and it is one of the strongest Indian pharmaceutical companies exporting its products to the United States. I sometimes tell the team that we should reflect on why we are still inferior to others in exporting pharmaceutical products to the United States given that we think we are stronger in all aspects. In these areas, we can learn a lot from our Indian counterparts. To invest in this enterprise means we should not only learn from India's experience but should also open up the American market. In this way, Fosun can link China, the United States and India, the world's three largest pharmaceutical markets. Of course, this is not an easy thing to do and requires heavy investment. Now, Fosun should focus on doing such right and important things. Because it is important, we must concentrate on it. In addition, Fosun United Health Insurance has recently won approval from the CIRC [China Insurance Regulatory Commission]. This is very important to Fosun. However, getting approval is only the first step. We still have to think about how to integrate health insurance with our medical care and health services so that we can form a closed loop. This is a right thing, an important thing and we have to try our best to make it happen. Indeed, sometimes I feel tired of doing such things and always feel bad. When you make investments, it is the case that the vast majority of people lack money and need your investments. However, if you go to a project where people don't need money, you have to persuade them to accept your investments, by convincing them that you can bring value to them. This is the key to our investment philosophy: we must make breakthroughs in our important areas.

Fourth, we pay attention not only to investments but also to post-investment management. Most of the time, qualifying for the investments we make depends on post-investment management. A lot of people are very happy and enthusiastic when they invest, but they will neglect the post-investment management. It's just like giving birth to your children without caring for them. In fact, the key to children's wellbeing lies in the cultivation and discovery of their talents. If you invest in a project with genius genes, can you create value for it? Therefore, post-investment management is very important. The key to investment is how you cultivate your acquisition after the investment. Give it sunshine when it needs sunshine, and give it water when it needs water. In the past two years, Fosun has also patiently cultivated some programs. For example, this year we won the payment licence, but how will the payment develop?

How do you open it? How can we grow when we obtain a health insurance licence? This is a big problem, and we should do it step by step. One of the most common mistakes that investment companies make is to take a shortcut. We always feel that everything will be fine as long as we buy the right one. In fact, investment is only the beginning. Beyond investment, it is more important to spend energy to develop the industry and train employees step by step. This is something that other investment enterprises do not have but Fosun has. We must have depth and background in the industry. We must penetrate our main pain points by investment. After that, we have to form a closed loop and then gradually cultivate and strengthen it. This is what we have to do.

TO DEVELOP THE GROUP IS TO DEEPEN ITS GLOBALIZATION

On 25 August 2016, the 13th Summer Summit of the Yabuli China Entrepreneurs Forum was officially opened at the Jinjiang International Hotel in Xi'an. Guo attended the forum and delivered a speech:

The next step is to deepen globalization. I would like to talk about the history of Fosun's overseas investment enterprises: H & A, a German private bank that Fosun invested in, was established in 1796. It has a 219-year history and is now wholly owned by Fosun. Fidelidade, a Portuguese insurance company invested in by Fosun, was established in 1808 and it has a history of 208 years. Silver Cross, a famous British baby stroller brand invested in by Fosun, was established in 1877 and has a history of 139 years, and is now wholly owned by Fosun. The Championship club Wolves, which it has been announced will be invested in by Fosun, was a founding member of the English Football League and was founded in 1877, having a history of 139 years. India's Gland Pharma pharmaceutical company, invested in by Fosun, was established in 1978 and has a history of 37 years. The Canadian Cirque du Soleil, invested in by Fosun, was established in 1984 and has a history of 32 years. The Israeli skincare brand AHAVA, invested in by Fosun, has a history of 28 years. Fosun, however, only has a history of 25 years.

The history of these enterprises invested in by Fosun is undoubtedly very short compared with the ancient capital Xi'an. However, compared with the enterprises led by leaders today, including Fosun, the histories are very long. In my opinion, all great enterprises have "endured long and then survived." So does globalization. Step by step, great enterprises are created from the lessons of blood and tears. Fosun began its globalization process in 2007 and is now proposing a plan to deepen this globalization. For Fosun, globalization and "deep globalization" are two different concepts.

First, one aspect of deep globalization is complete localization. Fosun will establish fully localized investment teams all over the world. This so-called complete localization is not about sending Chinese employees to our global offices but about finding independent local investment teams around the world. These teams have accumulated more than ten years of regional experience in these local areas and they agree with Fosun's culture and investment logic. In the past two years, we have found such teams in Russia and Brazil, and previously in London, England, and Tokyo, Japan. Their investment results are excellent. Fosun will continue to build such localized teams around the world. One member of Fosun's Rio Bravo team in Brazil, the former president of Brazil's Central Bank, is very experienced. Only a team with such excellent talents can be said to be a truly in-depth localization team.

Second, another aspect of deep globalization is to deepen industrialization. Deep globalization was previously proposed to consist of global investment, but different places have inherited different situations. For example, in the pharmaceutical industry, the forefront of scientific research and innovation must be in the United States, so Fosun set up three research and development laboratories in Silicon Valley seven years ago. But recently, Fosun has invested in India's Gland Pharma. Why did we invest in Gland Pharma? It was because India has done better than China in innovative medicine. Gland Pharma was certified by the FDA [US Food and Drug Administration] 25 years ago and has accrued no bad records for 25 years. This enterprise performed very well when investigated recently by US regulators. Through the investment in Gland Pharma, Fosun has further deepened its industrialization in the pharmaceutical field, for it can combine the advantages of scientific research in the United States with the low-cost but high-quality manufacturing in India and the huge market demand of China. Hence, the respective advantages of the three markets can be brought into full play. It is this road that gives me full confidence in Fosun Pharma's future. We can become the most competitive enterprise in the world. We can use the advantages of the United States, India and China. Fosun's next step is to deepen globalization, not simply make investments.

Fosun should be a responsible global enterprise. In the process of globalization, there will be cultural and other related differences. However, some so-called cultural and other differences between enterprises and countries are actually differences between good and bad enterprises. The world's good corporate cultures are similar: they are all entrepreneur-oriented, pay attention to efficiency, emphasize product power and care for employees. These are the universal principles. But bad enterprises are also similar: the government and the business collude, and the business pays no attention to efficiency and bureaucracy. Is there any difference between the United States and China? Therefore, there must be some cultural differences. But we shouldn't think of the differences between good and bad enterprises as the differences between countries. This is my first point of view.

My second point of view is that we should understand each other. How would the Chinese feel if an American or European company had bought 85% of the stock of China's largest insurance company 20 years ago?

Fosun spent €1 billion to buy about 85% of Portugal's largest insurance company in 2014. Its market share in Portugal is about 30%, including life insurance and property insurance. Although the government has approved the deal, it is normal that people and other organizations will disagree. We must understand the local people's thoughts. Therefore, I think we should actively abide by the rules, be a responsible citizen and do more for the local society. Therefore, when Fosun learned that young people in Portugal have employment problems, we decided that we would support the youth in starting up businesses. For a while, we were under a lot of pressure from public opinion in Portugal, but now things are getting much better. Therefore, encountering problems is common in the process of enterprise globalization. We should not blame others or ourselves, but nor should we be arrogant. We should be neither humble nor pushy but gain understanding and recognition through our actions.

Insurance is the most unusual road Fosun has chosen. Fosun is not so brave and fierce as some enterprises. We don't have 20 years of experience like Taikang. Fosun did not know about the insurance industry at first, so it suffered losses for several years. Only after several years of investment did it begin to develop. To keep up with the development of this industry, it is necessary for Fosun to acquire and merge, look for talents, and constantly learn and improve. Fosun Insurance should take its own unique road. Therefore, Fosun has just obtained a health insurance licence and will definitely make efforts in health insurance. In addition, the global structure means that there are more opportunities for us to develop in other countries. We should speed up our own development through foreign insurance companies.

TO PRODUCE GOOD PRODUCTS IS THE SOUL OF A GOOD ENTERPRISE

From 24 to 26 August 2018, the Summer Summit of the Yabuli China Entrepreneurs Forum was held in Nanchang, Jiangxi Province, with the theme of "Chinese Economy: Initiation and Restart." At this summit, more than 600 well-known entrepreneurs, scholars and government officials gathered to discuss the initiation and restarting of China's economic reform.

At the summit, Guo stated:

Most people want to know the secrets of business and also want to get shortcuts that others do not know. However, it has been 26 years since the founding of Fosun, and I feel more and more confident that there is no secret in business. If one must sum this up, it must be "products" and "product power." A good product is the soul of an enterprise, especially a good enterprise. For example, Alibaba is an e-commerce company, but its most amazing product is Alipay; Tencent, without WeChat, would not surpass its competitors by much; Taikang, led by Chairman Chen Dongsheng, develops step by step based on its good products. Some friends, when encountering various obstacles and problems, will complain about the impact of e-commerce, channels and the market. But in fact, there is something wrong with the product. How can an enterprise be good without good products? It is the same for Fosun: products are the base of an enterprise and enable it to achieve sustainable development and make every family in the world happier.

How to make good products? Good products must first be accumulated over time. Therefore, the first aspect of making good products is to endure loneliness and continuously carry out innovative research and development. For example, nine years ago, we acquired a bio-innovative pharmaceutical enterprise, Henlius. After ten years of hard work, we have become the world's leading unicorn in the biopharmaceutical industry. Moreover, the core goal of Henlius is to make cancer a chronic disease and to make its treatment affordable. Aitrox, an in-house innovation that Fosun supports, helps doctors to read data and diagnose illnesses using AI and big data. When the task of reading data is taken over by AI, the accuracy and level of medical diagnosis in the whole of society will be greatly improved. Fosun and Kite Pharma jointly established Fosun Kite in Shanghai, focusing on the application of Car-T technology in cancer treatment. The second aspect of making good products is that we must keep improving and polishing the world's good products with ingenuity. Good products can speak for themselves. Fosun has a clear requirement internally: its products must be top quality. The burden on the earth is already very heavy; if something is not a high-quality product, why do you make it, as there is so much garbage on the earth? We would rather not do it. Therefore, we must keep improving and making good products.

A good product is 28 Liberty Street in New York. It was once the headquarters of JPMorgan Chase Bank and was carefully built by Mr [David] Rockefeller. Another building that he built with the same energy was the Rockefeller Center in New York. This building has a history of more than 60 years, and is very classic now. I am shocked by the strength of this product and his pursuit of excellence. This is also one of the reasons why I am determined to make good products. Recently, we opened a restaurant with the best scenery in New York on the 60th floor of this building. One has to queue up three months in advance to make reservations. This is the power of good products, because real estate can directly reflect the level of polish in a product. Another good product I want to talk about is our office in Shanghai: the Bund Finance Center. Anyone who has ever been to the Bund would evaluate it highly ...

A good product is not necessarily a building or a physical object. A good product may also be good service, a life experience or a way of life. Therefore, to make good products, as a service provider, one must do something others dare not do and create a unique and happy life for our customers. For example, in our Club Med, the room is not particularly beautiful or luxurious, but children will be very happy there and want to enjoy it again. Parents will also be happy, so family customers will enjoy unforgettable holidays at Club Med. This is what others don't own and what people dare not do. Earlier this year, Atlantis Sanya, built by Fosun in five years, officially opened. This is not a hotel but a tourist destination including an aquarium, a water park, a dolphin theatre, etc. Even in summer, the off-season, the occupancy rate of Atlantis is very high. Therefore, I deeply feel that as long as we make good and distinctive products, there will be a good response.

To make good products, we should be smart! Football players need to be smart, and so do those who do business. Because of the World Cup, everyone is talking about football. For me, football is attractive because it is like business. For example, before Rúben Neves, Wolves" star, plays a free kick (a very beautiful curve-ball), he must carefully observe, think and judge in order to be as accurate in hitting his target as a surgeon who uses a scalpel. This is to "be smart"! So if we want to make good products, we should also be smart. It is useless to buy or spend money foolishly. To make good products, we need to do research and development, but research and development also require smart investment. The bigger the company is, the greater the investment in research and development is. Why do so many people buy technology instead of just doing whatever they want to do themselves? Why are big enterprises mainly engaged in mergers, acquisitions and buying? Because the efficiency of the investment in research and development is very low. Therefore, if we are to make good products, we still need to make smart investments. No matter how complicated the situation is, to avoid anxiety, we must stick to our original initiative and make good products.

After chatting with many friends recently, I found that many were not in a good mood and their economic situation was not good, and that they worried about problems such as Sino–US trade. But I think, no matter how complicated the situation is, no matter what problems we encounter, the best way to avoid anxiety for an enterprise is to find pleasure. What is my personal pleasure now? I am more and more interested in products, more and more fond of thinking about products, their links, how to create a better way of life, etc. Therefore, I think the solution to anxiety is to find a good way forward. For a member of an enterprise, the best way forward is the product itself. I am very happy that after more than 1,000 days of hard work, the first movie of Fosun's Studio 8, Alpha: The Solutrean, *has finally been released globally and will come to China on 7 September. I have watched it four times. To be honest, I was a little disappointed during the first screening. But after the screening, our team summarized all kinds of opinions and then polished and adjusted more than 20 versions. In their words, all of a sudden the movie became sublime. Therefore, they invited many viewers to watch it several times with full confidence and I was with them. The movie finally shown now, with epic prehistoric pictures and stories about love, warmth and courage, can be enjoyed over and over again.*

Making good products is not easy, but it is a great achievement. I enjoyed it.

FOSUN'S PRODUCTS WILL BE THE BEST IN THE WORLD

On 14 September 2018, Fosun joined Jeve, the auto battery industrial company in Tianjin, in hosting the conference "Green China Star Action" at the Fosun Art Center in Shanghai. Fosun officially announced its investment in Jeve and fully empowered Jeve to become a leader in the green energy battery industry in China and even in the world.

At the press conference, Guo expressed his views on the new energy automobile industry:

First, the business we are doing is great. New energy vehicles are an opportunity for China and a strategy that China must follow, because we are short of oil and the environment is already very fragile. Our technology in the new energy vehicle has developed relatively. This will indeed be China's next business card with great opportunities.

Second, industries that rely on subsidies will not last forever. A few years ago, Jeve and Fosun did not enjoy large subsidies for new energy. However, I personally have a basic idea that only the enterprises that win in the market can really develop in the long run. Solar energy is still subsidized, even in Europe. Once Europe reduces its subsidies, it will be a disaster for our entire solar energy industry. When Fosun has invested in an industry, it certainly does not focus on the short-term interest. Why are we so interested in this industry? Basically, it is because now is the time to capitalize on the market's struggle.

Third, why is Fosun investing in Jeve? Because we are well matched. Fosun's strategy is to improve step by step. In recent years, we have proposed to deepen the industry; focus on the concept of "health, happiness and prosperity" in household consumption, our globalization strategy, and our scientific and technological innovation; and increase our technological investment. The happiness of any family cannot be separated from the overall environment. Our investment in Jeve to help the development of China's electric vehicle industry is also inseparable from our strategy.

I believe no success can be achieved without experiencing hardship. Just as Zheng Yonggang, the group chairman of Shanshan, mentioned earlier, he has invested in the cutting-edge development of batteries for 19 years. And this is exactly what makes Jeve remarkable. When I communicated with the team of Chairman Guo Chuntai and General Manager Wang Chiwei of Jeve, I respected them very much, because what they had persisted in doing over the past decade is not easy. Although they have gone through many detours, they still persist. I am very touched by this spirit. Jeve already has good products and a good technical foundation. From Fosun's point of view, if the products are not good, relying solely on Fosun's investment, amplification and industrial operation will not be sufficient to achieve success. If the team is not good, no matter how rich it is, it is useless. But Jeve already has good products and a good technical foundation, so Fosun can help Jeve develop further.

I understand that Jeve will definitely do better in several aspects in the future. First, it will increase investment in technological research and development and continue to increase investment in innovation. Second, I believe we will keep cooperating with upstream and downstream companies. Just now Chery's Chairman Gao [Gao Xinhua] mentioned that electric cars do not make money, but battery factories do. Chairman Gao can invest in our battery factory and we can make money together. We will build more joint ventures with more upstream and downstream enterprises, especially good automobile factories. The third aspect is scale. Scale is still very important. I think our goal can be higher and we will develop faster in the future. In order to achieve this goal, I value talents most. We are very happy that not only is the original team good, but Jeve has also recently been recruiting across the whole industry. We have the honorary dean of the research institute led by an academician. I believe our technical team, development team and operation team will get stronger and stronger. In addition, there will be no shortage of money. Fosun will provide strong backing for Jeve and will definitely not allow its development to slow down due to insufficient funds. The fourth aspect is how globalization is structured, including the global distribution of talents and ecosystems. Our team has been doing this part, as Nanjing Iron & Steel has now set up research and development Centers in Britain and Japan. We also need to set up a global strategy for Jeve's technology. Jeve will also integrate into Fosun's ecosystem. Fosun has already invested in Koller, a lightweight material factory in Germany in the auto-related industries. Jeve can cooperate with them in many parts in this big ecosystem in the future. We will give Jeve support in terms of talent, global strategy and integration into Fosun's ecosystem.

Fosun is indeed an enterprise with investment genes, but we are definitely not satisfied with being an investor. We need to deepen our *industry. We are very patient in this respect. Everyone envies Fosun's holding of Nanjing Iron & Steel now, but before 2015 it lost ¥2 billion to ¥3 billion every year. Industry always has ups and downs, so we should have patience. Since we have chosen this industry and Jeve, Fosun and our team will be very patient in deepening the industry. No matter what the future of this industry will be, I believe those who can persist in innovation, have team spirit, global vision and sufficient funds will eventually create a strong enterprise and a great enterprise. We will all work hard for this.*

On 20 September, just after the announcement of the investment in Jeve, Fosun's FOLIDAY, an Alpine holiday town project, was officially launched in Taicang city, Suzhou, Jiangsu Province. At the project's commencement ceremony, Guo spoke highly of Fosun's product strength. He said:

Fosun's mission is to create a happy life for billions of families around the world. We realize this vision through three major sectors: health, happiness and prosperity. Especially in the past few years, we have grown very quickly in the "happiness" sector, bringing more laughter to many families. In this area, Fosun Travel has made great contributions. Fosun Travel has established 69 resorts and Club Med sites in 20 countries and regions around the world. Particularly, in April this year, we held a grand opening at Atlantis Sanya, Hainan, and it has become a benchmark for "Tourism 3.0" in Hainan and even in China. More importantly, Fosun Travel is also building an ecosystem to provide one-stop solutions for family vacations around the world.

Starting with Atlantis, we have made a request to the team, including Fosun itself. Fosun's products must be world-class products. Our products must not only be good products but must also appeal to others. I believe good products can speak for themselves and appeal to others by themselves—just like our Atlantis, which had great success when it was established in July this year. With the success of Atlantis, Fosun's product power has been recognized by families around the world, and Fosun's colleagues will continue to create high-quality products. Returning to the mentality of starting up a business, we continue to create products. Whether in medicine, sports or other fields, we are making good products for everyone around the world. In particular, the FOLIDAY, the Alpine resort town that officially launched today, will also be built according to such a pattern of thought.

10

CHAPTER

REPAYING SOCIETY, FOSUN COMMITS ITSELF TO PUBLIC WELFARE

SUPPORTING MEDICAL ENTERPRISES IS FOSUN'S DREAM FOR HEALTH

As we know, Fosun is a private enterprise that has seen long-term success and has competitive advantages in the healthcare field. What can Fosun do in light of the state's basic strategy of "poverty alleviation with precision"? Guo Guangchang, who as a child once saw "barefoot doctors" in rural areas deliver medicine to homes, said: "We should support medical treatment as we support education, and support rural doctors as we support rural teachers, so that the vast majority of rural people will no longer worry about diseases. When it comes to the crucial moment of overcoming poverty, Fosun cannot lag behind."

Most poverty is caused by illness; the rate of returning to poverty is rising instead of falling, and rural medical teams are facing three challenges: recruitment, employment and retainment of doctors. At the end of 2017, the Fosun Foundation jointly launched the massive Rural Doctors" Health and Poverty Alleviation Project with relevant organizations such as the Health News agency and the China Population Welfare Foundation, aiming at empowering rural doctors, improving the management of primary health and the medical services system, and contributing to the "medical care guarantee." Through the implementation of this project over the following three to ten years, the social security, technical ability and medical conditions of rural doctors in poor counties at the national level will be improved, and the incidence rate of key diseases in poor areas will be reduced. Rural doctors involved in the project will cover 100 poor counties nationwide, bringing the total number of local beneficiaries to more than 15 million.

In order to implement the Rural Doctors" Health and Poverty Alleviation Project, Fosun selected 38 outstanding employees to form a Poverty Alleviation Team to work in frontline poor villages. The areas reached by Fosun's Poverty Alleviation Team covered 37 national poverty-stricken counties in the central and western regions of Sichuan, Shaanxi, Gansu and Yunnan. By January 2019, team members had visited 485 health Centers and 4,083 village clinics. On the basis of investigation and visits, 5,082 instances of helping local doctors were recorded. The work of the Poverty Alleviation Team has accumulated extremely valuable raw materials for the project, and these will be connected to the China Social Service Platform for Serious Diseases.

In line with the actual situation encountered in the implementation of the Rural Doctors" Health and Poverty Alleviation Project, measures have been taken at various levels, including social security, serious illness relief, renovation of smart clinics, award packages for public service contracts and honor incentives. Additionally, the Five Ones project has been carried out, involving a rural doctor guarantee project, an award package for health poverty alleviation and chronic illness contract services, a social service platform for serious illness, the selection of warm-hearted rural doctors and knowledge upgrades for a number of rural clinics.

Thanks to the joint efforts of Fosun and relevant organizations, the Rural Doctors" Health and Poverty Alleviation Project has issued 10,659 accident insurance policies and 1,326 heavy disease insurance policies, with a total coverage of nearly ¥280 million. More than 49 training sessions for village doctors have been organized, with 4,476 village doctors participating. In total, 276 smart clinics have been built with a total investment of over ¥800,000, and 52 cases of serious illness relief have been launched with total fundraising of nearly ¥330,000. Additionally, ¥6.52 million worth of medical office equip-ment has been given as gifts, and a ¥5 million reward fund has been established for the management of chronic diseases of rural doctors. All of this makes Fosun's slogan loud and clear: "We protect rural doctors, and rural doctors protect everyone."

On 16 February 2019, the 19th annual meeting of the Yabuli China Entrepreneurs Forum, an annual event in China's economic circles, was ceremoniously opened in Yabuli, Heilongjiang Province. This annual forum has become China's most influential platform for the exchange of ideas, attracting numerous business elites and industry leaders to come together and hold discussions.

Surprisingly, a special award ceremony—Top Ten Warm-Hearted Rural Doctors and Directors of Health Centers in Townships in 2018—was an important agenda of this influential entrepreneur forum. That night, Yang Tiankui, Zhang Ruiting, Bai Meimei, Ma Jinhua and the remainder of the ten village doctors and ten heads of township hospitals stepped into the spotlight, becoming the focus and the esteemed representatives of the Yabuli China Entrepreneurs Forum. They came from remote villages in the central and western regions of Sichuan, Shaanxi, Gansu and Yunnan, representing a huge team of 1.5 million rural doctors. They had also gradually changed from being beneficiaries of the Rural Doctors" Health and Poverty Alleviation Project to facilitators of health poverty alleviation.

The 20 village doctors and heads of health centers in townships who were commended had long been rooted in the countryside and served there. Behind each person, there are endless stories and these stories are full of hardship and bitterness.

Yang Tiankui, director of the health center in the town of Shangduke in Rangtang County, Sichuan Province, had served Tibetan villages on the Qinghai–Tibet Plateau for more than 30 years. He suffered from pulmonary oedema due to overwork in anoxic areas all year round, but he still insisted on working on the front line. Bai Meimei came to work at Bai Yunxiang Health Center in Pingbian County, Mengzi Prefecture, Yunnan Province, after graduating in maternal and child health in 2010. She served as vice dean for more than a year and as dean since 2014. She gradually established an obstetrics and gynaecology department. She asked the health authorities in the county to send an old pickup truck as an "ambulance" for emergency and home visits.

The deeds of these village doctors and the directors of township hospitals all reflect their dedication and their greatness.

At the award ceremony, Ma Jinhua, a village doctor from Guo*yuan* in Dongxiang County, Linxia Prefecture, Gansu Province, was extremely excited. She was 26 years old and was affectionately known as "Dr Ga" by the villagers. In 2018, a mountain torrent washed away Dr Ga's village clinic and the three-wheeled motorcycle used for home visits. The working group of the Rural Doctors" Health and Poverty Alleviation Project put out an appeal and raised ¥467,686.65 within 24 hours, thus ensuring the reconstruction of the clinic, upon which 1,300 villagers in Guo*yuan* rely. The reconstruction of Dr Ga's health clinic is only a microcosm of the implementation of the Rural Doctors" Health and Poverty Alleviation Project.

In the year following the implementation of the Rural Doctors" Health and Poverty Alleviation Project, Fosun and the associated organizations delivered medicine to poor villages in central and western regions, striving to implement the campaign objective of "a healthy China without sickness in villages."

On the night of the award ceremony, a kick-off ceremony for the Rural Doctors" Guardian Alliance was also held. Guo, together with Chen Dongsheng (chairman of the Yabuli China Entrepreneurs Forum and chairman and CEO of Taikang Insurance Group), cut the ribbons together to jointly launch the Rural Doctors" Guardian Alliance. A number of entrepreneurs participating in the Rural Doctors" Guardian Alliance said that they would use their social resources to the greatest extent possible to promote more institutions, enterprises and individuals to participate in rural doctors" health and poverty alleviation actions and to try to find sustainable solutions for rural medical care. Only by keeping public welfare as public welfare and commerce as commerce can poverty alleviation actions mobilize social resources to the greatest extent possible and encourage more organizations, en-terprises and individuals to take joint action, thus seeking sustainable solutions to rural medical problems.

In fact, to some extent, Guo has promoted more and more entrepreneurs to participate in the Rural Doctors" Health and Poverty Alleviation Project, which has become an important symbol of Chinese entrepreneurs" desire to devote their efforts to improving China's basic medical care.

TO GO OVERSEAS IS TO HELP THE WORLD WITH COMMITMENT

From 21 to 22 June 2018, the Forum for Economic and Trade Cooperation between China and Portuguese-Speaking Countries (MACAO) was held in Lisbon, Portugal. More than 400 representatives from the business sectors of the mainland of China, Macao and Portuguese-speaking countries attended the event.

For a long time, Fosun has organically combined its development strategy with China's mutually beneficial and win-win opening-up strategy and the Belt and Road Initiative, actively expanding its business in Portugal, Brazil and Portuguese-speaking African countries. Since 2014, Fosun has successively invested in projects such as Fidelidade (Portugal's largest insurance company), Luz Saúde (Portugal's largest medical group) and BCP (Portugal's largest commercial bank). With a total investment of €2.15 billion, Fosun has become one of the largest international investors in Portugal. Fully respecting Portuguese law and corporate culture, Fosun has continuously strengthened its integration with these enterprises and achieved success, providing strong support for Portugal's economic development.

Fosun entered the Brazilian market in the second half of 2016 and invested in Rio Bravo, one of the leading asset management companies in this region. In addition, Fosun has been actively looking for opportunities to invest in areas such as health, energy, minerals and industries characteristic of the region. In Portuguese-speaking countries in Africa, Fosun actively conducts relevant business through the insurance and banking enterprises in Portugal. At the same time, the products of Fosun's Guilin Nanyao–China's largest artemisinin-based antimalarial drug manufacturer–have been registered and sold in nearly 40 countries, including Portuguese-speaking African countries. It is known that Guilin Nanyao's antimalarial drug has benefited nearly 20 million severely ill patients worldwide and saved about 100,000 lives, mostly those of African children.

It is gratifying that Guo has never forgotten his social responsibilities and international responsibilities in the process of going out to Portuguese-speaking countries. Over the years, Fosun has held two instances of the global innovation and entrepreneurship competition Protechting, whose birthplace is Portugal. Through cooperation with Portugal's native business incubators, Fosun has helped young people to innovate and start up their businesses. All indications show that Fosun will also make use of its unique advantages to conduct more public welfare activities in the fight against malaria in Portuguese-speaking African countries.

By 2018, the MACAO forum had been successfully held 13 times, and its influence has been continuously expanding. It has become an important platform for economic and trade exchange and cooperation between China and Portuguese-speaking countries, and has played a positive role in consolidating and deepening economic and trade relations between Portuguese-speaking countries and improving the level of economic and trade cooperation between China and Portugal.

Although Fosun has become a large multinational enterprise, in Guo's eyes, there are still many people who cannot live and work in peace and contentment at home and abroad. Fosun is needed to "help the world" and help people lead a happy life through establishing a career. For this reason, Guo changed the philosophy of "cultivating the moral self, regulating the family, maintaining the state rightly and making all peaceful" in *Great Learning* to "cultivating the moral self, regulating the family, maintaining the state rightly and helping the world." He made this Fosun's mission and core values. Under the guidance of the idea of "helping the world," Guo has gradually established a very grand mission to make every family in the world happier and to use all his effort to achieve this goal.

In June 2018, Guo said in a special speech titled "Six Reasons Why Fosun and I Can Survive":

When I look at the young people in the big cities who work late at night for a better life, the children running happily with their families in the park, the old people who are accompanied and guarded by their children in the hospital, and the parents who are worried about their children's food, clothing, health and education in poor mountainous areas, I know there are too many things in the world that Fosun and I need to do. To sum up, Fosun's mission is to make every family in the world happier. This is by no means empty talk. In Fosun's eyes, we are in the best era because of the 40th anniversary of reform and opening-up, the integration of China with the world and the innovation of global technology. At the same time, standing at the forefront of the best times, Fosun and I are longing for the future.

We see that consumers" time is becoming more and more precious. The speed of technology transformation into products and industries is getting faster and faster. The boundaries of each participant in business links are more blurred. Flexible industrial intelligence has been realized. Because of new technologies such as the mobile internet, the internal management of organizations is more efficient and thorough, which will make Fosun's global cross-border integration possible.

Based on this, Fosun has redivided its business into three major sectors—health, happiness and prosperity—and has made "taking root in China, serving one billion family customers around the world and building a healthy, happy and prosperous ecosystem" our new corporate vision.

The reason why we focus not on an individual but on a family customer is because the family is the smallest unit of happiness in our world. No matter what stage of life you are at, the company of your family is an indispensable part of your happiness. The themes of health, happiness and prosperity basically cover all the needs of a happy family, and the industries corresponding to these three needs are also the fields in which Fosun has been operating for many years. The reason why Fosun wants to take root in China and serve the world is that Fosun has always firmly believed in China and that China's future will be better because of its huge market potential. At the same time, with the globalization of China's industry, Fosun also has to take more and more global responsibility. The reason why it is a happy ecosystem is that a family's needs for health, happiness and prosperity are interrelated. Fosun's products and services for family customers are not separate, but an organic ecosystem, a C2M [customer to manufacturer] ecosystem in which customers and intelligent builders are closely related with each other, which provides a set of customized solutions centring on customer needs.

Fosun will keep in mind its initial intention of "helping the world" and will help more people. For example, the Rural Doctors" Health and Poverty Alleviation Project has helped 1.5 million rural doctors in China to live with more dignity and serve the local villagers in a better way, and we have conducted a project based on artesunate to help the world eradicate malaria completely. Fosun is already on its way. We have to do the right thing, the difficult thing, the thing that needs time to accumulate, and we will stick to it. I will use my whole life's efforts to realize Fosun's mission and fulfil Fosun's responsibilities. Because of

Fosun, every family in the world will live a happier life.

In recent years, Fosun has actively expanded its overseas public welfare undertakings and has successfully launched various public welfare activities in Lisbon, Berlin and New York to benefit local families.

TO PROTECT WITH CARE AND LOVE IS TO REPAY SOCIETY MORE

Guo knows very well that, as an entrepreneur, he should be grateful to society because the growth of an enterprise cannot be achieved without the support of society. For this reason, for many years Guo has led Fosun's people with love, giving more feedback to society where it is within his power to do so and making countless donations to social welfare.

On 25 July 2007, Guo donated ¥13 million to the China Guangcai Foundation. Huang Mengfu, chairman of the AllChina Federation of Industry and Commerce, accepted the donation from Guo.

On 12 May 2008, a strong earthquake occurred in Wenchuan, Sichuan Province, causing serious losses. Upon hearing of the disaster, Fosun immediately extended a helping hand and announced an initial donation of ¥10 million. At the same time, Fosun established air transport channels to quickly send disaster relief medicine to the disaster areas. On that occasion, Fosun donated more than ¥40 million in materials and its employees gave more than ¥3.6 million in personal donations.

On 17 April 2010, another strong earthquake occurred in Yushu, Qinghai Province. Guo and Fosun Pharma donated disaster relief medicine worth ¥1 million and the medicine was immediately sent to the disaster area by a Hainan Airlines special plane. At the same time, Fosun Pharma's manufacturing and sales outlets in Chengdu and

Chongqing organized emergency supplies of relief medicine to support disaster areas.

An outstanding enterprise must be an enterprise with gratitude. Fosun cannot advance today without the support of the whole of society. Therefore, Fosun has not set an end point on the road to public welfare. Guo has said: "Our life expectancy is limited, but the spirit can be inherited. Buffett created the myth of the investment world, and I understood it and used it for myself. Now, I will also con-tinue to develop it and let more latecomers understand it."

The dates 26 November to 8 December 2018 marked the sixth anniversary of the founding of the Fosun Foundation. On this occasion, the foundation (jointly with the Fosun family) solemnly launched a public welfare week with the theme "Fosun for Love" and called on Fosun employees around the world to participate in the activities. In this themed public welfare week, more than 40 enterprises within Fosun organized more than 60 activities in more than 50 cities in eight countries and attracted the participation of more than 30,000 Fosun employees around the four major themes: "be grateful to others," "restrain oneself," "do one's best" and "cherish things." In recognition of Fosun employees" good deeds in the public welfare week activities, awards such as Top Ten Star Public Welfare Projects, Top Five Charity Groups and Top Five Public Welfare Stars—with recipients selected by the Fosun Foundation Public Welfare Week Organizing Committee— were announced on the evening of 8 December.

In addition, at the evening party, a Special Award of the Year for Public Welfare was presented to all 37 full-time members of the Rural Doctors" Health and Poverty Alleviation Project to commend them for their perseverance in implementing the project.

At the party, Li Haifeng, chairman of the Fosun Foundation and senior vice president of Fosun International, said: "This year's Fosun Public Welfare Week is only the beginning. This activity will become a

Fosun public welfare tradition and will be held as scheduled in the last week of November each year."

He further said: "There is no end to the road to public welfare. Fosun's employees will gather for and act for good. Do not forget your original aspiration, persist in it, and pass on love and charitable deeds year after year. The pace of running for love will never stop. Every story of love is the motivation for the next good deed. We believe that Fosun's public welfare undertakings in the future will certainly move in a greater direction. Let's pay tribute to every public welfare person! Let Fosun's public welfare light up more happiness. Let all meanings be more meaningful because of love."

TO STRIVE FOR BUSINESS IS ULTIMATELY TO HELP THE WORLD

Since 2001, Fosun has been investing ¥500,000 per year to set up the Fosun Award to Respect Teachers in Jiulong Model Middle School in Shanghai. The award is specially designed to reward the teaching and administrative staff of the school for their outstanding performance in education, teaching and management services. On Teachers" Day, Guo always leads Fosun's executives to the school to give awards to the winners of the Fosun Award to Respect Teachers. Guo even takes the time to speak to teachers and students about "growth and ideals," bringing them endless spiritual strength. Fosun's corporate philosophy of "cultivating the moral self, regulating the family, maintaining the state rightly and helping the world" deeply affects the teachers and students of Jiulong.

As a model of successful entrepreneurship among college students, Guo has never forgotten to return to his alma mater. In 2006, Fosun set up the Fosun Medical Scholarship for Fudan University's School of Life Sciences to support various undertakings, such as teaching, scientific research and talent team-building. A total of ¥1 million in scholarship and teaching grants is dedicated to rewarding outstanding students from poor families and young teachers who have made scientific research and innovation achievements. The goal is to help award-winning teachers and students make greater strides in their research.

In June 2017, Fosun and Hong Kong University of Science and Technology's Creating a Happy Life Start Up Plan was officially launched. According to the plan, Fosun cooperates with this well-known university in Hong Kong to cultivate the entrepreneurial spirit of Hong Kong students and encourage them to start their own businesses. Fosun's rich network and resources are used to jointly design excellent entrepreneurial plans in finance, science and technology, health, tourism and insurance.

Starting from 2013, Fosun has held the Fosun & Prudential Youth Community Volunteer Award every year in Jiangsu. The award is based entirely on voluntary community service. It aims to attract and encourage more young people to carry out public service by finding and recognizing young volunteers who have made outstanding contributions to the community. By 2018, it had received nearly 2,800 valid applications and had recognized 225 high school students who had made outstanding contributions to public welfare.

On 21 January 2018, in Sanya Club Holiday Village, a group of more than ten high school students born after 2000 held a special "Me and Hainan's Future" symposium with Guo. The students were from the affiliated high school of Hainan Tropical Ocean University and were supported by a Fosun education grant. In order to promote education in Hainan Province and solve the schooling problems of poor high school students with excellent academic performance, in 2007 Fosun set up the Fosun Guangcai Education Award Fund to assist outstanding students from high schools in Hainan to complete their studies every year.

Guo recalled his childhood and said to the students: "My family was no better than yours when I was a child. Hardship in life is not what we seek, but you should regard it as one of the best aspects of your life. Difficulty in childhood is a kind of wealth and it is a good exercise for your will and character." He said: "Fosun and I have always had deep feelings about education. We should give everyone more equal opportunities, especially the equality of educational opportunities. At present, poverty is caused by two factors. One is that without education one cannot keep up with updates to knowledge. The second is because of illness and the inability to improve one's life. Education and medical care problems are issues Fosun's public welfare efforts should strive to solve."

Guo suggested to students: "In college life, you should study hard, play fewer games and take part in more sports. You must develop the habit of sports and reading. It will be useful to you for life. In short, college life can be a little more colourful, and the ability to learn by oneself is very important."

In Hainan, Fosun has supported 4,840 students over 11 years with total funding of ¥7.26 million. Students from nine ordinary high schools have been assisted: Hainan Middle School, Hainan Overseas Chinese Middle School, Wenchang Middle School, Jiaji Middle School, Hainan Normal University Secondary School, Qiongzhou College Secondary School, Guoxing Middle School, Changjiang Middle School and Wanning Middle School.

Guo said: "Fosun will further expand its education incentive fund in Hainan and fully carry out assistance activities. In combination with Fosun's project team in Hainan, Fosun will carry out more teaching expansion initiatives in addition to providing grants."

On the evening of 19 January 2019, participants in Fosun's annual meeting of global managers enthusiastically held an event titled "Round-the-Stove Night Talk on Corporate Social Responsibility," sponsored by the Fosun Foundation. More than 100 Fosun employees from around the world gathered to brainstorm and talk about love and public welfare.

It is known that the annual global managers" meeting is a golden moment for Fosun members and helps them to define their vision, focus their wisdom and brainstorm. During the meeting, Fosun held a total of three round-the-stove night talks, one of which was the aforementioned event sponsored by the Fosun Foundation.

From the host's speech, one can feel Fosun's people's spirit of participating in public welfare: "This night is destined to be extraordinary. Here, we listen to warm stories. Here, we listen to everyone's views on public welfare. Here, we think about how public welfare projects can develop continuously. ... Watch with love, help with your heart, little by little, trickle by trickle, and eventually an ocean of love is formed. I only hope that more people will join this big family and pass on this warmth together."

During the event, Fosun's employees gathered together and shared their initiatives. For example, Yang Bin, chief operating officer of Sunlight Printing Network, talked about how the company's environmental protection packaging containers and boxes would not only protect the environment but also improve production efficiency.

Qiao Baihua, chairman of Donglun Media, said that the company had sent a reporting team to go deep into the front lines of the Rural Doctors" Health and Poverty Alleviation Project and would start shooting a TV series about rural doctors to let more people know about them.

At the event, Fosun CEO Wang Qunbin said in his speech: "Fosun's ultimate goal in all its efforts is to create value for society. Of course, there are various forms of contribution, including globalization, technological innovation, product innovation, public welfare model innovation, etc. We need to benchmark, learn and cooperate with the world's best public welfare funds. Fosun's people have always been on the road to public welfare and we hope everyone can provide more valuable suggestions and grow together."

Guo also took part in the corporate social responsibility activity and called for more people to join in public welfare undertakings. He said: "You have love and you create for society. The whole society is positive and moving upward. Only in this way can life be better."

APPENDIX

GUO GUANGCHANG'S CLASSIC SPEECHES

MY SELF-REFLECTION AND SELF-CONFIDENCE IN FOUR ASPECTS

On 1 December 2018, the annual meeting of the Zhejiang Entrepreneurs Association was held in Hangzhou. At the meeting, Guo Guangchang, vice president of the association, delivered a speech:

This year marks the 40th anniversary of reform and opening-up. In the past 40 years, we, businesspeople from Zhejiang—with the "4,000 spirit," hard work and continuous endeavour—have achieved considerable success. In the past few years, although every year we said it was difficult, we actually "passed year after year." But this winter, it seems to be a little different. In particular, many entrepreneurs have had problems this year, and they are not small enterprises. Some of them are very good, and some are even listed companies with a market value of tens of billions RMB.

I am thinking, what's going on? Just now Professor Chen Long gave us detailed information on the changes in the external environment. What about ourselves? Over the years, we have been saying that we want to change ourselves. How much have we changed?

So here is my view on the current economy.

First, the economy will indeed be very difficult. This winter will be very cold.

Second, if there is a saviour in the world, that will be the market. In the market, only you can save yourself.

Fortunately, the party and the state have clearly seen these problems and difficulties and have issued a series of policies and measures for the development of private enterprises. Therefore, I think the future will be better. But whether we can survive this winter depends on ourselves.

As for ourselves, one thing we must do now is reflect on ourselves. I think now we must seriously think about what problems we are facing and what we did in the past five years.

I have asked myself the following four questions in recent years.

First, we have to ask ourselves: how much time have we spent on our customers? How much time have we spent in learning about our products? How much time have we spent in upgrading product services?

Every chairman should first be the chief product experience officer of their company. Is the product good or not? Is the customer satisfied or not? We should know them best ourselves. However, this understanding must not rely on your preference and intuition. You need to spend more time communicating with customers. Especially when the sales volume of the products is not good and there is a lot of competition in the market, you need to spend more time experiencing the products.

At present, I spend most of my time researching products and I basically think there are two ways to make good products: one is to make platforms, but there are a few companies, like Ali and Tencent, [that already do this]. The second is to spend more time thinking about how to make good products.

But if we are to make products, I must emphasize: we must make high-quality products, we must work hard and we must create value for our customers.

Second, we often have to ask ourselves: how much money have we spent on research and development?

How much time do we spend studying new formats? How long does it take to feel the new trends and directions? I believe that now everyone attaches great importance to the mobile internet. But I want to ask: how many people in our manufacturing enterprises really understand the mobile internet? Does the mobile internet just mean selling things on Taobao? Jack Ma has made Ali, an internet company, so well, but he still spends a lot of time studying offline commerce and physical manufacturing.

Therefore, we must not stop studying even though we have made achievements. Only when we learn faster than others can we move better and further than others. At present, the needs of customers are changing very quickly and we have entered an era in which scientific and technological research and development can be rapidly transformed into products. In such an era, the progress of technology, industry and market forces us to study continuously.

On the other hand, we must attach importance to scientific research and innovation. Although many of our enterprises that are in trouble are large enough, most of their products are still homogeneous and low-tech, and they used to rely on low gross profit to continuously expand their sales. However, everything is changing so quickly today that it is very likely that what you produce will no longer be products but inventory. Therefore, it is especially important to use scientific and technological innovation to lead the way now.

Third, we should ask ourselves: how much energy have we spent on organizational upgrading and personnel training? How much energy have we spent recruiting senior talents? How much energy has been spent on young people? Have we learned anything from people born in the 1990s and 2000s?

Organization and talents are definitely the core assets of an enterprise, because everything needs to be done by the right person. Moreover, according to the development and changes of the market, our organization needs to be upgraded continuously, and the talents of enterprises need to be changed continuously. We must absorb people with high energy levels, who are in the right state and who are eager to succeed. We all have our own teams, but how much effort have we made to upgrade those teams?

Let me give you an example. Fosun's Wolves Group has entered the Premier League from the English Football League Championship this season. However, I suddenly realized that although we played well in the Championship, we are encountering many problems in the Premier League. Why? Because the Premier League requires a different quality from our players. No matter what happens to the economic relationship between China and the United States, it will be a relatively long-term and difficult problem. However, regardless of how we solve it, China's economy is already participating in the global competition. Objectively speaking, we are already playing in the "World Cup." At this time, wouldn't it be strange if your talents remained in their original state and still no problems occurred?

Fourth, we have to ask ourselves: are we willing to slow down?

After 40 years of the reform and opening-up, China has enjoyed fast development and we are accustomed to it.

For example, we saw President Ma build a world-class enterprise in over ten years and everyone wants to copy his path.

However, there is only one Jack Ma in the world. If everyone is like him, what will the world be? So you need to know what you should do and whether you are focusing on doing what you should do. I have a feeling that the style of many enterprises is to go "all in"—in other words, "gambling." By "gambling" I do not mean going to casinos; I mean that being an enterprise is very much like gambling. Over the past 40 years, because the whole market has been developing, one has had a good chance of winning one's bets. But you must not regard the general trend of the economy as your own ability. What will happen if the market is not good? "All in" will be great in the short term, but then what's next?

I believe we really need to settle down and do the right thing, the difficult thing and the thing that needs time to accumulate.

Of course, after talking about so many difficulties and problems, I am still full of confidence in the future.

I firmly believe that the degree of marketization in China will become higher and higher and that the business environment for our private enterprises will be better and better. I believe that tax cuts will be made in the near future to reduce the costs of enterprises and stimulate their vitality.

I firmly believe that Chinese entrepreneurs, especially businesspeople from Zhejiang, can well endure hardship. As long as we really focus on innovation, we will develop faster in the future.

I firmly believe that we will integrate into the world. For us, businesspeople from Zhejiang, this is an important direction for the future. We are not afraid of global competition. In an increasingly open and standardized market and in the integration of globalization, businesspeople from Zhejiang will only get better and better.

This is just like Chinese football. If Chinese football means playing in the World Cup, only by letting our players play around the world instead of just letting them get high wages in the Super League can we get real success.

I firmly believe that businesspeople from Zhejiang have this expectation and ability. So let's work together.

THE COMMON SENSE OF BUSINESS: KNOW HOWS

On 25 April 2019, at the annual meeting of China Green Companies held in Dunhuang, Gansu Province, Guo delivered the following keynote speech:

Recently, I have been thinking about a question: why do many of our actions violate the common sense of business? Frankly speaking, people who work in enterprises are often very smart. The bigger the enterprise is, the less likely it is to make mistakes in technical matters. But why are there still problems in enterprises every year? I have found that most mistakes are made because they violate the common sense of business.

What is the common sense of business?

The common sense of business is the basic knowledge that every enterprise should understand and possess, all of which is based on the most basic business rules.

For example, doing business must be profitable. However, some people feel that profit is not that important and money should be "burned" first. When all the competitors have been "burned" to death, all of the market will be theirs and money will naturally be made. But let's think about this: do monopolies still exist?

Another example is controlling the liabilities of enterprises. However, some enterprises just feel that they need more debts. The more debts they have, the more people will be afraid of them. They believe in this familiar view: "If a company is big enough, it won't fail."

In addition, we say we should focus on customers, which is also common sense in business. However, many people are keen on attending all kinds of meetings and parties but spend less time on customers.

We also say that good products are made. However, some people think that selling in recent years has been hard because e-commerce has made competition fiercer in sales channels. But they have never thought about whether their products are bad or outdated.

There is another very important aspect of common sense in business: if we want to survive in the future, we must invest in the future. Therefore, in addition to thinking about our current profits, it is very important to invest in scientific research and personnel training.

Why is it difficult for us to stick to common sense?

Why is it so difficult for us to stick to what seems very clear and simple? I have been thinking about this problem and realize that there are some very clear reasons.

There are always weaknesses in human nature.

For example, when the stock market reaches 5,000 to 6,000, we should be more cautious, but often we are extremely greedy and think we can reach 10,000. When the stock market is at 2,000 or 3,000, the value of the investment has actually emerged although we may still be losing money. We should be brave, but people are often very scared instead.

There are always too many temptations around us, making us greedy.

There are also too many negative things that make us scared. These are all weaknesses in human nature and we always have to fight against these weaknesses.

There is another factor: self-judgement and expectations.

Sometimes we have too much confidence in ourselves, because during the 40 years of reform and opening-up, some people have "gambled" every time and have "gambled" on the right thing every time. So they might think, why am I wrong this time? But the world has changed. The original principle is no longer working. If you continue to "gamble" and go "all in" every time, will you not lose?

There are also some people who are completely the opposite and are excessively insecure. They were originally overconfident, but as soon as the internet came, they were immediately beaten down and felt that everything Jack Ma said was right, and they did not know what they wanted to believe. And then they violated common sense in many ways.

Of course, there are still some cases where they simply feel tired.

Some people who have been working for 20 or 30 years are tired and have begun to slack off. They begin to look for a group of people who are very experienced or highly educated, so-called successors or airborne troops. In fact, this is just an excuse for inaction and laziness.

How to avoid these human weaknesses and mistakes regarding common sense?

Often, success depends on how we stick to the common sense of business by doing what we should do and making efforts every day after finding the right direction. There is nothing particularly profound in this re-gard. But how can we avoid these human weaknesses and mistakes regarding common sense? In this regard, I also have some ideas.

One is the methodology of thinking.

I believe that anyone who has achieved business success has good business intuition and can feel sensi-tively what the customer needs and where the business model should go. However, our intuition will be dis-

torted for various reasons. Therefore, it is not enough to have intuition alone. There should be a perfect foundation of business logic behind intuition. Most of the time, we will attach more importance to intuition than business logic, which is a very bad weakness.

However, once we have achieved the unity and balance of intuition and logic, we also need to know what is the given condition at this moment. Because any-one can achieve a goal under given conditions. This includes what kind of situation we have inherited and the kind of environment in the outside world.

Therefore, business intuition, logic and external given conditions are indispensable growth factors. On this basis, we can formulate our own strategic plan.

However, we also need to know that more, stronger, faster, better or more beautiful strategic planning is not everything. Instead, strategic plans must conform to the organization's own positioning. We must imple-ment them into the organization, talents, culture and so on step by step, so as not to deviate from common sense but to take us on the right path.

There are also some technical means to avoid violating common sense as much as possible.

First, we should set up more suitable performance indicators. Once there was an overseas enterprise whose business development was not always good. After we went through the business, we found that one of the major reasons was that the main assessment index of the enterprise was only focused on sales, so the management team worked hard to expand sales, regardless of profits, technology, talents and other factors. This way just did not work, so Fosun changed it. Now, "profit + research investment" is a very important indicator. If profit is very high and scientific research isn't, the indicator is not met.

Second, we should pay attention to the grey scale within enterprises and encourage internal competition and cooperation. Many enterprises, *especially large ones, are likely to transmit some distorted and incomplete information, which makes it easy to violate common commercial sense. Therefore, we encourage the existence of a grey scale and internal competition and cooperation, which is intended to break the inefficiency of communications that strictly adhere to a hierarchical personnel structure. Doing so aims to realize the transparency of internal information and the most efficient use of resources.*

Third, we should frequently review our trades and pay special attention to failures. At present, Fosun has more than 50 global partners and the most important task for all of us is to face the things we haven't done yet. The weaknesses in human nature always tempt us to listen to good news, but looking at failure drives us to develop continuously. We need to know very clearly where the failure arose and force ourselves to know where our weaknesses are. Therefore, it is very important to review our trades.

There are also two other good working skills: one is to brainstorm and the other is to make full use of more efficient communication tools, such as DingDing. Now I spend more than half of my time on DingDing, and we have many working groups on it. Anyone in the company can pull me into a group at any time as long as they think the discussion is related to me and they want me to be informed. It's really efficient.